"Understanding a complex organism requires understanding of its genetic inheritance and its developmental dynamic including its embryological history. The re-emergence of China on the world stage is a complex phenomenon with a long evolution. It is not surprising for those who see only a few snapshots of China to imagine all kinds of futures for China including some fearful ones. Those who study China in its earlier incarnations know that China's growth and behaviour are in fact constrained by its past and civilizational character, and therefore not altogether unpredictable. Chandran Nair has authored a useful book for those who seek to have a sense of what China will become in the coming years."

—**George Yeo Yong-Boon**, *Former Foreign Minister of Singapore*

"China's swift and resourceful rise has scrambled the knowledge systems of the West, confounding their existing intellectual frameworks and making hostile speculation the main unit of analysis. Those looking for a picture undistorted by ideology and resentment of how China reshapes the world can do no better than read this impressively researched and detailed account."

—**Pankaj Mishra**, *Author of* From the Ruins of Empire: The Intellectuals Who Remade Asia

"Chandran Nair's *Understanding China: Governance, Socio-Economics, Global Influence* is a timely and essential work that offers an insightful and balanced perspective on one of the most significant transformations in modern history. At a time when a nuanced understanding of China's rise is urgently needed, this book provides a comprehensive analysis that cuts through the noise of media narratives. It serves as an invaluable resource for policymakers, academics, and anyone seeking to grasp the complexities of China's governance model, economic evolution, and growing global impact. Additionally, it fosters informed dialogue and deeper international understanding."

—**Bernard Charnwut Chan**, GBM, GBS, JP. *Chairman and President of Asia Financial Holdings and Former Convenor of the Executive Council of Hong Kong SAR*

"Where to go for a one-stop, comprehensive, balanced, and thought-provoking analysis of China's rapid rise over the last few decades? This book!"

—**Daniel A. Bell**, *Author of* Why China's Ancient Political Thought Matters

UNDERSTANDING CHINA

This book offers a long-overdue, balanced, and objective perspective on China's transformation from a constrained economy in the late 1970s to a leading global power in 2024.

It examines the political motivations behind China's rise through a detailed contextualisation of the reforms and opening-up policies of Deng Xiaoping, its governing principles, and the implications of its ascent for the world.

For readers interested in China's evolution over the past 50 years, this book is a valuable resource for policymakers, business professionals, academics, and students of contemporary Chinese studies, international relations, global political economy, and governance.

Chandran Nair is the founder and CEO of the Global Institute for Tomorrow, an independent Pan-Asian think tank that explores the dynamic relationship among business, society, and the state, as well as the rules governing global capitalism.

Jorgen Randers is Professor Emeritus of Climate Strategy at the Norwegian Business School, specialising in climate issues, scenario analysis, and system dynamics.

Jinfeng Zhou is Secretary-General of the China Biodiversity and Green Development Foundation.

Frederick Charles Dubee has an extensive background in international education, development, and strategy. He joined the UN in 2000 as Senior Officer and later Senior Advisor for the UN Global Compact.

Routledge Contemporary China Series

259 Modernization in Eastern Tibet
Leviathan the Forager
Su Hu

260 Inside The Expressive Culture of Chinese Women's Mosques
'This Turmoil of the Soul'
Maria Jaschok

261 Exploring China's Religious Sites
Digital and Spatial Insights
Zhaohui Hong

262 Cultural Bifocals on Chinese TV Series and Diaspora Fiction
Sheng-mei Ma

263 Chinese Educated Youth Literature
Ambivalent Bodies and Personal Literary Histories
Gabriel F. Y. Tsang

264 Performance Across Chinese Borders
Wei Zhang

265 Heritage, Homemaking, and Identity Formation in Migrant Workers
An Ethnographic Study of Yi Migrants in Shenzhen
Junmin Liu

266 China's State Ideology and the Three Gorges Dam
The Political Theodicy of Development
Yuen-ching Bellette Lee

267 Understanding China
Governance, Socio-Economics, Global Influence
Chandran Nair, Jorgen Randers, Jinfeng Zhou, and Frederick Charles Dubee

268 The Transformational Role of Dramaturgy in China's Performing Arts
Proactive Engagement with Multi-Stakeholders
Ting Zhang

269 Chinese Diasporic Writers and Artists
Reimagining Identity and the Self Beyond and Without China
Edited by Kwok-Kan Tam and Lily Li

For more information about this series, please visit: www.routledge.com/Routledge-Contemporary-China-Series/book-series/SE0768

UNDERSTANDING CHINA

Governance, Socio-Economics, Global Influence

Chandran Nair, Jorgen Randers, Jinfeng Zhou, and Frederick Charles Dubee

Routledge
Taylor & Francis Group
LONDON AND NEW YORK

THE CLUB OF ROME

Designed cover image: Tay Chin Lun

First published 2026
by Routledge
4 Park Square, Milton Park, Abingdon, Oxon OX14 4RN

and by Routledge
605 Third Avenue, New York, NY 10158

Routledge is an imprint of the Taylor & Francis Group, an informa business

British Library Cataloguing-in-Publication Data
A catalogue record for this book is available from the British Library

ISBN: 978-1-041-08057-2 (hbk)
ISBN: 978-1-041-08056-5 (pbk)
ISBN: 978-1-003-64354-8 (ebk)

DOI: 10.4324/9781003643548

Typeset in Galliard
by Deanta Global Publishing Services, Chennai, India

CONTENTS

LIST OF ILLUSTRATIONS

FOREWORD

China has emerged as the world's largest economy in terms of purchasing power parity (PPP), achieving a remarkable ascent from its historically low economic base to global preeminence. It is now the world's largest industrial, manufacturing, and trading nation, with the world's largest middle class. Extreme poverty has been completely eradicated, and life expectancy is currently two years more than in the United States. With a speed of accomplishing almost one industrial revolution every decade since the early 1980s, China is now at the forefront of the Fourth Industrial Revolution with big data, artificial intelligence (AI), and quantum technologies. It is now the only country still capable of providing goods, services, and experience which spans the four Industrial Revolutions to the whole world. All of this has changed the global landscape and the framework of the existing global order.

Yet the narratives shaping global perceptions of China are still distilled through narrow media frames, usually with a Western ideological bias. They reduce China's governance model to such labels as "authoritarian" or "abuse of human rights". China's dynamic approach to technological innovation, climate change, and social-economic transformation is often framed through a lens of suspicion rather than analysis, ignoring its unique blend of meritocratic policymaking, adaptive governance, long-term strategic thinking, rather than short-termism so prevalent in the West today.

Furthering such perceptions has a high cost, as they fuel geopolitical tensions, trade wars, stifle climate cooperation, and exacerbate military brinkmanship. They also hinder people-to-people trust, discourage cross-cultural exchanges, and undermine global solutions to shared challenges.

This book therefore arrives at a critical juncture as anti-China rhetoric reaches fever pitch in some quarters, and global audiences increasingly recognise that neither demonisation nor uncritical admiration will suffice. The book offers a balanced, well-reasoned and accessible framework for understanding China and its complexity, a civilisation by itself. It will hopefully empower readers – particularly the younger generation – to engage critically with the rise of China and the extensive implications for the world. It resists stereotypes and interrogates oversimplified narratives. Its brevity is deliberate: complex themes like China's hybrid governance, AI ethics, or "common prosperity" policies are explored with adequate depth and clarity to allow for further inquiry.

It does not seek universal agreement – a futile aim in any discussion of a nation as vast and dynamic as China. Instead, it provides a structured framework for dialogue, one that acknowledges contradictions and invites curiosity as well as debate. The truth, as the book shows, lies in the interplay of historical context, cultural values, civilisational wisdoms, and pragmatic problem-solving. Ultimately it will help fuel the curiosity of readers who desire to understand the trajectory of the evolving 21st century and China's role in shaping it.

Indeed, *Understanding China: Governance, Socio-Economics, Global Influence* is ideal for those seeking to develop a more balanced and holistic understanding of this complex and fast-changing nation. We all owe an intellectual debt to its authors Chandran Nair, Dr Jorgen Randers, Dr Zhou Jinfeng, and Dr Frederick Charles Dubee for their valuable insights and the endeavour itself.

The rise of China is not merely a geopolitical event – it is a catalyst for rethinking how we engage with differences in a multipolar world and how we share wisdom and practices for building a better society and a better world. This book invites us to begin this journey together.

Zhang Weiwei,
Dean, China Institute, Fudan University
April 28, 2025

PREFACE

Understanding China and the multi-polar world

We live in an increasingly multi-polar world – one that is defined by the crumbling of the ageing post-colonial Western-dominated world. It is also one shaped by the growing presence of and interaction between countries with disparate geopolitical, economic, and strategic interests. The biggest of these said countries is of course China – the second most populous nation in the world, as well as the second-largest economy in nominal GDP terms.

The mission of the China Association for the Club of Rome (China CoR), amongst other things, is to promote international understanding and cooperation between China and the rest of the world. In its most distilled form, the mission is to reduce geopolitical tensions surrounding the rise of China and to contribute to creating the conditions for friendly and peaceful co-existence.

There exists a void today in the understanding of China, despite the clear need for the rest of the world to do so. Almost all the discussions about China and its role in the 21st century take place along deeply divided ideological lines and differences. Interventions and contributions are invariably viewed as either pro-China or critical towards it. This book is an attempt to fill this void and contribute to reducing said tensions in the process.

In order to build a middle ground of common understanding amongst globally divided opinions, China CoR decided to write this book. It should be viewed as a primer; a presentation of insights and facts to establish a new perspective from which the reader can continue a journey of discovery. Naturally, the authors are well aware of the difficulties of writing a book about China that satisfies the diverse interests of the intended global audience.

The aim is to provide readers with insights into China based on available information that is objective and factual, relying on both Chinese and international sources. It also draws on the experience gained by the founders of China CoR, who have many years of experience working in China and reflects their views. Needless to say, there has been some level of interpretation during the writing of this book, but at all times the commitment has been to seek balance and to remain impartial.

Given that so much of what is written about China over the last decade has been driven by ideological differences, the authors are conscious that the absence of (often-repeated) criticism of China on certain (well-known) issues may be viewed as a (disturbing) bias.

Therefore, we would like to state that we have tried very hard to make the book as precise and balanced as possible whilst avoiding the trap of getting enmeshed in and repeating well-trodden and unproductive debates. In this manner, it is our hope that the book will be viewed as neither pro- nor anti-China. Getting this nuance right has been the most challenging aspect of writing this book and it is our firm conviction that the book is balanced and provides a sound basis for anyone interested in understanding China and its impact on the world.

Chandran Nair
Jorgen Randers
Zhou Jinfeng
Frederick Charles Dubee
Members of the Board,
The China Association for the Club of Rome

1

INTRODUCTION

Most people in the world recognise China as a country that has rapidly grown from one with a sizeable population yet constricted economy in the 1970s, to one of the leading economic powers in the world as of 2025. After the four decades since the country undertook the monumental decision to "reform and open-up", China today stands as a prominent regional and global power, as well as an "economic super-connector" with extensive economic ties and influence over a large number of states – especially states historically neglected by the Western liberal order. Understanding China comprehensively – its past, present, and future; its shortcomings and strengths; its opportunities and risks – is pivotal to anyone who seeks to engage with serious international geopolitical analysis and enhance international cooperation.

This book submits that China's rise, on net, is in the interest of the world and yields positive global impacts. The ascent of the country has lifted a sizeable proportion of the global population out of poverty;[1] it helped consolidate the world's supply chains and vastly enhanced its own technological capacity and efficiency. It has promulgated critical scientific and technological breakthroughs, as well as opening up the largest consumer market – in mankind's history – to foreign investment, trade, and business (for graphical depictions of China's development over the last 40 years, please see the Appendix). Nevertheless, with its rise has also come a plethora of critical issues – the perception of its, at times, adverse overseas sociocultural influence, the sustainability of its growth – and discussions over its unique political structure and distinctive governance system. These issues must be dealt with through intensive and respectful dialogue, understanding, and cooperation for global progress – and not become the substance of confrontation.

DOI: 10.4324/9781003643548-1

Whilst perhaps not always inevitable, the economic and technological rise of China has proven to be both staggering in pace and inexorable in trajectory. This neither calls for mindless optimism and zealous embracing of all that the country has to offer; nor, of course, should the world respond with hasty dismissal and alarmist rejectionism that embeds the understandable – albeit mistaken – assumption that, "Only the West, can be best". The path forward requires all parties to partake in constructive engagement, collaboration, and organic liaison – and to resist the temptations to conclude, erroneously, that the past four decades of internationalisation and globalisation have not helped China reform for the better. They certainly have – and the upcoming chapters of this very book will seek to show how.

China – in many ways – constitutes an enigma for the West. As a country rooted in a multi-millennia civilisational history, Chinese politics is imbued with and populated by consistent references to the past, to historical ideals and figures, and to the incredible achievements that successive Chinese dynasties had accomplished. As a contemporary nation-state and economic powerhouse, China offers a serious, albeit by no means exclusive and adversarial, alternative to the Western liberal democratic order – which, despite having continually served the West and its citizens in a largely functional manner, is increasingly riddled by problems and challenges of its own. The Chinese government, whilst by no means flawless and immune from criticism, is largely responsive to public needs, interests, and wills, without being directly elected at the highest levels by its citizenry. Some term this model of governance an instance of autocracy; others portray it as self-evident meritocracy.

Any talk of a holistic, independent China Model remains premature. Some scholars have termed the approach to governance instantiated in the country today a form of "directed improvisation" – directions are given from the top, with improvisation by mid-ranking and junior officials, as well as members of the private sector.[2] Others have characterised China's institutions as resilient in delivering *performance legitimacy*[3] – even in the absence of electoral democracy in the Western sense – in virtue of their ability to reflect public opinions and popular demands, whilst coopting opposition that is non-inimical to the political stability and continuity of the regime. One may not agree with the claim that these political practices are uniquely enduring, optimal, and applicable only to China. Indeed, one may not even see these interpretations as wholly reflective of how China works.

Yet what is hopefully fairly uncontroversial is the view that understanding China requires an appreciation of the lenses and values of its government, people, civil society, economy, and all stakeholders invested in the country's trajectory. China is not an enemy or a threat – it does not proactively export its governance model, for one. The international community, particularly the West, should ideally respect the diversity of governance systems that can flourish in the world – and the Chinese system is indeed just one amongst many.

Short of such respect, indeed, it is imperative that the world at least develop an accurate understanding of the governance system adopted by China, and its origins, rationale, and shortcomings, without being sidetracked by political quibbles and emotive rhetoric from all sides.

Where the West sees poles of power and spheres of influence, the Chinese sees elements within a continually evolving *tianxia* – an all-encompassing civilisational concept "under the Heaven", comprising self-governing, sovereign states underpinned by their own governance logics, yet economically and socially embedded within networks connecting them with China. China views global interconnectivity and autonomous governance not as mutually exclusive, antithetical poles, but as complementary forces – it is perhaps this worldview, too, that renders its actions and gestures often construed, and at times with good reason, as being economically expansionist. Yet such perceptions cannot be conflated with reality: China may act in an expansionist manner, but its interests remain deeply rooted in and is centred around the preservation of political unity and governmental stability in its own territory, as well as its own peaceful rise.[4] In our view, it is territorial integrity, not expansionism, that undergirds Chinese actions – both domestic and abroad.

For scoping purposes, this book will focus predominantly on China since Deng Xiaoping's announcement of "reform and opening-up" at the Third Plenum of the 11th Central Committee in 1978, to January 2025, which was when the second inauguration of President Donald Trump took place in the US.[5] The case for such focus is as follows: contemporary China's economic and social infrastructure was predominantly fomented and shaped through the era of rapid modernisation and liberalisation under Deng Xiaoping; whilst Mao Zedong certainly played a pivotal role in establishing the national ethos of modern China, the primary period in which contemporary China took form and shape remains the years since Deng's ascent to power. Pre-1980s periods will be referred to, both as a historical backdrop, and to contextualise and inform the world's understanding of incentives and rationale of contemporary actors today.

As for why the cut-off of 2025 was chosen, the logic is substantially simpler. The preparation of this manuscript took place in the first half of the 2020s, coinciding with a persisting rhetorical and theoretical drive to frame the Sino–US competition as a contest between "democracy" and "autocracy" by former US President Joe Biden. In the interregnum of almost four decades between 1978 and 2025, the Chinese government has continually undertaken reforms with the aims of accomplishing the dual objectives of improving governance efficiency and maximising economic dividends for its citizens – thereby aligning the interests of the ruling party and the public at large. With respect to the latter, a particular focus has been placed upon improving the lot of the people and to end poverty within the country.[6] Yet the country has also been riddled by a series of structural challenges and calamities – the most "obvious" ones being the slowing growth rates it experienced during COVID-19 and given a series of contentious economic decisions undertaken in the first half of the 2020s; the risks of over-isolationism in international trade and politics, the volatile relationship between state and private sector in the country, and the environmental and sustainability-related challenges that accompany its rise.

This book is evidently interested in a variety of questions, beyond unpacking the above quandaries concerning China's governance ethos and first principles. In Chapter 2, it delves into the structural causes and roots of China's rapid rise, as well as diagnosing the motivations that drive decision-makers and veto players in national, provincial, and local politics. China's extensive history, robust and diverse intellectual ideas, and entrenched emphasis upon the role of the academe and knowledge in driving its economic progress, will all be surveyed and considered as important tenets of its governing practice and methodology.

In Chapter 3, this book explores the internal strengths and weaknesses of Chinese governance, grappling with the measurement and evaluation of how China is performing across the multitude of dimensions tracking governmental competence. In Chapter 4, this book grapples with the question of how China is governed, dispelling and addressing existing misconceptions concerning its distinctive and complex system of governance.

In Chapter 5, the book delves into the implications and consequences of China's ascent for the world at large – the benefits, challenges, and prospective gains that China has and continues to offer the world. This chapter also offers an evidence-informed prognosis that seeks to identify the forces steering the country's growth in the short to medium-term, as well as its likely long-term trajectory, and proceeds to a discussion of how international perceptions of China have changed, especially in view of the country's precipitously trenchant foreign policy and the COVID-19 pandemic.

This section also briefly surveys China's interests and motives in its interactions with core regions and entities such as the Five Eyes Alliance, the European Union, the Association of Southeast Asian Nations (ASEAN), Africa, and the Middle East. Chapter 6 closes with recommendations and prescriptions on how states – especially those in the West, including the European Union – ought to engage with a country that encapsulates 20% of the world's population. Chapter 7 offers concluding reflections.

At critical times like these, it is all the more imperative that the world and China alike cultivate a sustainable, convivial, and successful set of working principles through which mutual interests can be enshrined – as opposed to confrontation and conflict. These principles will serve to hopefully address many of the perceptual and actual sources of tensions discussed in Chapter 7, as well as reflecting concerns and key interests from both China and the West.

We hence propose the following working principles in the international community's engagement with China. The hope is that with these principles, existing and future tensions can be adequately defused, with prospects for mutual benefit and collaboration identified and pursued. These foundational propositions should not be sidelined by entrenched ideological posturing. Instead, they ought to be continually debated and reflected upon – with inputs from all sides of the table and the world at large:

1. *There is more in common between China and other countries in the world – the West, particularly – than separates them.* Both China and the world at large are confronted by challenges ranging from public health crises, domestic and international terrorism, climate change, and the challenges posed by nascent technologies. It is precisely the embracing of these common and shared interests that the Chinese government has advanced the notion of a "community of shared future for mankind"[7] (人類命運共同體) – in full cognisance that in an era of globalisation, it would no longer be possible for national interests to be carved out and compartmentalised in narrow silos.
2. *China is "crossing the river whilst feeling the stones".*[8] Its actions and gestures should not be read as definitively embodying the intentional steps undertaken to accomplish a monolithic political vision. Understanding China requires us to appreciate both the successes and flaws of the present regime.
3. *Working with each other requires China and the West alike to see the world through the other's lenses – though this by no means implies acceding fully to the other's wants and needs.* Understanding China requires the rest of the world to get to grips with China's point of view, which cannot be accurately interpreted and understood through the lived experiences, analogies, and literature familiar to only the West.
4. *China should not be viewed as a state that seeks to become like the West – nor should it be reasonably expected to.* On the other hand, indeed, we must also guard against views and narratives that portray China as innately bound to exist in antithesis to the West (or reacted to in this light), whether it be out of nationalistic sentiments or skewed confidence in its own institutions. China has much to learn from the rest of the world too, a fact that Chinese leaders often express openly – and premature or overzealous jubilation at its successes could risk undercutting its government and people's ability to correct its mistakes and limitations.
5. *At the same time, whilst there exist fledgling contours of a China Model, the talk of a distinct China Model remains premature* – in interpreting China, there is an active need to return to the basics of incentives that drive its senior politicians, bureaucrats, burgeoning civil society and middle class, and its sizeable grassroots population. In seeking to make sense of how

China governs internally, it is equally important to note that China does not seek to export its model of governance.[9]

Only through empirically informed analysis delving into the country's institutions and people – drawing upon both culturalist and materialist lenses – can the world fully understand China today. China is not a threat. However, given its size, scale, and vast potential, its rise will inevitably generate challenges. In tackling and resolving these challenges *with* China, the international community, as a collective, improves and grows. An inter-civilisational dialogue between China and the world is not only an imperative for academics, but critical for world leaders and thinkers striving towards a more peaceful world.

Notes

1 World Bank (2024) The World Bank in China – Overview. Available at: https://www.worldbank.org/en/country/china/overview
2 Ang, Y.Y. (2022) *How China escaped the poverty trap*, Ithaca: Cornell University Press.
3 Yang, H. and Zhao, D. (2014) Performance legitimacy, state autonomy and China's economic miracle, *Journal of Contemporary China*, 24(91), pp. 64–82. doi: 10.1080/10670564.2014.918403.
4 Pathak, S. (2015) The "peace" in China's peaceful rise, *E-International Relations*. Available at: https://www.e-ir.info/2015/10/15/the-peace-in-chinas-peaceful-rise/#google_vignette
5 Vogel, E.F. (2013) *Deng Xiaoping and the transformation of China*, Cambridge, MA: The Belknap Press of Harvard University Press.
6 Huaxia (ed.) (2021) How China has lifted nearly 800 mln people out of poverty – xinhua | english.news.cn, *Xinhua*. Available at: https://web.archive.org/web/20241129135958/http://www.xinhuanet.com/english/2021-04/06/c_139862741.htm. Retrieved from Archived URL.
7 Shengchao, H.E.F. (2024) *Building a community with a shared future for mankind: A Chinese answer to a changing world*. Embassy of the People's Republic of China in the Federal Republic of Somalia. Available at: http://so.china-embassy.gov.cn/eng/zsgx_1/202403/t20240314_11260772.htm.
8 Mitter, R. and Johnson, E. (2021) What the west gets wrong about China, *Harvard Business Review*. Available at: https://hbr.org/2021/05/what-the-west-gets-wrong-about-china
9 Nair, C. (2020) America fears competition. It's time for a non-US led world order, *South China Morning Post*. Available at: https://www.scmp.com/week-asia/opinion/article/3104000/us-fears-competition-its-status-head-global-order-must-now-be; Reuters (2017) President Xi says China will not export its political system, *Reuters*. Available at: https://www.reuters.com/article/world/president-xi-says-china-will-not-export-its-political-system-idUSKBN1DV4UZ/; Wong, B. (2021) Why is China insisting it is a democracy? *The Diplomat*. Available at: https://thediplomat.com/2021/12/why-is-china-insisting-it-is-a-democracy/

2

CHINA'S RISE

Economic and political ascent

How are we to make sense of the bipolarity in popular narratives that China's rise is "inexorable", "astronomical", or – on the opposite end – "peaking" or "kneecapped"? To do so behoves us to have a fair and unbiased understanding of how the world has changed, where dominance by the West is decreasing as others rise and in this context how China has evolved over the past four decades. The following chapter seeks to explore the extent to which China has risen, as well as the underlying factors that enabled its astronomical expansion and growth as an economy and global power. China's rise can be observed and tracked across a multitude of areas – including but not limited to, the economic, the political, the military, and, finally, its global and international reach. As impressive as the country's achievements may be in these areas, key bottlenecks and obstacles remain – and pose serious concerns for policymakers and critical stakeholders alike.

2.1 Measuring China's rise

One could often hear the phrase "China is rising", or "China has risen". Yet it remains less than clear what this phrase in fact, specifically, *means*. China's *ascent* as global economic power and a regional military power is a multi-decade process, with its growth and surge straddling a multitude of spheres: the economic, the political, and the military.

Economically, China's rise should be interpreted contextually through the particular lenses of its economy's rapidly increasing pre-eminence in global industrial, investment, production, and consumption chains. China accounted for 1.6%[1] of global economic GDP in PPP terms in 1987, rising to 18.7% of

DOI: 10.4324/9781003643548-2

the world's GDP in 2023 (cf. Figure 2.1).[2] Between 1978 and 2005, the country maintained an average annual growth rate of 10%[3] – reaching a historic high of 15.2% in 1984 and relative low of 3.9% in 1990, for the period.[4]

The past four decades saw the national economy transition from a state-driven, Maoist planned economy to a hybrid economy that synthesises, through a delicate balance, sectors fuelled predominantly by private investment through de-regulated, laissez-faire systems of capital consolidation, and state-driven sectors of critical and strategic importance, in which protectionist and interventionist governmental policies play a more substantial role in steering industrial directions and strategies.[5] The total volume of inward flow of Foreign Direct Investment (FDI) in China increased by a factor of over 150 between 1983 ($916 million USD[6]) and 2022 ($189bn USD[7]), with particularly pronounced surges in the early 1990s – coinciding with the country's second wave of liberalisation and opening-up. China is now the second largest economy in the world in real GDP terms, and the first in PPP terms (overtaking the US in 2017).[8]

Whilst it is imperative that countries around the world address China's political ascent, valid questions can and indeed ought to be posed over how

FIGURE 2.1 China's share of global GDP, adjusted for PPP, from 1980 to 2023, with predicted trajectory until 2029.

Source: Textor, C. (2024) *China: Share of global gross domestic product 2029 | statista*, *Statista*. Available at: https://www.statista.com/statistics/270439/chinas-share-of-global-gross-domestic-product-gdp/

such a rise can be measured. It is easy to exaggerate China's global political influence, especially given the ideologically charged nature of contemporary debates. Yet fundamentally, China's rise as a regional or global political actor is perhaps best captured through two proxy indicators: its presence and participation in international and multilateral organisations, and the extent to which its government is supported and endorsed by its own (expanding) population.[9]

On the first, China substantially increased its formal and informal powers across multilateral institutions, in the decades that followed its economic opening-up. In 1977, China had belonged to 21 international organisations, though few Chinese nationals, if any, held significant sway in them. Deng's and Jiang Zemin's economic liberalisations saw China join international institutions such as the International Monetary Fund (IMF), Asian Development Bank, and the World Intellectual Property Organization.[10] Yet it was not until 2006, that the first Chinese national was elected to head a top-tier international organisation – Margaret Chan (HKSAR, China) was nominated and elected as Director-General of the World Health Organisation (WHO), a remarkable first. Between 2010 and 2024, China's vote share rose from 4.4% to 5.9% at the World Bank.[11] The country's financial contributions towards the United Nations (UN) have steadily increased over the same period, surpassing Japan in 2019 to become the second largest contributor to the UN budget, per a UN General Assembly resolution adopted in 2018.[12] This moment was touted by many as evidence of China's surging strength at the highest echelons of international institutional power – though domestic commentary has downplayed the significance of the numerical crossover.

China has accrued substantial influence as a global economic engine and powerhouse throughout the past decades, playing a pivotal role via its substantial interconnectivity with networks of natural resources, human capital, financial capital, and labour. In November 2012, in the aftermath of the 2008 economic recession, China surpassed the United States to become the world's largest trading nation in terms of the number of trade partners considering China as their largest trading partner. That number, as of 2023, stood at over 120.[13] China's focus on importing raw materials and parts, and exporting finished, high-end, or manufactured products has lent it a distinctive niche and edge as compared with counterparts with distinctly costlier factors of production – e.g., the United States.

As for the second, the Chinese government has continually entrenched its popularity and mass support amongst its population – through a combination of robust economic results and resounding sociocultural solidarity. An Ash Centre survey with results published in 2020[14] found that the overall level of satisfaction amongst citizens towards the central Chinese administration had increased from an average of 3.16 (out of 4) in 2003 to 3.31 and 3.3 in 2015 and 2016, respectively. Similar increases have been observed on the township and provincial levels, with an increase from 2.32 to 2.8 for the former between 2003 and 2016, and 2.89 and 3.1 for the latter.[15] The resilience and durability of the Chinese administration have increased substantially throughout the past decades – and were certainly amplified by the country's handling of the first two years of the pandemic.[16]

Finally, when it comes to the military, metrics of measuring strength ought to be multidimensional, encompassing not only considerations pertaining to expenditure, but also relative strength and scope of military influence. As a military power, China has progressively sought to streamline and specifically enhance its armed forces' capacities. Through substantial reductions in the number of actively enlisted personnel (from 3.9 million in 1985 to 2.7 million in 2018), the army significantly raised the volume of capital invested into each member of the active force.[17] The overarching strategy of Deng's and his successors' military reforms has been to improve working efficiency whilst minimising the volume of resources consumed by the army – despite the latter, the country's defence expenditure has steadily increased over the past 50 years, and it is now the second largest military spender in the world, second to only the United States – per unofficial estimates by Stockholm International Peace Research Institute (SIPRI), whilst the United States spent $916bn USD on the military in 2023, China's spending amounted to around $296bn USD (cf. Figure 2.2).[18]

With respect to maritime capacities, China launched its first aircraft carrier (*Liaoning*) in September 2012, with the second (*Shandong*) launched in 2017. From a largely continental and territory-centric approach to its military inherited from the days of Mao, the country has taken on a distinctively more outward-looking position in its foreign security projection – though claims that China is thereby a hegemonic actor seeking global dominance or projection are erroneously exaggerated: as of today, China has only one overseas naval base in Djibouti, with talk of potentially establishing a foothold in Cambodia, as compared with the US, which maintains nearly 800 bases in over 70 countries and territories.[19]

What the above demonstrates, therefore, is that China has risen across a multitude of facets. In 2020, the Chinese government declared that it had successfully eradicated extreme poverty – lifting hundreds of millions of its denizens out of the direst of circumstances.[20] It is tempting to reduce China's ascent to purely raw economic and materialist terms – yet doing so would neglect the substantial level of hard power and international strength, as well as the internal advancements to the livelihood of its citizens, that the country has accumulated over the years.

It also behoves actors seeking to understand China to contextualise the country's governance records and inadequacies in the context of its steep developmental curve – for a country whose GDP per capita has increased by almost 25-fold (from 1985 to 2025) across the last four decades,[21] whilst its

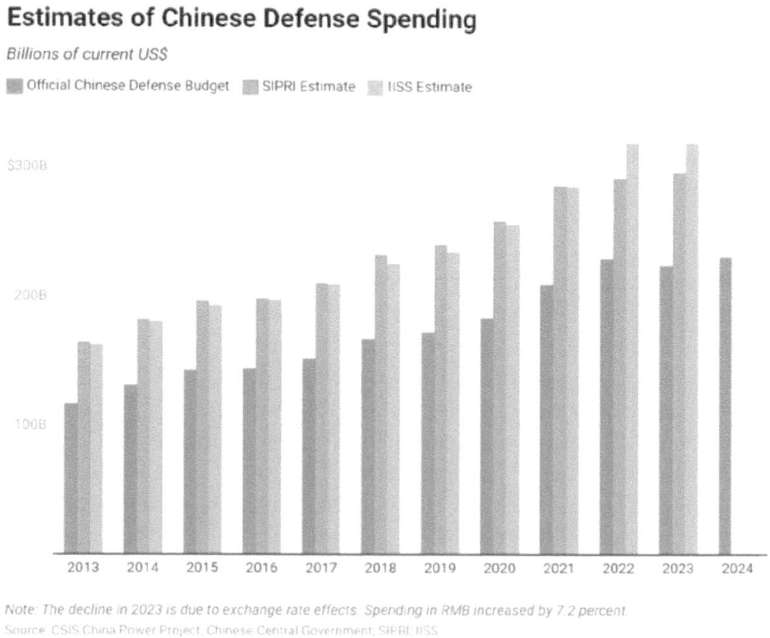

FIGURE 2.2 China's estimated defence spending over the past decade. The data is drawn from both official Chinese sources and the Stockholm International Peace Research Institute.

Source: Chinapower 2017 (2025) *What does China really spend on its military?*, *ChinaPower Project*. Available at: https://chinapower.csis.org/military-spending/

governance track record is by no means perfect, the numbers speak for themselves: China has come a long way.

2.2 Factors underpinning China's rise

What are the factors that could explain China's rise since the early 1980s? The following seeks not to provide an exhaustive list of accounts and hypotheses, but to instead outline the most significant explanations and variables for consideration.

2.2.1 Productivity-centred economic reforms and improvements

China's economic "miracle" – substantial growth, accelerated improvements to quality of life, and radical boost to capital stock and investment – was largely propelled by a series of productivity-centred economic reforms, undertaken with the objective of sustaining the country's contiguous growth. Chinese productivity increased at a paltry annual rate of 1.1% per year during 1953–1978, which rapidly tripled to 3.9% per year during 1979–1994, upon the introduction of market-centric reforms. By the early 1990s, productivity gains constituted over 50% of output growth, whilst the share contributed by capital dropped below 33%. To put this in perspective, the American productivity growth rate was only 0.4% per year during 1960–1989.[22]

Deng's market reforms spurred productivity[23] surges in three distinctive ways – first, through reforms that allowed producers to retain surplus profits gained from selling their products, they stimulated competition and innovation in rural collective enterprises and small, private, independent businesses (*getihus*). Second, in decentralising (especially during the 1980s) economic governance and relaxing controls over establishment and operations of business ventures, these reforms liberated businesses from the shackles of excess bureaucratism and statist interference. Finally, the relative liberalisation of internal capital markets within China enabled firms to raise funds – through borrowing (in the 1980s and 1990s) and, upon the establishment of stock exchanges, IPOs and partnering-up with foreign investors (in the late 1990s onwards) – to fund their long-term-oriented innovation and research. The upshot was – it was through qualitative improvements in ***human capital*** (labour) that China achieved its successes in the early days of the Opening-up and Reform Era.[24]

Admittedly, the past two decades have seen a gradual slowing to China's productivity growth – at least, as measured through conventional economic metrics. Between 1978 and 2022, China's Total Factor Productivity (TFP) saw a growth rate of 2.73% per annum, contributing almost 30% to its economic growth.[25] Yet further decomposition would find that China's average TFP growth rate had declined from a previous 4% in the 2000s to 1.8% in the 2010s. Some have rightfully raised concerns over a decelerated and unproductive Chinese economy.[26] Yet it is worth noting that in the last eight years (2016–2024) since the start of the trade war and other sanctions imposed by the Trump administration in 2017 and maintained by the Biden administration, China's GDP has grown by about 60% and in PPP terms by around 90%.[27]

In response to productivity bottlenecks, however, the incumbent administration has expounded the concept of "new quality productive forces", a form of "advanced productivity freed from the traditional economic growth mode and productivity development paths".[28] In practice, this would entail significant investments into and commitment towards the bolstering and development of China's cutting-edge technological sectors – especially industries that are artificial intelligence-centric or adjacent, including, but not limited to, quantum computing, advanced robotics, hybrid digital infrastructure, and renewable energy powered by AI research and large language models.

Recent years have seen Chinese firms emerge with exceptional breakthroughs in productivity and efficiency. In January 2025, a start-up hitherto unbeknownst to many in the world, DeepSeek, managed to accomplish what many of its counterparts and rivals in the West had accomplished – at a fraction of their costs. Whilst it would be premature and erroneous to portray China as having "won" or scored a victory in a purported Sino–American technological race, what remains relatively clear is the enduring tenacity and entrepreneurial creativity on the part of the private sector in China.[29] Indeed, it is such qualities that have enabled them to weather the systematic attempts to kneecap their rise through the introduction of restrictions on access to advanced semiconductors and related technologies, by the United States. Despite the best efforts to curb Chinese firms' ability to access frontier technologies, private actors on the ground have proven the adage time and time again: it would be a mistake to bet against Chinese ingenuity and determination, especially under substantial levels of stress. What is also noteworthy is that the new generation of tech entrepreneurs were invariably born, raised, and educated in China, a testament to the quality of education in leading universities such as Tsinghua and Zhejiang.

2.2.2 Intense and substantial investments into infrastructure

Productivity improvements have always mattered, yet by no means suffice in accounting for the miraculous transformations to China's economic performance. Indeed, whilst there apparently exist variations and differences over time, as well as nuances, a core engine of China's inexorable contemporary rise comprises its significant and intense investment into infrastructure – which precipitated the investment-led growth that it had experienced all the way from 1990s through to the 2000s.[30] China has benefited substantially from its state's intense and considerable infrastructural investments. The average Chinese citizen has experienced significant progress – especially over the past four decades – in spheres ranging from education, health, energy supply, housing, and sanitation to the opportunities to travel within and beyond the country. In particular, travel infrastructure has served as the backbone to the national government's ongoing quest to fully connect and embed the countryside, cities, and suburbs across provinces and national corridors within the cross-country transport networks.[31]

China's railway – the primary basis of long-distance transport within the country – has expanded considerably since the PRC's establishment in 1949. Estimates have placed this total length of China's railway network, as of 2023, at 159,000 km, second only in the world to the United States, whose railway network stood, as of 2019, at 220,044 km long.[32] The total length of the country's high-speed railway reached 45,000 km by the end of 2023.[33]

China spent up to 9% of its GDP on infrastructure in the 1990s and 2000s, which contributed substantially to the stimulation of economic growth, employment opportunities, and development of a robust and sophisticated network of capital (loaners, borrowers, and banks). Many have argued that China's willingness to expend substantial volumes on improving its internal infrastructure, has enabled the country to pull ahead of proximate rivals such as Brazil and India (there, infrastructural investment occupies no more than 2–5% of their national GDP).[34]

Infrastructural investments have served three pivotal functions in relation to China's developments – (1) in stimulating internal consumption and demand for resources and equipment within the country, (2) in advancing productivity and improvements to the production and distribution of goods and services (see Section 2.2.1), and, above all, (3) in creating employment opportunities for individuals with low- to mid-level education backgrounds.

With respect to (1), infrastructural investments have – through the multiplier effect – vastly enhanced the supply of capital and liquidity within the Chinese economy: firms and contractors who benefited from constructing such infrastructure, have in turn grown to act as primary engines of economic growth in the country, whether it be through the production and sale of consumer goods, importing and exporting of commodities related to construction, or, indeed, piggybacking off the enhanced interconnectivity between cities and the countryside to distribute a wider range of products. Additionally, enhancements to transportation have also facilitated rapid urbanisation and sub-urbanisation across large tracts of the country. This has in turn proven to be crucial in mobilising untapped human capital and transforming it into harnessable labour for the country's highly concentrated economic developments in the city. Indeed, the returns from investment into infrastructure have been broadly lucrative and promising – infrastructure investment's share of China's total fixed asset investment (in terms of value and net worth) has steadily increased over the years, from no more than 5% in 2007, to nearly 30% in 2019.[35]

The productivity boost through (2) is equally apparent. Advanced transportation networks enable the transfer of goods, services, and human capital at relatively efficient rates. Indeed, aviation traffic has expanded considerably in the country – China is currently the world's second largest and fastest growing aerospace and aviation services market – in 2019, the value of China's aviation industry output stood at $53.3 billion.[36] In 2009, passenger throughputs of all airports in China stood at 486 million;[37] in 2020, despite the then-ongoing COVID-19 pandemic, the number had risen to over 850 million passengers.[38] The substantial volume of passengers and air freight is pivotal in not only enshrining the country's status as a leading aviation hub in Asia and the world at large, but also in facilitating and expediting internal supply and consumption of goods within the country. The productivity gains from improved interconnectivity are likely to continually sustain China's ascent as an economic powerhouse – through the streamlining of supply chains, consolidation of human capital, and optimising exchanges in personnel and equipment within the country.

Finally, Chinese investments into infrastructure have created vast employment opportunities for millions in the country (3). Indeed, by 2017, a vast majority of employees in the construction industry in China were informally hired rural migrant workers – as opposed to urban workers with formal employment contracts (although concerns could and should be raised over the safety and legality of their employment conditions).[39] This proposition equally applies to beyond jobs in relation to construction and transportation. Infrastructural investment is hence clearly a significant pillar of China's economic expansion and growth.

As heralded by the Third Plenum in 2024, the Chinese state is keen to implement much-needed reform policies targeting investment into human capital. The focus on infrastructure enabling rural-to-urban migration, as well as prospective alterations to the hukou system in the country, point to a government that is keen to unleash the immense potential in urban workers who must currently grapple with the challenges of a dearth of legal (due to their possessing the "wrong" hukous for the cities where they work) and welfare protections for said workers.[40] Infrastructural investment does not solely take the form of hardware investment and refinement, but could also play out through "software upgrading" – namely, via investing intensely and strategically into refining and bolstering human capital, and thereby improving the quality of life and productivity of the country's workers. It is high time that observers recognised the shifting winds in investment and how such directions of travel could well shape the most investment- and capital-friendly industries in China, for the decades to come.

Observers of China should also consider how the state undertakes public financing[41] – in supporting its substantial state spending. The Chinese economic miracle succeeded without excessive dependence upon foreign debt, loans, and taxes, through a dexterous synthesis of creative central bank policy and prudent fiscal policies designed to prevent superfluous inflation. Per economist Jorgen Randers, the Chinese adopt a combination of high taxes (especially in urban centres and areas of relative economic development) and rigorously controlled monetary policies (e.g., printing money and quantitative easing) as means of financing its operations. The Chinese governmental model of financing prioritises delivering welfare improvements for the public, as opposed to generating dividends for private shareholders and capitalists, as its core objective. The emphasis is placed distinctly upon a creative and dynamic synthesis of bonds, loans, and production of new money in order to support state-owned enterprises and dominant private sector firms on their significant financial undertakings. As compared with alternatives – raising interest rates and taking on substantial national debt, this is certainly a relatively sustainable and risk-free approach to public financing, which nevertheless could only be adopted by states where public reluctance and resistance to monetary and capital controls is minimal.

2.2.3 Emphasis upon strategic, intense technological research

As wages appreciated during the late 2000s and throughout the 2010s – with, as a result, factories and firms relocating out of the country's increasingly expensive production ecosystem – the Chinese administration recognised that the productivity surplus the country had been banking on previously was no longer sufficient in attracting foreign capital and sustaining its export-driven economic trajectory. Hence, as a means of diversifying its sources of productivity growth, Beijing began investing heavily into technological research.

The country's technological ascent can be observed across two distinct dimensions: the *input factor* (e.g., how much it invests, governmentally or via civil society, into technological research), and the *output factor* (e.g., how much it produces, via research undertaken endogenously or overseas). In the 1980s and 1990s, China overhauled its Academy of Sciences to fund pre-commercial research conducted by independent, peer-reviewed academic experts drawn in from across the world, based in their own universities. Concurrently, through a mixture of compact high-tech zones and top-down bodies such as the National Natural Science Foundation and the State Key Laboratory programmes,[42] the Chinese government took to promulgating technological growth and expansion in advanced research in sectors of both strategic and nascent importance. Between 2003 and 2012, GDP expenditure on technological Research and Development rose from 1.1% to 2% per year;[43] by 2023, the figure reached 2.59% per year.[44] Beijing has worked closely with the private sector in funding its research – with 77% of total research expenditure in 2015 coming from private enterprises.

On the question of output – in 2009, China's share of the total number of patents filed worldwide was 17%; by 2019, it had leapt to 44% – with 89% amongst Chinese patent applications filed by residents, as opposed to non-residents.[45] Per Figure 2.3, China's office received more than twice the amount of patent applications received by the US in 2019. In 2023, China filed 69,610 patent applications, a small dent of 0.6% relative to the previous year. The United States came in at a respectable second, with 55,678 applications – a 5.3% drop on 2022. Despite American export bans and restrictions on Chinese tech companies, leading Chinese tech giants Huawei Technologies remained the top filer in the world by far, with 6,494 published patent applications in the year.[46]

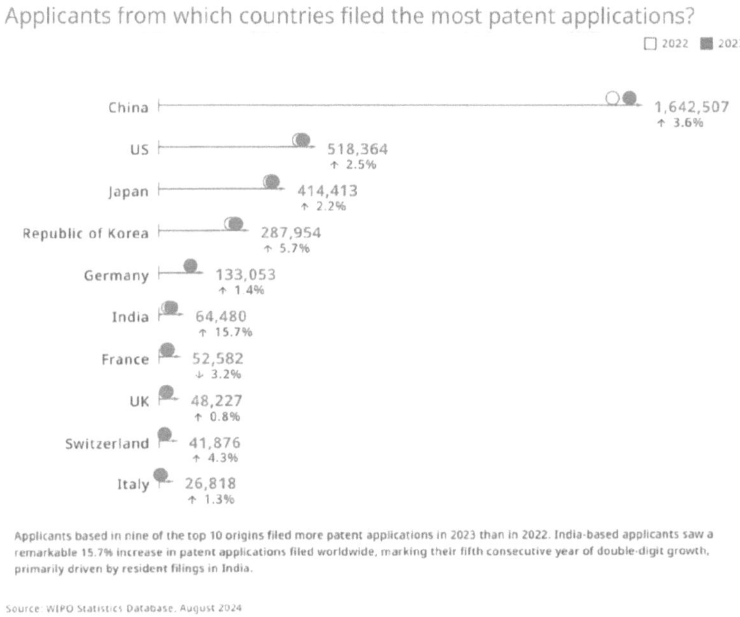

FIGURE 2.3 Top ten countries in the world by number of patent applications as of 2023.

Source: 陳平 (2012)「中國道路的本質和中國未來的選擇」，《經濟社會體制比較》Comparative Economic & Social Systems. Available at https://ias.ahu.edu.cn/_upload/article/files/d0/19/27ea340743ec9161ca1d5a956343/a7ff143c-af88-4a2c-8498-9fb2d6783a9c.pdf

Additionally, as an educational power, China has sought to play a constructive role in strengthening its exposure and access to top talents who had received their education abroad, in world-leading institutions. In truth, China has benefited hugely from waves of overseas "returnees" – individuals who had studied abroad and sought to return to and build in the country for a roster of reasons, including the job opportunities available, the hostility of foreign states' visa regimes and civil societies, and the slowing economic growth rates and stagnating quality of life in leading "alternatives", such as the United States and Europe. Indeed, the Chinese leadership's heavy emphasis upon technological breakthroughs in semiconductors, artificial intelligence, quantum computing and other forms of hard technology has plausibly played a pivotal role in driving the country's growth since the early 2000s.[47] Such breakthroughs were bolstered and reinforced by the streamlining of the industry-academia-research pipeline.

2.2.4 Distinctively communitarian, collectivist civic culture

Culturalist explanations argue that the successes of China can be attributed to the distinctive cultural mores and values adopted by its citizens. Senior Fellow at the Centre for New Political Economy at Fudan University Chen Ping posits that the Chinese emphasis upon discipline, compliance with the laws of the land, and deeply ingrained industriousness are pivotal factors that account for the country's economic rise.[48] Other voices have suggested the distinctive blend of materialist individualism and post-materialist, nationalist collectivism has acted as a critical coagulant that holds together the collective fabric of a society that has selectively and tactically embraced individualist ideals on matters of individual consumption, employment, career progress, and production – whilst concurrently acceding to the need for sacrifice *for the greater good.*

These culturally enshrined dispositions have played a critical role in ensuring widespread acceptance of governmental steering and policies amongst the country's population. Yet it had also lent normative legitimacy and credibility to the relatively high taxes levied by the Central Administration, as well as acceptance of national edicts and policies legislated in Beijing, implemented and prosecuted with a large degree of fealty by provincial and local governments. Yet such collectivism should not be conflated with Confucianism – whilst Confucian ideals and values have remained somewhat salient amongst the Chinese masses, the charge that the country's leadership and civil society are underpinned largely by Confucian thought is both overstated and anachronistic.[49]

Culturalist explanations are parsimonious and plausible – though a caveat must nevertheless be included: they are often difficult to falsify or establish empirically, largely as a result of the ambiguities involved in determining what counts as a valid indicator or reflection of a particular cultural "genome" or type. There exists innate underdetermination in terms of how one may interpret particular behavioural tropes; the Chinese could just as much be portrayed as "industrious", as be interpreted as simply "deferential to authority"[50] – both descriptions are equally supported by the (limited) empirical evidence that exists. Furthermore, the stark episodes of public backlash towards the draconian lockdowns implemented throughout 2022 are a reminder that even the most communitarian and publicly minded civic culture in the world has its limits – the fraternalism that binds Chinese society together, is also the very ethos that renders the public resistant towards the atomising, divisive measures implemented by regional authorities in their pursuit of "Zero-COVID".[51]

2.2.5 Long-termist political planning, stability, and coordinative efficiency

Whilst the case can be – at times – overstated, China is spearheaded by senior bureaucrats who regularly engage in long-termist planning, not just in economic terms, but also with respect to questions of political and institutional reforms. Economic policies are demarcated through five-year plans, which comprise blueprints that channel long-termist visions through short- to medium-term policy directives and decisions. More significantly, perhaps, since the end of the Cultural Revolution and Deng's ascent, China has placed substantially greater premium on the development of manageable, cogent, and practicable five-year plans, prioritising attainability over rhetorical flair or ideological zeal.[52]

Five-year plans are a pivotal element in Chinese governance. Since 1953, the Chinese administration has been regularly issuing "plans" on a five-year basis, shaping and moulding the country's economic policies and landscape through the regular plenums of the party's Central Committee – its highest-ranking decision-making organ. The party's senior leaders play a critical role in spearheading and overseeing the devising and construction of principles of development – directly and unambiguously setting growth targets, reforms, and policy targets for economic development.[53] Five-year plans enable the country to prioritise and cut through the silos in decision-making: rather than getting bogged down in endless, futile vacillations over policies, Chinese leaders engage in determinate and discrete decision-making – once the decision is made, the emphasis and focus of the bureaucracy shifts to expedient implementation of the consensus, as opposed to back-and-forth quibbling.

China's centralised planning is an anomaly amongst socialist economies – in that it readily incorporates elements of capitalistic economics, whilst ensuring that the state retains a firm grip over the institutional order and forces underpinning the economy. To dichotomously label China as either "socialist" or "capitalist" hence does no justice to the country – the government operates as a state-driven, socialist economy with capitalistic influences, where the degree of marketisation depends heavily upon the context and objectives by which the state's planning processes are driven. The involvement of skilled technocrats and experienced bureaucrats in the planning process ensures that the visions developed are not undermined by ideological overreach or untenable, dogmatic thinking. Such planning[54] also renders China comparatively more coordinatively efficient and responsive from a macroscopic point-of-view, whether it be in grappling with emerging crises and threats to the country's economic growth (e.g., the rising wages and dangers of inflation in the early 2000s; the slowing growth in the three years between 1989 and 1992), or in directing the country's substantial population in herculean economic endeavours.

The presence of a heavy-handed state, steering and spearheading institutions of change and reform, has been pivotal in ensuring that Chinese planning is both continued and contiguous. Now, some critics have pointed out that Chinese leaders remain susceptible to short-termist incentives – e.g., when it comes to the country's opting to deprioritise environmental protection in exchange for economic growth, or the state's inability to curtail spontaneous eruption of nationalistic sentiments that have threatened to derail its foreign policy.[55] Such criticisms are nevertheless misguided – the claim that China engages in long-term planning (somewhat successfully) is not akin to the postulation that Chinese officials and politicians do not engage in *any* short-term correctional or adaptive policymaking. Nor is it to say that Chinese leaders are flawless, meticulous executors who could never err. The bar for determining whether long-term planning in fact succeeds, ought not to be infeasibly demanding.

The question of freedom of speech is oft cited as a criticism of how China is governed. Certain viewpoints posit that China – as a country – practises substantial censorship, and that such censorship poses a fundamental threat to the country's ability to thrive as a creative, open, and amenable economy in attracting foreign talents. Additionally, the room for public dissent and criticisms of the government is also vastly constricted; critics of regime are occasionally prosecuted and imprisoned for their alleged sowing of "civil unrest".

Much of such critique has some grain of truth to it – speech is indeed curtailed and regulated, specifically across public spaces (e.g., online forums, streets, government billboards and communications, and mass media), where official censors often police and eliminate discourses deemed to be at odds with the objectives of "national stability" and "harmony". Censorship – both official and unofficial (enacted through chilling effect and self-censorship) – is indeed a ubiquitous phenomenon in China, especially as compared with certain liberal democratic states in Europe and North America.

It is nevertheless imperative that we consider the question of censorship in light of the wider contextual and country-specific considerations underpinning the administration's tight grip over public discourse (private discourse, on the other hand, is neither inhibited nor curbed through official regulations). For countries with population sizes and geographical spreads as vast and substantial as China's, the perils of fake news and misinformation cannot be overstated. This adage particularly holds for China, where hyper-nationalistic, jingoistic, and populist discourses, if amplified by an absolutely unfettered discursive/media space and social media platforms, could well induce highly undesirable policies from the governing politicians, posing substantial volatility and uncertainty for not only the country's 1.4-bn-strong population but also its surrounding neighbours.

Dissent and criticism of the state are – apparently, per above – curtailed. Yet this does not quite render it thereby impossible to criticise governmental policies, especially if decoupled from a fundamentalist and structural rebuking of the governing authority and legitimacy of the Communist Party of China. Leaders, administrators, politicians can be criticised, but such criticisms must necessarily invoke imagery, symbolism, and discourses that are accepted and deemed as publicly acceptable by the party. As noted by Kevin O'Brien and Li Lianjiang, "rightful resistance"[56] – a form of dissenting politics rooted in critiquing local and municipal officials whilst co-opting and adhering to the lines of the central authorities – has been an effective model of opposition embraced by civilians and Chinese civil society. Indeed, the partially co-opted Chinese civil society has thrived despite the constraints and restrictions upon speech and political organisation at large.

2.2.6 Effective population management policies

The Chinese government has – historically, since the 1980s – sought to reduce the country's dependency ratio, which denotes the ratio of individuals who are either too young or too old to work, to those of working age. This was achieved largely through the One Child Policy, which by and large curbed population growth rates and significantly constrained the pace at which the Chinese population expanded; administrators deemed this necessary as a means of uplifting average quality of life and preventing infrastructural overload. With dwindling numbers of new-borns, China's dependency ratio hence reached a historic low between 2005 and 2017, dropping to levels below 40%. The concentration and high proportion of working-age adults in the country have been credited as features that have rendered China economically competitive and lucrative for foreign investors and firms, looking to set up shop in the country.

China's dependency ratio has nevertheless steadily increased since 2017, as a growing problem of old-age dependency emerges, induced by improvements in average lifespan and the demographic "deficit" amongst working-age adults. How China copes with its demographic challenges; whether the declining birth rates will prove to be a catalyst for China's transition into an advanced, high-income economy, or a setback to its labour productivity, remains to be seen. With that said, the increasing emphasis placed upon stimulating consumption and developing a tenable inner circulation (內循環)[57] – a natural process and stage undergone by all nations that have successfully lifted a vast majority of their population from extremely low incomes to mid-incomes could well be a tenable path forward for China – for it would render the economy less dependent upon production or exports, and increasingly driven by consumption that is more easily and expediently recycled through the circular flow of liquidity in the economy.

2.3 China's rise as revival?

To conclude this section, a question must necessarily be asked: should the world view China's ascent as a "rise", or should its ascent instead be viewed through the lenses of a "revival", as argued by those who posit that the global community must couple the world's reading of China's current trajectory with an appreciation of its historical developments in the past?

China's economy was estimated to be the largest in the world in the period spanning the 15th century through to the early 19th century.[58] China had remained a leading cradle of commerce, technological innovation, and culture, throughout a vast majority of the past two millennia. It was not until the final decades of the 19th century that China was overtaken by the United States. Hence it is understandable that some would portray China's recent decades of economic growth as a "revival" or "restoration".

Indeed, the present Chinese state also tends towards narrating its own accomplishments and objectives through civilisational lenses – for one, the emphasis upon environmental sustainability, as articulated through the concept of ecological civilisation, is rooted in ancient Daoist thought that revered nature and wildlife. Alternatively, Xi Jinping's vision of a Global Civilization Initiative speaks volumes to the country's desire to share the fruits of its ancient wisdom with the contemporary world, disseminating – but not forcefully exporting – concepts that have been tried and tested for tens of centuries in the country's past.[59] This book shall withhold normative judgement on the matter – though it is indeed noteworthy that such thinking has become increasingly prominent amongst Chinese nationals and leaders, and is likely to play a pivotal role in steering how the Chinese public views and reacts to the world at large. Whether such exuberant sentiments evolve into a virulent form of revanchism – or a constructive force for China's peaceful co-existence, is a question over which all must reflect and contemplate carefully.

Notes

1 All figures in this book have been rounded to 3 s.f
2 Textor, C. (2024) China: Share of global gross domestic product 2029 | statista, *Statista*. Available at: https://www.statista.com/statistics/270439/chinas-share-of-global-gross-domestic-product-gdp/
3 World Bank Open Data (2023) GDP growth (annual %) – China. Available at: https://data.worldbank.org/indicator/NY.GDP.MKTP.KD.ZG?locations=CN
4 World Bank Open Data (2023) GDP growth (annual %) – China. Available at: https://data.worldbank.org/indicator/NY.GDP.MKTP.KD.ZG?locations=CN
5 Mitter, R. and Bayrasli, E. (2021) *The communist party of China at 100: By Rana Mitter & Elmira bayrasli*, Project Syndicate. Available at: https://www.project-syndicate.org/podcasts/the-communist-party-of-china-at-100
6 Davies, K. (2013) *China investment policy: An update*, OECD Working Papers on International Investment, 2013/01, OECD Publishing. http://dx.doi.org/10.1787/5k469l1hmvbt-en

7 Ministry of Commerce of the People's Republic of China (2023) Statistical bulletin of FDI in China. Available at: https://fdi.mofcom.gov.cn/resource/pdf/2024/03/14/564085296c88430c98e426696f3751e1.pdf
8 Xu, N. (2021) China's 2020 GDP means it will overtake U.S. as World's no. 1 economy sooner than expected, *Fortune*. Available at: https://fortune.com/2021/01/18/chinas-2020-gdp-world-no-1-economy-us/
9 Cunningham, E., Saich, T. and Turiel, J. (2020) Understanding CCP resilience: Surveying Chinese public opinion through time. Available at: https://ash.harvard.edu/wp-content/uploads/2024/02/final_policy_brief_7.6.2020.pdf
10 Huang, Y., Kurlantzick, J. and O'Neill, S. (2025) *China's Approach to Global Governance*, Council on Foreign Relations. Available at: https://www.cfr.org/china-global-governance/
11 Wroughton, L. (2010) China gains clout in world bank vote shift | Reuters, *Reuters*. Available at: https://www.reuters.com/article/us-worldbank-idUSTRE63O1RQ20100425/
Group, W.B. (2025) IBRD top 8 countries voting power – WBG finances one. Available at: https://financesone.worldbank.org/ibrd-top-8-countries-voting-power/DS01463
12 The State Council Information Office, PRC. (2018) China rises to 2nd largest contributor to UN budget. Available at: http://english.scio.gov.cn/internationalexchanges/2018-12/24/content_74308296.htm
13 China Briefing (2013) China passes U.S. to become world's largest trading nation, *China Briefing News*. Available at: https://www.china-briefing.com/news/china-becomes-worlds-largest-trading-nation-passes-u-s/
Green, M.A. (2023) China is the top trading partner to more than 120 countries, *Wilson Center*. Available at: https://www.wilsoncenter.org/blog-post/china-top-trading-partner-more-120-countries
14 Harsha, D. (2020) Long-term survey reveals Chinese government satisfaction, *Harvard Gazette*. Available at: https://news.harvard.edu/gazette/story/2020/07/long-term-survey-reveals-chinese-government-satisfaction/
15 Cunningham, E., Saich, T. and Turiel, J. (2020) Understanding CCP resilience: Surveying Chinese public opinion through time. Available at: https://ash.harvard.edu/wp-content/uploads/2024/02/final_policy_brief_7.6.2020.pdf
16 Wong, B. (2020) How Chinese nationalism is changing – The diplomat. Available at: https://thediplomat.com/2020/05/how-chinese-nationalism-is-changing/
17 Huisken, R. (ed.) (2009) *Rising china: Power and reassurance*, The Australian National University. Available at: http://dspace.cus.ac.in/jspui/bitstream/1/5539/1/Rising China Power and Reassurance.pdf
18 Tien, N. *et al.* (2024) *Trends in World Military Expenditure, 2023*, SIPRI Factsheet. Available at: https://www.sipri.org/sites/default/files/2024-04/2404_fs_milex_2023.pdf
19 Wang, H. and Beauchamp-Mustafaga, N. (2024) The threat from overseas Chinese military bases is overblown – The diplomat. Available at: https://thediplomat.com/2024/07/the-threat-from-overseas-chinese-military-bases-is-overblown/
20 Marques, C.F. (2020) China scores big against poverty but the poor haven't gone away, *NDTV Profit*. Available at: https://www.ndtvprofit.com/gadfly/xi-jinping-scores-big-against-extreme-poverty-but-china-still-has-its-poor
21 *GDP (constant 2015 US$)* (2024) World bank open data. Available at: https://data.worldbank.org/indicator/NY.GDP.MKTP.KD?locations=CN
22 Khan, M.S. and Hu, Z. (1997) *Economic issues 8 – why is China growing so fast?* International Monetary Fund. Available at: https://www.imf.org/external/pubs/ft/issues8/index.htm

23 This report takes productivity to denote the volume of output per man-hour. Khan, M.S. and Hu, Z. (1997) *Economic issues 8 – why is China growing so fast?* International Monetary Fund. Available at: https://www.imf.org/external/pubs/ft/issues8/index.htm; Ee, K.H., Poonpatpibul, C., Wenlong, L., Yong, F.S., Xinyi, S.L., Xinke, T., and Ekapirak, T. (2019) *China's reform and opening-up: Experiences, prospects, and implications for ASEAN,* ASEAN Macroeconomic Research Office. Available at: https://www.amro-asia.org/wp-content/uploads/2019/11/Chinas-Reform-and-Opening-Up_compressed.pdf
24 Deng, Y., Li, X. and Ye, A. (2024) *Research on total factor productivity in China's economic growth since the reform and opening-up*, EUDL. Available at: https://eudl.eu/doi/10.4108/eai.29-3-2024.2347395
25 Liu, Q. (2024) Total factor productivity growth a telling metric, *Chinadaily.com.cn*. Available at: https://www.chinadaily.com.cn/a/202408/05/WS66b02694a3104e74fddb86a6.html
26 Gaofeng Advisory Company Analysis – China's transformation over eight years from 2016 to 2024.
27 The State Council, The People's Republic of China (2024) China unleashes new quality productive forces in push for reform, innovation. Available at: https://english.www.gov.cn/news/202406/25/content_WS667a2943c6d0868f4e8e8835.html
28 Liu, J.Z.Y. (2025) *Deepseek and u.s.-china AI competition w/ Brian Wong – U.S.-China perception monitor*, U.S.-China Perception Monitor – Bridging the Pacific. Available at: https://uscnpm.org/2025/03/04/deepseek-and-us-china-ai-competition-w-brian-wong/
29 Yale University Press (2025a) *Trade wars are class wars*, Yale University Press. Available at: https://yalebooks.yale.edu/book/9780300261448/trade-wars-are-class-wars/
30 Ratings, M. (6667) Infrastructure investment will play a key role in China's economic recovery, *FinanceAsia*. Available at: https://www.financeasia.com/article/infrastructure-investment-will-play-a-key-role-in-chinas-economic-recovery/465372
31 World Population Review (2025) Railroads by country 2025. Available at: https://worldpopulationreview.com/country-rankings/railroads-by-country
32 The State Council Information Office of the People's Republic of China. (2024) China's operating high-speed railway hits 45,000 km. Available at: http://english.scio.gov.cn/chinavoices/2024-01/09/content_116928609.htm
33 Firzli, M.N. (2011) Infrastructure investments in an age of austerity, *OpEd News*. Available at: https://www.opednews.com/populum/page.php?f=Infrastructure-Investments-by-M-Nicolas-Firzli-110807-769.html
34 Ratings, M. (6667a) Infrastructure investment will play a key role in China's economic recovery, *FinanceAsia*. Available at: https://www.financeasia.com/article/infrastructure-investment-will-play-a-key-role-in-chinas-economic-recovery/465372
35 (2023) China – aviation, International Trade Administration | Trade.gov. Available at: https://www.trade.gov/country-commercial-guides/china-aviation
36 World Bank Open Data (2021) Air Transport, passengers carried. Available at: https://data.worldbank.org/indicator/IS.AIR.PSGR
37 China.org.cn. (2021) 27 airports report passenger throughput over 10m in 2020. Available at: http://www.china.org.cn/business/2021-04/14/content_77404626.htm
38 China Labour Bulletin (2019) Understanding and resolving the fundamental problems in China's construction industry. Available at: https://clb.org.hk/

content/understanding-and-resolving-fundamental-problems-china%E2%80%99s-construction-industry

39 DBS (2024) China: The 3rd plenum – deepening reform. Available at: https://www.dbs.com.hk/private-banking/aics/economics/templatedata/article/generic/data/en/GR/072024/240723_insights_china.xml

40 Hong, Y.-H. and Man, J.Y. (2011) China's local public finance in transition. Available at: https://www.lincolninst.edu/sites/default/files/pubfiles/chinas-local-public-finance-in-transition-chp.pdf
Wang, S. and Lou, J. (2008) *Public finance in China : Reform and growth for a harmonious society*. Open Knowledge Repository. Available at: https://openknowledge.worldbank.org/handle/10986/6360

41 王作跃 (2007) 近现代中国科技史研究：历史、现状与展望 *The Chinese Journal for the History of Science and Technology*, 28(4). Available at: https://www.cpp.edu/faculty/zywang/documents/wangchina2007.pdf

42 Schlegel, F., Schneegans, S. and Erocal, D. (2015) *Unesco science report towards 2030*. Unesco. Available at: https://web.archive.org/web/20171010135440/http:/unesdoc.unesco.org/images/0023/002354/235406e.pdf (Retrieved from Archives).

43 The State Council The People's Republic of China (2024) China's R&D expenditure exceeds 3.3 trln yuan in 2023. Available at: https://english.www.gov.cn/news/202403/05/content_WS65e6ff4dc6d0868f4e8e4b66.html (~USD459bn expenditure/USD17.7trn total GDP).

44 World Intellectual Property Organization (2020) *World intellectual property indicators 2020*, Geneva: World Intellectual Property Organization. Available at: https://www.wipo.int/edocs/pubdocs/en/wipo_pub_941_2020.pdf

45 Wininger, A. (2024) China international patent filings down 0.6% in 2023 but maintains lead as top filer, *China IP Law Update*. Available at: https://www.chinaiplawupdate.com/2024/03/china-international-patent-filings-down-0-6-in-2023-but-maintains-lead-as-top-filer/

46 Li, Y. (2018) Understanding China's technological rise, *The Diplomat*. Available at: https://thediplomat.com/2018/08/understanding-chinas-technological-rise/

47 WIPO (2024) Global IP filing activity in 2023. Available at: https://www.wipo.int/en/ipfactsandfigures/patents

48 Shi, T. (2020) *The cultural logic of politics in mainland China and Taiwan*, Cambridge: Cambridge University Press. Available at: https://ir101.co.uk/wp-content/uploads/2018/11/shi-the-cultural-logic-of-politics-in-mainland-china-and-taiwan-compressed.pdf

49 Crane, S. (2018) Why Xi Jinping's China is Legalist, not Confucian, *China Channel*. Available at: https://chinachannel.lareviewofbooks.org/2018/06/29/legalism/

50 Almond, G.A. and Verba, S. (1963) *The civic culture: Political attitudes and democracy in five nations*. Princeton University Press. Available at: http://www.jstor.org/stable/j.ctt183pnr2

51 Tone, S. (2022) Shanghai sets new 'zero-COVID' target, plans to reopen schools, *#SixthTone*. Available at: https://www.sixthtone.com/news/1010334/shanghai-sets-new-zero-covid-target%2C-plans-to-reopen-schools

52 Zhao, J. (2017) What can we learn from China's long-term national plans?, *China US Focus*. Available at: https://www.chinausfocus.com/society-culture/what-can-we-learn-from-chinas-long-term-national-plans

53 The Economist (2021) What is China's five-Year plan?. Available at: https://www.economist.com/the-economist-explains/2021/03/04/what-is-chinas-five-year-plan

54 Huang, H. and Arranz, A. (2020) Visual explainer: China's five-Year plans, *South China Morning Post.* Available at: https://multimedia.scmp.com/infographics/news/china/article/3085903/china-five-year-plans/index.html
55 Skidmore, D. (2019) China's reputation for long-range planning is wildly exaggerated, *The Diplomat.* Available at: https://thediplomat.com/2019/03/chinas-reputation-for-long-range-planning-is-wildly-exaggerated/
56 O'Brien, K.J. (1996) Rightful resistance, *World Politics*, 49(1), pp. 31–55. http://www.jstor.org/stable/25053988
57 Chernyak, M. (2020) Weekly investment update – 12 August 2020, *BNP Paribas.* Available at: https://www.bnpparibas-am.com/en-hk/intermediaries/front-of-mind/weekly-investment-update-12-august-2020/
58 Cox, W. (2015) 500 years of GDP: A tale of two countries, 500 Years of GDP: A tale of two Countries | Newgeography.com. Available at: https://www.newgeography.com/content/005050-500-years-gdp-a-tale-two-countries#:~:text=1500%3A%20In%201500%2C%20China%20was,GDP's%20of%20approximately%20%24100%20billion
59 The State Council Information Office of the People's Republic of China (2024) 3 things to know about China's global civilization initiative. Available at: http://english.scio.gov.cn/in-depth/2024-04/03/content_117103205.htm

3

THE PRESENT

On China's actual strengths, weaknesses, opportunities, and challenges

Understanding China today is no mean task. It cannot be accomplished in full within tens or even hundreds of pages. The following hence seeks not to be an exhaustive survey of China's current state of affairs, but instead only a cursory elucidation of its strengths, weakness, opportunities, and challenges.

The upshot of the following should be clear – China is indubitably an ascendant major power that the world should reckon with seriously, yet over-hyping its capacities and ambitions in taking over the world and superseding existing powers, would neither be in the interest of genuinely accurate analysis, nor be in alignment with the interests of parties who would benefit from engaging, liaising, and organically negotiating with China.

3.1 Economics

The Chinese economy is the largest economy in the world by GDP (purchasing power parity, PPP) in 2024, and the second largest in nominal GDP terms. Yet its GDP per capita remains modest – 68th in nominal terms, and 73rd in PPP terms.[1] There remains a reasonable distance between China and many of its global strategic counterparts and rivals, when it comes to its per capita GDP. With a population of over 1.4bn, the state's economy remains dominated by state-owned and mixed-ownership enterprises. Out of the top 100 listed firms in China, over 48.4% of China's market capital went to state-owned enterprises and 12.6% to mixed-ownership enterprises, as of June 2023. The proportion of non-public enterprises in the top 100 has correspondingly shrunken from the peak of 55.4% in June 2021 to 39.0% in June 2023.[2]

DOI: 10.4324/9781003643548-3

The Chinese workforce is now increasingly concentrated in the service sector, with 48.1% of its labour force working in the services industry as of 2023; in the same year, 29.1% of the workforce works in industry, whilst 22.8% works in agriculture.[3] With that said, the service sector remains low-priced, precarious, and susceptible to market volatility and shocks in many locations – it would be premature to conclude that services are now the primary promulgating factor behind China's continued economic growth. The renewed interest in advanced manufacturing under the incumbent leadership has seen a shift towards particular sectors of key strategic importance in the "green economy" and renewable energy transition – such as electric vehicles, photovoltaic cells (solar panels), and lithium batteries.

Indeed, these have become archetypally definitive components of China's new industrial strategy – as encapsulated by the "Made in China 2025" vision set forth by the government in 2015, which advocated that Beijing must achieve key breakthroughs in ten sectors: advanced information technologies, automation in robotics and tool usage, aerospace equipment, maritime equipment and high-tech shipping, railway modernisation, electric vehicles, power equipment, agricultural equipment, new materials, and bio-pharma and medical technological innovation.[4] In cohering with this overarching vision, the country has largely transitioned out of a primary sector-driven economic model, into one propelled predominantly by a mixture of trade and high-end services in urban areas, and heavy industry in rural areas.[5]

As it stands, state-owned enterprises play a critical role in not only boosting economic output, but also to create jobs, redistribute incomes, and spread economic activities throughout the country – including, of course, to areas where firms in the private market lack inherent incentives to serve or set up business. As we shall come to see, however, the predominance of state-owned enterprises may not necessarily always work to the interest of the Chinese state – and there have been progressive efforts adopted by senior Chinese leaders in spurring more competitive innovation and robust accountability on the part of state-owned and -backed firms. Indeed, the 2024 Central Economic Work Conference mentioned cracking down on "involution-style competition" – a much-needed and long-overdue effort to rein in the tendencies of select state-affiliated enterprises to pour most of their resources into singular industries, at the expense of their marginal productivity and the overarching balance of the economy.[6]

3.1.1 Strengths and opportunities

There are several distinctive strengths undergirding the Chinese economy that have enabled it to grow at very high rates over the past two decades – and continue to do so, albeit at a reduced and slowing pace, as of the early 2020s.

As sources of opportunities and openings for the country's future development, these strengths must be taken seriously – they include:

3.1.1.1 *Substantial and objective-oriented public spending*

The Chinese government allocates a substantial volume of its budget to targeted public spending. The ratio of government expenditure to GDP has increased between 2014 and 2021, rising from 29% seven years ago to an estimated 36% in 2021.[7] Whilst this could in part be attributed to the slowing GDP growth rates and the stickiness of state budgets, it should also be recognised that the Chinese state remains relatively proactive in its fiscal and spending policies, with a particular emphasis placed upon securing objectives such as poverty relief and inequality amelioration.

With respect to the former, the Chinese state spent 384bn yuan ($57.7bn USD in 2017 terms) between 2016 and 2019 to alleviate poverty; in late 2020, President Xi Jinping declared that between 2013 and 2020, nearly 100 million Chinese had been lifted out of poverty.[8]

One may ask – how does poverty relief exemplify economic strength? The answer has much to do with China's pro-poor development model since the early 2010s – one that prizes and focuses significantly on poverty alleviation (more precisely, as a part of Xi Jinping's approach to economic and developmental governance).

The more detailed answer is threefold – the first is that if economic strength is to be taken as tracking more than solely the gross GDP and net growth of a state, then the amelioration of inequality should and must count as a significant indicator in the appraisal of economic wherewithal and strength; the second is that through uplifting millions from poverty, the Chinese state in turn has embarked upon a path towards a genuinely middle-class society – a society where, nominally, no one lives under an absolute poverty line; finally, and from the second point here, the elimination of poverty would be instrumentally important in reducing the burdens on China's social welfare system, as well as facilitating the sustaining of a vibrant middle class, even in third- or fourth-tier cities and the countryside.

More fundamentally, China's successful campaign against poverty highlights that its public spending is hyper-efficiently targeted and aimed at providing genuine solutions to pressing problems. There may well be setbacks, but the concentration and focussing of resources instrumentally enables China to withstand economic contingencies and short-term market shocks. To put things into perspective (and to ground the above), in 2020, China spent 13% of its expenditure/budget on social welfare (e.g., transfer payments, social security, support for the poor, sick, unemployed, and pensioners)[9] – by no means a figure that stands out as compared with other states. Yet what sets China from other capitalist economies, is its heavy emphasis upon government, as compared with private, consumption of goods and services – during the 2010s, 70%–80% of the annual budget was allocated to purchasing goods and services.[10]

3.1.1.2 Embeddedness within global supply chains

China has also risen to become the most important component in most global supply chains. China remains the top sourcing location amongst Western producers, with 77% and 80% of US-based and Europe-based companies listing China as one of their top-three sourcing countries in 2021. Whilst this indeed marked a decline from the 96% and 100% in 2019,[11] it should be noted that such a decline stemmed less necessarily from fundamental changes to the Chinese economic infrastructure, and more from a mixture of the pandemic and the geopolitical flare-ups that have taken the world over the past two years.

Whilst China's share in backward Global Value Chain (GVC) linkages (e.g., the share of commodity and primary resource supplied to firms abroad) has indeed declined over recent years, especially between 2005 and 2015, its forward GVC linkages (e.g., the share of processing- and production-related value creation for firms abroad) have risen considerably during the same period. This suggests that China is shifting increasingly away from merely providing merchants and firms with raw materials and primary sector labour, towards higher value-added activities that enhance the country's ability to ascend the value chain ladder.[12]

In particular, China remains heavily integrated in supply chains in Asia. As compared with other regions, Asia has grown to be an increasingly important – indeed, the primary – trade and economic partner for China. The rise of regional trade agreements between China and its Asian-Pacific counterparts – such as the Regional Comprehensive Economic Partnership (RCEP) – has been instrumental in embedding China within the supply chains of many leading economies in the region, thereby consolidating its status as a leading supplier and production economy in the world.

Of course, there are challenges that must be acknowledged. China's stringent and dogmatic lockdowns at the beginning of 2022 – in response to the Omicron wave– had generated a substantial congestion-cum-bottleneck across many of its most prominent port cities, including Shanghai amongst them. Countries around the world are reassessing the extent to which they can justifiably and rationally continue to depend on China, with some calling for strategic reduction in dependence and others even adamantly recommending "de-risking" or partial decoupling from China. The Russian war in Ukraine and the ongoing war in Gaza have accelerated the pushes for "friend-shoring" and "near-shoring" by Western politicians and companies.

Yet much of such talk remains easier said than done – China's integral positioning within supply chains would take years, if not decades, to supplant and wean off; in the meanwhilst, it is likely that subsequent to the pandemic and given its sluggish pace economic recovery, Beijing would adopt more aggressive and proactive reforms to its supply chains policies, in ways that enhances its attractiveness to firms and producers heavily invested in advanced manufacturing. Hence the talk of decoupling from China remains fundamentally vacuous and exaggerated, backed by little on-the-ground evidence.[13]

Some observers may be rightfully concerned by the implications of the return of Donald J Trump to the White House for his second term. Since his second inauguration, Trump has rolled out a slew of deeply erratic and damaging protectionist measures targeting not just China, but also key trade partners with which the US experiences a negative trade deficit, such as Mexico, Canada, and India. Such moves have been touted by some to be cataclysmically destructive for China, which had long been dependent upon export-led growth as a core pillar of its national strategy. The imposition of stiff tariffs by Trump on a large number of countries has not only fuelled the persistently high inflation on the ground in the US – thereby contributing towards more obstinate-than-usual interest rates on the Fed – but also worries that China would be susceptible to the involuntary and haphazardly imposed trade decoupling under the American leader.[14]

Such worries are nevertheless overblown. Being actively aware of the American stated objective to contain China, policymakers have had several years to adjust and prepare. In response to Trump, Beijing has adopted a proactively pro-trade and pro-business foreign and economic policy, extending a substantive olive branch to countries such as India and Japan, which are of crucial geo-strategic and commercial significance to China, as key importers of Chinese goods.[15] As it turns out, the best antidote to the capricious and uncanny erraticism of Trump, is for China to solidify trade and supply chain ties with more receptive partners – both current and receptive.

3.1.1.3 *Mutually beneficial economic presence in developing countries – the Belt and Road Initiative, the Asian Infrastructure Investment Bank*

China maintains a significant and largely beneficial economic presence in developing countries, through schemes and institutions ranging from the Belt and Road Initiative (henceforth BRI) to the Asian Infrastructure Investment Bank (henceforth AIIB). Its extensive and dynamic collaboration and connections with developing countries pave a critical path for the country's economic and military hard power abroad – with the former especially prominent. These countries in turn supply China with critical goods, human capital, tourism destinations, sites for Chinese investment, markets for Chinese goods and services, and select-sector investment.

To exemplify this, consider the specific facts that China had overtaken the United States to become the world's largest FDI investor into Africa in 2013, and supplied over $2.7bn in 2019 to the continent of 1.3bn people (with a median age of 19.7, as of 2020).[16] Chinese investment has continuously expanded in Southeast Asia, with China emerging as the largest trade partner to ASEAN by 2020.[17]

China's international goodwill affords it access to both scarce and general resources in abundance, but also – more importantly, perhaps, capital and consumer markets that had been largely left unsaturated during the Cold War, including Southeast Asia and Africa. As shall be later discussed, especially in relation to Central Asia and Pakistan, China has also leveraged its abilities to deliver affordable infrastructure and accessible loans, as a means of generating and preserving political goodwill and capital amongst countries that collectively house a vast majority of the world's population.

It is nevertheless easy to over-state China's prowess and influence amongst developing economies. Doing so would risk ignoring the potential setbacks that Chinese investment has faced in recent years: from ensuring that its loans are enforceable and repaid in time, to stipulating that particular aid and investment be directed towards particular causes, Chinese investors have been confronted by significant practical hurdles.

3.1.1.4 Continuous commitment to deepening institutional reforms and transformations

Held in July 2024, the Third Plenum of the 20th Party Congress of the Communist Party of China, played a significant role in enabling China to advance initiatives rooted in its continuous commitment to deepening institutional reforms and transformations. This high-level meeting, echoing the Third Plenum convened in 1978 – which heralded the commencement of reform and opening-up, served as a crucial platform for the party to outline its strategic priorities and reinforce its commitment to comprehensive reforms across various sectors.

The Third Plenum provided high-level political endorsement for a series of institutional reforms, seeking to establish and develop clearly institutions that would allow for centralised coordination, leadership, and pioneering of innovation. High-level objectives were unveiled for institutional changes in areas such as governance, economic management, and social welfare and services. Additionally, in seeking to tackle the ongoing confidence malaise and deficit amongst Chinese entrepreneurs, one of the key focus areas was economic reforms aimed at enhancing market efficiency and resource allocation. Indeed, building off recent statements by the central leadership, the Plenum emphasised the need to streamline regulatory frameworks, reduce bureaucratic red tape, and promote private sector participation. This included measures to improve the business environment, encourage foreign investment, and support technological innovation.

In addition to economic and governance reforms, the Plenum highlighted the importance of constructing and maintaining a safety net for disadvantaged and disempowered communities. Senior party leaders spoke of the need to tackle the shrinking albeit fundamentally worrying inequalities between coastal and inland provinces, as well as urban and rural populations.[18] Indeed, some have interpreted the Plenum to be anchored in the doubling-down of top-down-driven industrial policymaking[19] – though such interpretations evidently omit the centrality of feedback loops and holistic planning undertaken by mid-ranking and frontline grassroots officials in spearheading what economist Keyu Jin dubs to be China's distinctive "mayor economy", one in which leaders of municipal polities take to fronting and steering the respective macro-economic and industrial policies in the regions for which they bear primary responsibility.[20]

3.1.2 Weaknesses and challenges

We must nevertheless not shy away from difficult questions and conversations that must take place over China's economic future. As of 2025, the prognosis is by no means sunshine and rainbows for the country. The Chinese economy is afflicted by a series of structural weaknesses and obstacles that, if unaddressed, could pose serious challenges to the country's growth and developmental trajectory. The following comprises a tentative survey of some of the conspicuous challenges that have and are likely to emerge.

3.1.2.1 Slowing economic and productivity growth

China's economic growth had been steadily slowing over recent decades – from the highs of 10–14% per year between 2004 and 2007, to around 6% per year from 2018 to 2019, and now slowing to the range of 3%–5.2% post-pandemic (in years 2022 and 2023) (see Figure 3.1).[21] Valid questions can indeed be asked over the root causes of such slowing growth – though some may argue that there has been a secular decline in growth rates across the world over the past few years. The Chinese government had openly acknowledged the fact of declining growth rates, noting that the declining growth numbers were a "new normal" – given the country's transition into a higher-income economy, though added that China must therefore shift towards a new growth model that depended less on fixed investment and exporting, and more on stimulating internal consumption and demand and maintaining what was dubbed a "double circulation" in official state parlance.[22]

FIGURE 3.1 China's quarterly GDP growth rates from 1989 to 2024.

Source: Data taken from the *National Bureau of Statistics of China*. Available at: http://www.stats.gov.cn/english/; graph taken from *Trading Economics. China GDP Annual Growth Rate*. Available at: https://tradingeconomics.com/china/gdp-growth-annual

China's declining growth rates could be attributed to a multitude of factors, which are impossible to exhaustively discuss and capture here, though worth outlining, nevertheless. First, demographic data reveal the fact that China's working-age population had been steadily shrinking – the latest official census (results published in 2021) revealed that as compared with 2010, China's working-age population had declined by 40 million, though remained strong at 880 million. The country's One-Child (later reformulated as Two-Child) Policy had steered the country's demographic approach for the better part of the past four decades, with the government only scrapping the policy altogether in May 2021.[23]

To compensate for the shrinking workforce, China could – in theory – resort to boosting its overall productivity, through a combination of technological innovation and capital consolidation per each member of the workforce. Yet Japan, with its ageing demographic, had struggled to improve its productivity post-1997, with productivity growth slumping to less than 1% per year; the vast majority of these gains came from the manufacturing sector, as opposed to the service sector. Similarly, prior to the pandemic, China's productivity growth rates had slowed to an average of 5.7% per year from 2014 to 2018, from a high of 16% per year between 1995 and 2013.[24] Estimates of China's post-pandemic productivity gains are perhaps premature. The declining productivity growth rates can in turn be traced to a multitude of factors – including productivity stagnation in industries in which the country held a comparative advantage, and the difficulty and dearth of innovation in a highly state-regulated private sector.

Through increasing the competitiveness and tenability of its exports, China has sought to pivot from an investment-driven growth trajectory to an export- and consumption-led developmental path – though this approach could well be hamstrung by another key pitfall that had plagued China for decades: the rising costs of production in China have rendered its exports less appealing as compared with other states in the region, including ASEAN member states; as well as the nascent manufacturing sectors of other BRICS (Brazil, Russia, India, China, and South Africa) states.[25]

On a more positive note, there indeed exist viable paths forward for China. A priority rests with seeking to bolster structurally the country's productivity, as aforementioned.[26] This could be achieved through a range of policies – some of which have already been adopted by the current government: from attracting overseas talents (including Chinese nationals who had emigrated abroad) to investing more in quality higher education, from liberalising and opening up private sectoral innovation to spurring organic competition within state-owned enterprises, there exists a plurality of ways through which China can and should push for productivity gains. To transition from a capital-intensive investment-led growth approach to a productivity-centred approach is by no means easy but is arguably China's best bet when it comes to regaining its economic momentum.

In defence of the Chinese approach – and as an important caveat that is oft-overlooked, there exist apparent welfare benefits and gains to be derived by the public at large from China's past five years of regulatory tightening. The Chinese government views its growth-curbing actions (e.g., crackdown on excessive concentration of power in the hands of a few Big Tech firms, as well as the recent calls for increased redistributive taxation by Beijing[27]) as worthy, on grounds that in doing so, it would be redistributing income and wealth to those who are in most need of the wealth, or labour and social security protections. Whilst increasing the GDP per capita had been an issue of priority throughout the past four decades, President Xi Jinping views equalisation as an equally – if not more – important prerogative. The governmental approach to macroeconomics has hence undergone substantial transformations under the present government – into one with a dual focus, on both the employment and directing of resources towards seemingly economically unprofitable collective goods (e.g., climate-friendly energy and sustainable development) and meeting the needs and demands of the underprivileged working and "sandwich" classes.[28]

As individuals save less and consume more (upon China reaching an upper-middle income country status), it is imperative for China to diversify in its sources of growth, to shift from investment-driven growth to innovation-driven growth. Yet this, in turn, behoves the country to possess a healthy, robust, and organic "economy of ideas".

The bank-dominated financial system has long favoured lending to predominantly state enterprises and corporations – which are significantly less productive and innovative as compared with their private counterparts. The debt-to-GDP ratio in China has been rising substantially since the global financial crisis – the debt being taken on, in other words, is not transduced into a satisfactory level of productivity; to the extent that such debts are used to finance state-owned enterprises, these are often "sunset" enterprises with substantial internal weaknesses and impediments that stifle their resuscitation of productivity.

China has poured in an impressive volume of capital (as aforementioned) into innovation and research and development. Yet the outputs – with respect to the country's public sector in particular – remain lacklustre. The state's more recent attempts to target particular industries, via the Made in China 2025 industrial policy, have sought to rejuvenate and invigorate particular sectors within the national economy – yet whether this forceful campaign will in fact succeed will depend heavily upon whether China can sufficiently rehabilitate and purge these companies free of rent-seeking behaviours and entrenchment of vested interests. That much remains to be seen.[29]

A further factor that has played a critical role in the economic development of contemporary China constitutes state-owned enterprises (SOEs). SOEs are government-owned corporations, either with the Chinese government as the sole or dominant stockholder, or with the state directly owning and administering the firms' operations by and large. The party formally takes a commanding role in all SOEs under Xi Jinping, with SOEs being required by state directive and prerogative to "execute the will of the party".[30] More fundamentally, SOE employees' wages are, in contrast to their counterparts in the private sectors, usually guaranteed through either formal ordinance and regulations, or informal norms that enshrine job security. Whilst some of the "iron-clad" protections for grassroots employers have been rolled back under China's economic liberalisation since the 1980s, much of the undergirding logic – that the state provides and guarantees the welfare of its employees – has remained intact and constant. SOEs should also be contrasted against private enterprises, such as Jack Ma's Alibaba and Dewang Cao's Fuyao Group, where ownership stakes remain predominantly with private investors and funders.[31]

Why are SOEs still inefficient in China today? For a short period under Deng, the liberalisation of labour movement, the installation of internal performance indicators and external competition (through the establishment of a private sector), and the importing of technologies from advanced industrial democracies, went a long way in improving the efficiency of SOEs. Yet most of these gains have been stunted – even rolled back – over recent decades, as SOEs have become over-leveraged and structurally packed to the brim with political clutter and abused, unproductive loans (i.e., loans preferentially offered to these companies on the grounds of their political importance). The over-regulation of select sectors has also driven out competitive private enterprises, leaving SOE-led industries uncompetitive and unproductive.

A rejoinder to the above logic may, again, be one that draws upon the doctrines of socialism and egalitarianism enshrined in the Communist Party of China' official ideology – whilst economic growth and expansion of the raw size of the pie may be *somewhat important*, China is, at its core, relatively uninterested in playing the numbers' game for the sake of it. A dual-sector (service and manufacturing) economy with full employment and equal income distribution, is by all means seen as preferable to a GDP-chasing/maximising service economy that leaves out far more than it serves. What is clear is that China seems less willing to put all its faith in neoliberal ideas, such as trickle-down economics.

Yet in response to this view, note that even public-oriented services and infrastructure in China have come under heightening risks of being captured by rent-seeking activities. It is imperative that issues such as corruption, inefficiencies, embezzlements, and lack of transparency over expenditure of funds and capital, be addressed promptly and expeditiously, so as to ensure a smoother transition towards a more equal and fair society within the country. What increases GDP may not increase well-being – though there exist problematic structures that inhibit growth across both dimensions. These structures are to the detriment of both growth and development alike.

3.1.2.2 SOE corporate debt

Does China have a debt crisis? The answer would be tentatively to the negative when it comes to household debt – household debt growth in China slowed down considerably in 2023, with the debt-to-disposable income ratio rising from 112% in 2022 to 115% in 2023.[32] With that said, when couched in terms of the debt-to-nominal GDP ratio, household debt amounts to around 61% of GDP.[33]

A slightly more worrying issue rests with the country's corporate debt – standing at 134% of its GDP as of 2022, China's non-financial corporate debt-to-GDP ratio was almost twice of that of the United States. Even then, the number was comparable to that of both Japan and Korea.[34] With the handful of corporate default incidents over the past few years, speculation and worries have arisen over the extent to which the country's corporations are capable of repaying debts and discharging loans. The worry is amplified by the fact that with the increasing liberalisation of capital and investor markets, the primary holders of corporate debt are no longer merely state-controlled banks or the

Chinese state itself, but also private consumers and investors actively engaged in the corporate bond market.[35]

Whilst the risk to the international financial system is moderate – albeit certainly present, the corporate debt crisis would be to the detriment of, first and foremost, China itself. Should SOEs default *en masse*, not only could this pose a fundamental threat to the country's banks and financial institutions, but it would also vastly undermine the country's credibility and credit standing in relation to sovereign debt, and other forms of financial commitments. Such interconnectivity uniquely stems from the disproportionate concentration of SOEs and state-affiliated companies as debtors. If China is to continually fund its economic ventures and international commitments abroad, it must ensure that it steers clear of the debt trap. Boosting productivity and efficiency, lowering debt uptake, streamlining and improving loan allocations process – these are pivotal steps that China must and should take in averting what could otherwise be the largest economic crisis in the country's contemporary history.

3.1.2.3 Trade wars and geopolitical tensions with international partners

China's frayed relations with international trade and economic partners – particularly in the West – could also pose a substantial obstacle to the country's continued growth and successes. For one, the United States–China trade war, initiated by US President Donald Trump in 2018, saw the United States (then China's largest trade partner) impose substantial tariffs and trade barriers on China – with the alleged aims of compelling the country to adjust its "unfair trade practices" and intellectual property theft.[36] Trump's successor, Joe Biden, for domestic political reasons, had largely continued with the same policies. China thus currently faces a substantial wave of growing backlash and trade retaliation from Western states, especially the United States. How China navigates its fraught ties with states upon which it depends significantly for commodities and consumer markets, will be essential in determining the future economic trajectory of the country.

Geopolitical headwinds against China have strengthened considerably throughout the past five years. International alliances ranging from AUKUS to the Quad have been established and bolstered, with the implicit objective of constraining Chinese presence and expansion within the Indo-Pacific, and beyond. The Russo–Ukrainian War that broke out in February 2022 further compounded the potential risks befalling the Chinese economy. As China seeks to continually deepen its reform and opening up, it must grapple with the contingencies and risks that emerge from its greater interconnectivity with the global financial and economic systems at large. The key question is, to what extent could geopolitical and ideological divergences be set aside in light of the realignments taking place in reaction to the ongoing war in Ukraine, as well as in favour of shared economic interests across countries – this is a question that China alone cannot sufficiently address. India's position, carefully hedging between the West and the Global South, offers pointers on how new alliances can be built, with old alliances up-ended and revamped; China will no doubt be a key player in these configurations as the West is deemed by some to have overplayed its geopolitical cards vis-à-vis the unfolding situation in Ukraine.[37]

Indeed, the last point is particularly pertinent, given the drastic U-turns and changes-in-stance by the Trump administration towards Ukraine. The White House spat between US President Trump and Ukrainian President Volodymyr Zelenskyy spoke to the increasingly tenuous appeal of the American state to observers and allies around the world.[38] As compared with the highly dramatic vacillation between different policy stances and options over Ukraine – no less from the same administration – the Chinese administration's stance certainly offers a greater sense of certainty and clarity, in a relative sense. The extent to which such clarity could be converted into forging a path for peace, on the other hand, remains a challenging question that can only be answered by China's foreign policy leadership. Yet the hope is that Beijing can and will strike a balance between maintaining its long-standing commitments to and engagement with Russia on one hand and standing with the sovereignty and territorial rights of smaller nation-states, such as Ukraine. Navigating this conflict with success will prove to not just be a key challenge for the country's diplomats, but also a fundamental litmus test for the country's leadership – on the Grand Strategy that is to characterise China's position in the world, for the decades to come.

3.2 Domestic and global politics

The following section is primarily interested in questions of strengths and weaknesses of the Chinese government in the *contemporary era* – i.e., with a heightened emphasis upon the past 15–20 years or so of political transitions. This section should hence be read as mapping the culmination of the trajectory in the country's political developments, and an appraisal of the "product" of the past four decades of liberalisation, modernisation, and governance reforms.

3.2.1 Strengths and opportunities

What makes the current Chinese governance system *work*? There are primarily three areas that are worth exploring – in addition to what has been covered. They comprise China's recent, sustained crackdown on corruption, the substantial popularity of the Communist Party of China and the transformations to the judiciary and legal system undertaken over recent years.

3.2.1.1 Anti-corruption efforts and crackdowns

Since his rise to power, Xi Jinping has undertaken an extensive crackdown on corruption across the country. His tenure has been marked by his emphasis upon cracking down on "tigers and flies" – from high-level officials to local civil servants, corruption has been at the forefront of governance reforms over the past decade. Xi's anti-corruption campaigns had resulted in over 100,000 individuals being investigated and indicted for corruption – symbolic of the party's leadership's resolve to tackle systemic challenges of malfeasance and malign rent-seeking that had long plagued the country.

Whilst critics have dismissed the campaign as driven plausibly by ulterior political motives, many others have praised the campaign for serving as a critical cornerstone of a wider project of systemic political reform that had sought to restore the CPC's public mandate and perceptual legitimacy. Other voices have noted that the campaign against corruption was pivotal in streamlining governance and spurring party cadres to focus on delivering quality governance – as opposed to dabbling in dangerous rent-seeking.[39] Scholar Cheng Li[40] noted that the anti-corruption efforts had restored substantial laundered or siphoned-off monetary gains into the hands of the state, which facilitated the country's re-orientation towards boosting its long-term productivity, a process that had been stunted by the short-termist behaviours and calculus of corrupt officials. The campaign has also had the support of the significant majority of Chinese citizens, especially low-income groups who are vastly disillusioned at the exploitative practices of the officials in local and regional administrations.

The anti-corruption crackdown has also prosecuted and held to account party leaders at the highest levels – including former Politburo Standing Committee leaders Zhou Yongkang, former Central Military Commission Vice-Chairmen Xu Caihou and Guo Boxiong. Other senior officials, such as Su Rong and Ling Jihua, were dismissed and prosecuted in high-profile trials that served to highlight Xi's determination in enforcing party discipline.

These moves have had modest positive impacts. From assuaging public worries over an intransigent, arbitrary government propelled by narrow self-interests to enhancing governmental efficiency and ensuring that centralised decisions were effectively carried out at the local or provincial level, Xi's purge of insubordinate, corrupt officials has brought about welcome changes to China's gargantuan political machine.

3.2.1.2 Widespread popularity and public buy-in

The Chinese government enjoys a very high level of buy-in amongst its denizens. In 2014, Pew Global Research found that 92% of the country's respondents had confidence in the country's leader, Xi Jinping. Multinational polls and surveys regularly find a "high level of regime support"[41] in China, even when the possible problems of preference falsification or underreporting of dissent are factored into consideration. Some of this can indubitably be attributed towards the government's successful track record at eliminating poverty and reducing relative deprivation – a distinct political objective and priority for senior party leaders.

Fundamentally, the percentage of individuals who remain optimistic over the Chinese government's performance and ability to deliver upon critical social goods has remained high in the country. In 2013, over 80% of respondents felt that children – at that time – would be financially better-off than their parents. The figure rose to nearly 90% in 2015. To put things in perspective, only slightly over 30% of American respondents said the same across those two years. A vast majority of Chinese citizens remain fundamentally impressed by and committed to the ideals and operating principles undergirding the contemporary Chinese state, which has seen an explosion in access to consumer goods, installation of critical infrastructure, under the continued cultivation of a national ethos that encourages hard work and collective interests. The quality of life for Chinese citizens has materially improved over the past decades, and it is no wonder that Chinese denizens remain overwhelmingly in favour of their government's continuation.

China is known for its willingness to engage in pragmatic and open reforms as a means of improving its governance – this is also why Chinese administrators often trial/"test-run" or pilot governance policies on a small scale, locally, prior to rolling them out on a larger scale. An example of this could be found in the Special Economic Zones (SEZs)[42] – zones with laissez-faire and liberated capital controls, introduced in the 1980s, as a pioneering programme under China's opening-up reforms. These zones have played a pivotal role in elucidating how a socialist market – like China's – could rapidly acclimatise and render itself amenable to not only international investors, but also domestic capitalists and industrialists seeking to raise funds and cultivate competitive businesses. The SEZs were piloted in Southern China, and have since paved the way for the introduction of "economic zones" in regions ranging from Shanghai to Hainan.

Sceptics have posited that these figures are merely the results of the state's successful brainwashing – yet this view does not, rather unfairly, take sufficiently seriously the agency and autonomy of the Chinese people; nor does it sit well with the fact that the Chinese middle class has become exponentially more educated and informed over the past decades – without a corresponding drop in approval for their government. Indeed, in the aftermath of the government's largely successful and swift tackling of the COVID-19 pandemic, support for the government has only increased – as opposed to declined (though further polls must be carried out to verify incidental reports that strongly suggest this thesis).[43]

Yet considering China's substantial population size and the challenges uniquely associated with governing a country of its size and terrain, the enduring and warm reception towards its ruling government must not be overstated. Such popularity and mass support are indeed a key hallmark of successful governance – at least on the perceptual level – under China's central leadership. However, there is also the risk that should the country's economic performance falter considerably, such that its ability to deliver upon general stability, certainty, and predictability of rule is called into question, the implicit social contract holding together state and people would thus fall apart, culminating in rising public discontents and anger. This powerful warning concerning the preservation of the social contract has been made by prominent thinkers on China such as Minxin Pei[44] and Yasheng Huang[45] – in relation to the formal and institutional shortcomings in political representation within the country.

3.2.1.3 Continued and sustained legal reforms that are pragmatically outcome-driven

A third and relatively under-discussed strength of the Chinese government is its emphasis upon outcome-driven reforms to its judiciary and rule of law that render its governance compatible with both demands of the law and of economic realities.

Major progress has been made in two particular spheres – first, in rendering the country's jurisdiction more accessible and open to foreign businesses and investors, and second, in China's stepping up to become a leading mediation and legal adjudication hub for international disputes between and with countries involved with the Belt and Road Initiative. On the latter, Chinese courts resolved approximately 15,000 foreign-related civil disputes in 2013–2017, with BRI-related cases being a major component. Courts have adopted the equal protection of litigants as a guiding principle, notwithstanding their countries of origins.[46]

With respect to the former, the Chinese government introduced the Foreign Investment Law in 2020, which served to open up substantially more nascent opportunities for foreign investors. Judges handling foreign-related disputes have been trained and legally mandated to render their adjudication and processing of court cases more accountable, fair, and accessible to foreign residents in China. For one, foreign litigants are assigned to English-speaking judges who could engage with and explain the body of Chinese law to international expatriates and firms operating within China. In 2019 alone, China's arbitration commissions presided over 487,000 cases.[47]

Per legal expert Grenville Cross,[48] there exists an increasing emphasis upon the protection and upholding of the rights and interests of locals, especially via closer attention being paid to the needs and difficulties encountered by grassroots citizens in suing dominant companies. An increasingly robust set of consumer laws and regulations concerning manufacturing, production, and distribution of goods has offered consumers the safety net and means through which they can hold abusive vendors and suppliers accountable. These are all very much welcome changes to China's judiciary.

3.2.1.4 Fostering of context-sensitive and context-specific ties with developing countries through civil society, economic, political, and institutional exchanges

A factor that is often neglected when it comes to China is not only the extent to which it enjoys substantial popularity amongst developing countries – especially those who have been typically eschewed or locked out of international economic superstructures; it is also the fact that the country's foreign policy and diplomatic strategies are highly context-sensitive and adaptive.

During the pre-COVID period, countries ranging from Latin American military strongman states to Southeast Asian democracies welcomed Chinese economic supplement, investment, and aid – not just in pure economic terms, but also as an effective means for China to court political support and backing abroad. There is nothing inherently wrong with the deployment of economic resources as a means of courting favours – indeed, this is standard, established practice in international economy. China simply does it in a manner that is more comprehensive and thorough than many in the Western Hemisphere, especially when it comes to expediency and urgency.

The international reception of Chinese outreach efforts has certainly been mixed. Whilst the country's reception in African, Latin American, and some (not all) Southeast Asian states has seen a predominantly positive secular rise over the past two decades, Central and Eastern Europe states have cooled considerably on China in the wake of Russia's war in Ukraine, as well as the perception – perhaps inaccurate – of Chinese sympathies towards Russia.

It is the dexterity and strategic savviness of the Chinese government that renders it by far a more mature and developed power than the USSR – to which inopportune and ill-fitting analogies have often been erroneously drawn. Yet China should also avoid the very pitfalls and flaws that the USSR has committed, as noted by renowned political economist Chandran Nair.[49]

3.2.2 Weaknesses and challenges

Chinese governance, obviously, is not bereft of weaknesses, challenges, and problems. Should these problems be left unaddressed, not only would they pose a fundamental obstacle to China's continued economic success – they could also jeopardise the country's socio-political stability and sustainability on the whole.

3.2.2.1 Absence of consistent, transparent succession norms and rules

The Communist Party of China operates through an intricate combination of meritocratic appointment, technocratic selection, factionalist intrigue and bargaining, and intense contentious politics within the party. To characterise the party's selection and succession norms as the product of despotic whims would neither be accurate nor helpful in the world's understanding of the country's distinctive political norms and matrices. On the other hand, it would be equally erroneous to posit that the country's succession norms and rules need no further refinement or improvement. Till this date, the Party remains afflicted by the structural worry of a lack of stable, transparent succession norms undergirding its highest echelons of leadership.

To be very clear, the Chinese administration does have succession *norms* – the notion of succession planning was embodied and established by Deng Xiaoping as he revived China from the abyss of volatility and instability he inherited from the dying days of Mao Zedong's rule. As afore-discussed, succession in China has evolved to become progressively more merit-based and the product of balancing of competing interests and considerations, and less the product of factionalist horse-trading and anti-meritocratic politicking. All of that is fair and square, and it would be erroneous to ignore this.

Yet this fact alone does not imply that these norms are *stable*. The number of Standing Committee members, the *de jure* term limits on Presidency (the title is nominal only, for real power rests with the General Secretary, for which there has never been any term limit), and the powers and portfolios held by Standing Committee members have varied considerably throughout the tenures of Deng Xiaoping, Jiang Zemin, Hu Jintao, and Xi Jinping. Without delving into the merits and drawbacks of each and every leader's decisions with regards to the composition of the Standing Committee and Politburo, as well as the rules that were introduced under their tenure – one thing is clear: China lacks a succession pattern that can be transcribed and explicated clearly through codified rules.

Stability matters – especially when the government is seeking to root out abusive and corrupt practices amongst the elite. Stable rules – whether they be codified or informal yet enforced through binding, coercive mechanisms – are necessary in order for conflicts and dissent over "political" decisions (e.g., personnel appointment, removal, investigation, and dismissal) to be accepted with minimal backlash. Elsewise, the efforts of the anti-corruption campaign, whilst noble in intentions and theoretical scope, would be largely futile, as it descends into a series of factionalist struggles and vying for power.

Now, one may argue – somewhat plausibly – that the search for codifiability reflects itself a "Western bias" in the imagination and conceptualisation of how governance ought to operate. It is not a tradition that China has historically adopted, for there to be clear and concrete succession rules. Yet this claim, setting aside its Orientalist assumptions concerning Chinese political culture and history (and the fallacious view that Chinese governance must necessarily be *different* from the West's, and is *therefore desirable*), is empirically erroneous. Throughout vast swathes of Chinese history, the ruling Emperor passed on the rights over the dynasty – typified as the "Heaven's Mandate" – to their, often his, heir, who is often his son or nephew. Interruptions, exceptions obviously exist – yet they are by no means the rule. In other words, China has had a largely transparent succession rule (*quasi-primogeniture*) undergirding its rulers since the beginning of formal history.

In contrast, the Party defers to a basket of variables – ranging from compatibility with the respective factions, political acumen and experience, to age and credentials – in selecting its leader. Chinese leaders are not appointed unilaterally by unitary figures; nor are they selected through arbitrary processes. Yet these selection criteria have not and are not codified in a manner that ensures that they will indeed be applied consistently. To the extent that they have, this has been largely because of the convergence of the self-interests of the involved selectorate and these tacitly enshrined and celebrated virtues.[50]

The lack of transparency and consistency over selection metrics also transpires at lower levels – whether it be at the Politburo/national, provincial/ministerial, or equivalent tiers of leadership. As aforementioned, the Chinese civil service is an extraordinarily competitive institution, with personnel decisions approved and vetted by multiple individuals overseeing the more junior posts. In practice, the overlapping chains of command have produced substantial tensions and conflicts between factions – e.g., the "tiaos" and the "kuais".[51] To resolve such disagreements and disputes, it is imperative that China develops clearer, more concretely outlined, and enforceable criteria concerning personnel decisions – so as to preclude the low, albeit extant, possibility of unaccountable or incompetent party officials and leaders.

Doing so would also render the Chinese civil service more accessible and open to individuals who are seeking to enter government via a "revolving door" – whether it be from senior ranks in academia, business, technology, or other sectors; pathways into government certainly exist for talents in these fields, but are inevitably intertwined with political considerations that may not duly reflect the overarching interest of the country.

3.2.2.2 Tarnished international image amongst certain developed countries

China has suffered setbacks to its global reputation over recent years, on grounds ostensibly to do with the country's human rights record and handling of its internal affairs in regions or cities such as Xinjiang, Hong Kong, and Tibet. The country has also been criticised for its alleged exporting of authoritarian values abroad. As one shall come to see in Chapter 6, many of these assertions rest upon mistaken assumptions concerning China's ambitions, governance, and approach to internal, domestic problems.

The characterisation of China as a ruthless, anti-rights, totalitarian government bent on oppressing human rights has indeed taken root amongst certain international circles, in ways that are neither reflective of reality, nor particularly conducive towards improving the conditions of those who in fact reside in the country, nor, indeed, the introduction of measures needed for the genuine improvement of international relations. One thing is clear: China has an image problem[52] – amongst certain countries.

There is a substantial and extensive Western media campaign being waged against China, with the overarching objective to portray China, and states similar to China as inherently repressive, immoral, and evil. This campaign, coupled with China's significantly stultified soft power capacities and inability to push back against both misrepresentation and fair criticisms, has had a substantially negative impact on China's image abroad. On Xinjiang, UN Human Rights Commissioner Michelle Bachelet's visit in 2022 has provided some degree of clarity and conclusiveness to the situation on the ground, in which she raised concerns over "the application of counter-terrorism and de-radicalisation measures and their broad application – particularly their impact on the rights of Uyghurs and other predominantly Muslim minorities".[53]

Throughout the West, unfavourable views of China have reached significant heights, with the percentage of individuals with no confidence in the Chinese leadership[54] to "do the right thing" surging by over 15% across countries such as the UK, Germany, Australia, the Netherlands, and Italy at the beginning of the pandemic. Attitudes towards China have also soured considerably in America, with a majority viewing China as either a "competitor" or "enemy" – though, noticeably in the aftermath of the Russo–Ukrainian war's outbreak, the number of American citizens viewing China as a direct threat has declined considerably.[55] Additionally and increasingly, China has struggled to assuage the worries and concerns of the publics of EU member states, where backlash from segments of their civil societies towards China over the latter's governance, industrial policies, and stance on Russia are threatening to undermine the substantial goodwill and bilateral benefits that had arisen from the country's opening up to European firms and investors.

Taking a step back, China has persistently faced challenges from secessionist forces who have sought to undermine national and territorial integrity, through a combination of lone-wolf terrorist attacks and violent protests. Regions such as Xinjiang and Tibet have seen an escalation in frequency and intensity of altercations between minority secessionists and local denizens. In Xinjiang, for instance, East Turkistan Islamic Movement (ETIM)-backed terrorists and rebels have engaged in elaborate violence against civilians and local government representatives. The actions of a small minority of ethnic Uyghurs had induced substantial casualties upon both Uyghur and Han populations residing in Xinjiang alike. Some of the more severe and destructive attacks included the 1992 detonation of a bomb on a public bus in Urumqi by Uyghur separatists, and the attack on a hotel in Kashgar in the same year;[56] more recently, lone-wolf attacks on civilians by knife-wielding assailants have renewed the state's interests in enforcing strict compliance with the law in Xinjiang.[57]

From 2014 onwards, the Chinese had adopted a series of counter-terrorism measures in Xinjiang, with the aim of rooting out local security risks and insubordination, and tackling the manifestations of extremist ideology amongst local citizens. Concerns have been raised internationally over the proportionality, scope, lack of transparency and accountability of the state response – with allegations ranging from the existence of gross human rights abuses to charges of ostensible "genocide".[58] Yet as aptly noted by *The Economist*, the label of "genocide" should not be trivially and flippantly slapped onto the events unfolding in China (in the absence of further evidence and substantiation);[59] charges as exaggerated and radical as these must be treated with extreme care – lest they be misapplied to contexts for which they are ill-fitting. It is not implausible to suggest that human rights criticisms levelled at China may be exaggerated or selectively used without context to further negative views of the country. It seemed that for China's detractors, even the United Nations' verdict was not legitimate enough.

With that said, there remains a reasonable possibility that restrictions of civil liberties – especially restrictions upon freedoms of speech and movement – have occurred in Xinjiang. Such possibility merits more thorough, non-partisan, and politically non-skewed investigation (such as the visit by the United Nations High Commissioner), as well as greater transparency from Beijing – as argued by investment banker Shan Weijian and political economist Chandran Nair in their respective pieces for the *South China Morning Post*.[60,61] For those who seek to understand China through relatively unfiltered and objective lenses (to the extent that is indeed possible), it is imperative that they get the grips with the context in which China has implemented the stern, draconian regime it has in Xinjiang. It is equally vital that individuals recognise that much of the existing debate concerning the Xinjiang is packed to the brim with information that lacks institutional verification and credibility. Indeed, the Islamic world itself has largely not supported these charges.[62]

A particularly poignant part of the conversation on Xinjiang revolves around corporations that find themselves caught in the crosshairs. One of the most prominent and renowned commercial enterprises operating in Xinjiang today is the Esquel Corporation – a leading global textile manufacturer that found its subsidiaries on the Entities List by the Department of Commerce, on grounds that it purportedly engaged in unethical labour practices and allegedly used "forced labour" in its manufacturing processes.[63]

Such allegations fly explicitly in face of all evidence that points to Esquel's standing and role recognised within the industry internationally as a highly socially conscientious and responsible employer – one who sought to provide its employees in Xinjiang with upward economic mobility, upskilling opportunities via employment, and social transformation. Even despite the endorsements by leading US policy experts, industry experts, and academics, Esquel found itself effectively cut off from erstwhile clients, as a result of the stigmatising effects of being included on the entities list. It had little choice but to downsize and trim its operations – as well as shifting its primary clientele market to mainland China.[64] Whilst the transition had by no means been easy, the tenacity and persistence of Esquel also speak to a broader point about China's reputation abroad – beyond state-sponsored and -supported media campaigns, much of China's soft power has to do with the imaginative successes and impressive achievements of private Chinese enterprises and businessmen, which have been pivotal in driving forward the "China Story" on the international level. Whether Beijing can overcome the diplomatic and perceptual scepticism towards its political stance and rhetoric on contentious issues, could well turn on the ability of private Chinese firms to highlight the room and space for organic diversity and accommodated differences within the Chinese ecosystem. The economic is also political – and vice versa.[65]

3.3 Military

In Chapter 2, this book tentatively explored – in some detail – the quantitative and statistical aspects of China's rise as a military power. What has been less extensively discussed, however, constitutes the qualitative aspects of its military – especially in light of recent reforms – that render it a potent force in the world today. The following sections aim to track more contemporary, recent developments in the Chinese military, which would shed insight into the unique successes and obstacles currently confronting the military.

One comment that must be noted – from 2012 onwards, after Xi's ascent to power, he had mounted numerous military reforms that radically transformed the country's army, far more than his predecessors. Xi Jinping spearheads the Central Military Committee, and has openly committed to producing a "world-class force"[66] that is due to dominate the Asia-Pacific and "fight and win" wars on a global scale by the mid-point of this current century. Whether his vision would in fact succeed, would depend heavily upon the factors to be discussed as follows:

3.3.1 Strengths and opportunities

China has considerably consolidated its strengths in the military arena since Deng's resolved decision that the country's army be modernised and streamlined to reflect the changes of the times. As it stands, Chinese military policy is demarcated by several crucial strengths:

3.3.1.1 Continued expansion and improvements to quality of the country's navy

China has 252,000[67] active service members in its navy – charged with policing the country's near seas and oceans, as well as supporting long-distance operations ranging from counter-terrorism operations to personnel evacuation campaigns. The Chinese Navy is now the world's largest naval force in terms of ship numbers. It commissioned 18 ships in 2016, as compared with five by the US Navy.[68]

The navy's quality has also steadily improved over the years, with 70% of the fleet – per RAND Corporation estimates – "modern" in 2017, as compared with less than a half in 2010.[69] Other ongoing modernisation efforts include commissioning nuclear submarines, aircraft carriers (a third carrier is due to be operational by 2022), and the incorporation of artificial intelligence and advanced surveillance technology into navy apparatus.[70]

The opportunities afforded by China's navy growth can be viewed through two lenses – from China's perspective, and from the perspective of global security. With respect to the former, a bolstered Chinese Navy is of vital importance to China's ongoing, broader vision of consolidating its defences of territories and waters deemed crucial to national interest – including the South China Seas, in which China faces significant disputes over territories such as the Spratly Islands; as well as the Taiwan Straits and East China Sea. China's consolidated navy strength also serves as a critical deterrent against regional military competitors – e.g., Japan and Korea; though some have posited that China's military modernisation has in fact served to spur calls for re-militarisation in the former.[71]

As for the latter, a more competitive and equipped Chinese Navy could play an instrumental role in facilitating crackdowns on terrorists, pirates, and insurgents in open seas. There exist plenty of opportunities for genuine collaboration between China and other states – as integral pillars of the international community – in tackling common challenges that jeopardise the safety of the open seas. It is worth noting that even on areas that China takes as being of paramount importance in the South China Sea – e.g., access to islands and territories it has historically accessed and possessed – the country is keen to resolve its differences with neighbours through peaceful negotiations, and managing its military presence in the seas. This should and must be juxtaposed against the equally significant presence of the American navy in the seas – despite the fact that America has no legitimate or formal claim to any portion of the South China Seas.[72]

3.3.1.2 Streamlined management and centralised command

Since his rise to power, Xi Jinping has implemented substantial, structural changes to China's military, with the primary aims of streamlining its operations and management, as well as developing a centralised core of command coordination. The army shrunk to under one million troops, even whilst the other prongs of the military continued to expand. Reforms have reduced the average unit size – to reduce the unwieldiness and inefficiencies involved in the command structure, as well as devolved more powers to mid-tier commanders and officers. Soldiers deemed unfit for deployment have been asked to retire, as a means of improving capital intensity (i.e., the volume of capital per unit of labour). Lines of reporting and duty have been "clarified", with chains of command significantly de-cluttered to facilitate easier management and reporting.[73]

In late 2015, the Chinese government implemented drastic reforms that consolidated the former seven military regions into five new theatre commands (TCs), as well as abolishing the various "general departments" and forming the Strategic Support Force to spearhead the country's space, cyber, and electronic warfare developments.[74] The military regions were predominantly administrative entities with limited to no operational control over air, naval, and missile forces in peacetime. In juxtaposition, theatre commanders are endowed with the rights to draw on conventional forces within their respective regions to plan and execute operations – even during peacetime. The expansion of remit for military region leaders also came with the legitimation of their prerogatives – subordinates could no longer defy centrally issued commands on grounds that such commands exceeded the default scope of responsibilities for their superiors.

These reforms have in turn played a pivotal role in improving the overarching competitiveness and strength of the Chinese army. The shift to theatre commands reflects the country's ongoing advancing of an "Information System-based System of Systems Operations" – a paradigm that emphasises consolidation and pooling of information, such that it could be readily manipulated and wielded as weapons in the country's ongoing military efforts. The paradigm shift connotes, in turn, a greater emphasis that is placed upon *true jointness* and *unity* in military operations; hitherto, military operations have been largely individualised and segmented into departments – driven by "section leaders" with incentives that pull in different directions. By nudging the People's Liberation Army (PLA) commanders and staff to "think in terms of joint training rather than combined arms training", these reforms have critically strengthened the extent to which senior military commanders are *open and motivated* to work with one another.[75]

More fundamentally, a less inefficient Chinese army could prove to be a pivotal stabilising factor in the region. As exemplified by the series of high-level corruption probes and subsequent prosecutions since 2023,[76] military corruption and insubordination – coupled with factionalist struggles, internal disputes, and mutual vying for power – had long been a cause of potential conflict, both within the country and between China and neighbouring states: this is because the less centralised the military command is; the more heterogeneous the range of actors involved in military decision-making, the less likely it is that such decisions are undertaken exclusively with the country's best interests in mind. Instead, tensions between regional and local or sub-local command could well yield unintended conflicts that went against the instructions from the highest tiers of command. By reducing the communicative distance between the Central Command and frontline officers, Xi's reforms have vitally addressed the problems of clogged communications and plausible deniability that had previously existed. Such is another strength of China's army in 2021.

3.3.1.3 Substantial military spending

The Chinese government devotes a significant volume of its budget towards its military. Estimates have suggested that the Chinese defence budget had increased in absolute terms by over sevenfold in 20 years – from $31bn in 1998 to $239bn in 2018[77] – and clocked in at $296 billion[78] in 2024, a 6.0% growth relative to the previous year. Such growth has rendered China therefore the second largest nation by total military expenditure in the world, behind only the United States. Whilst military expenditure as a proportion of the country's official GDP has considerably fallen from 2.5% in 1989 to roughly 1.6% in 2021 (a small percentage of a rapidly growing GDP/pie at large) (cf. Figure 3.2),[79] estimates have suggested that the amount may in fact be larger – given the substantial number of military-affiliated and military-controlled SOEs, whose revenue does not count towards the official state military budget.

All of this is to say that China spends – on absolute and proportional terms – *a lot* on its military. Such spending in turn enables China to devote substantial volume of resources into expanding its sphere of influence over the Pacific, as well as upgrading its defences in anticipation of threats from

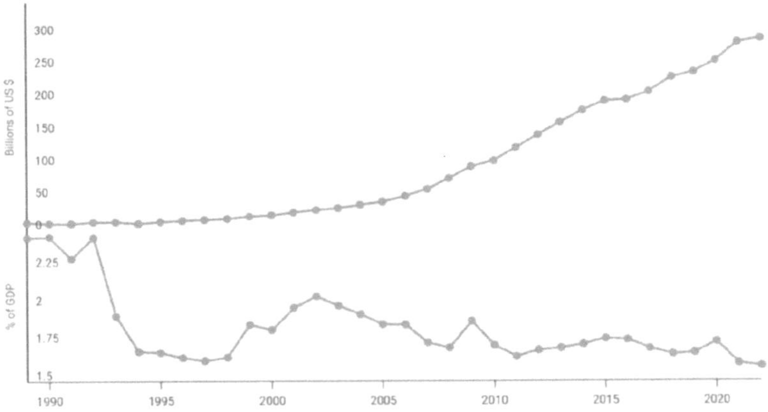

FIGURE 3.2 China's military spending as a percentage of total GDP (1989–2024).
Source: Macrotrends, (2025), China Military Spending/Defense Budget, Macrotrends. https://www.macrotrends.net/global-metrics/countries/CHN/china/military-spending-defense-budget

neighbouring countries or the United States – should they opt to undertake provocative moves within the East Asian sphere. Xi's aspirations are for China to become a leading military power in the Asia-Pacific, as a means of securing China's sovereignty, territorial integrity, and vital development-cum-economic interests. Concurrently, there also exist the secondary objectives of shoring up the army's role in nation-building and tackling emergencies, especially in regions with limited or a dearth of robust infrastructure in face of adversities. As such, the expansion in military budget cannot be decoupled from China's broader economic vision and geopolitical strategy – in addition to, of course, mainland China's irridentist quest for reunification with Taiwan.[80]

3.3.2 Weaknesses and challenges

China's military may be on the ascent in terms of its net quality and total strength, yet it remains ridden with structural problems that – if untreated – could severely hamper China's vision of becoming a modern military power. These obstacles bring about huge challenges for both China's military commanders and the country's top political leadership. Resolving them requires both acumen and swiftness, attributes that may not be shared – despite their presence at the upper echelons of Chinese government – by the mid-tier management and commanders of the PLA.

3.3.2.1The Chinese Navy's lack of top-tier hardware

China certainly has the world's largest navy by the sheer number of ships (as aforementioned). Yet its navy also suffers from a dearth of top-tier "hardware" – that is to say, its overarching competitiveness is inhibited by its disproportionate reliance upon smaller classes of ships.[81] Most estimates of the PLA navy size tend to include small coastal patrol ships and miscellaneous transports ships in it – which lead to a partially inflated estimate of the navy's substantial strength: many of these ships are neither designed for combat, nor combat-ready.

To put things into perspective, as of the early 2020s, the PLA navy's force comprised two aircraft carriers, one cruiser, 32 destroyers, and 86 missile-armed coastal patrol ships, amongst others; its submarines included 46 diesel-powered attack submarines and six nuclear-powered attack submarines. In contrast, the US Navy possessed a fleet that includes 11 (nine more) aircraft carriers, 92 cruisers and destroyers, and 50 attack submarines, 14 ballistic missile submarines, and four cruise missile submarines.[82] More fundamentally, the predominant majority of the PLA navy comprises coastal patrol ships – which have limited capacity to project beyond China's near seas. All of this is to say that the PLA pales in comparison against the US army with respect to its "top-tier" hardware – specifically, aircraft carriers and destroyers.

3.3.2.2 Command inefficiencies and barriers

Centralisation, as afore-discussed, yields plentiful benefits when it comes to eliminating the room for local insubordination and fragmentation. Yet it could also pose a substantial hindrance for the PLA as it seeks to improve overarching efficiencies. Central command has its upsides – it enhances coordinative efforts, it enables greater sense of unity in decision-making and planning processes, it allows for the attribution of responsibility to agents in an unambiguous and effective manner. Yet if left unaccompanied by reforms to informational processes, centralisation could also fundamentally weaken the responsiveness and dexterity of the PLA, in a way that inhibits internal innovation, competition, and checks and balances against the failures of top-down leadership.

In 2016, President Xi Jinping introduced a series of structural reforms that institutionalised and bolstered the Communist Party of China 's direct control over the PLA. Some critics have panned this move as a shift towards politically driven top-down leadership in the army, further entrenching the Party's authoritarian grip over power;[83] setting aside the political-ideological criticisms, it is apparent that without the necessary reforms to the way military command is carried out, the heightened adherence to central control could pose great liabilities for Beijing's military ambitions. The flipside to reduced command "clutter", is the very much real and pressing possibility of information overload and over-concentration in the hands of a few. All of this is to say that should efficiency enhancement be the primary motivation of recent transformations to the military, the software and governance infrastructure matter just as much – if not more so – than reducing bureaucratic red tape and the distance between Command Central and the frontlines.

Further barriers to command range from the lack of transparency over personnel promotion and demotion decisions,[84] to the outdated, anachronistic training received by its ground forces – which render the enactment and implementation of modern military strategy cumbersome at best, to the generational gap that has emerged between the military chiefs and younger generation of soldiers.[85] Modernisation takes a group effort – and China needs all hands on deck in order to advance genuine, thorough reforms.

3.3.2.3 Lack of "military soft power" - deficiencies in quality of human capital

Since 2015, President Xi Jinping has sought to tackle what he termed the "Five Incapables" – systemic deficiencies in the judgement and aptitude of military officers, who have struggled to "judge situations, understand higher authorities' intentions, make operational decisions, deploy troops, [or] deal with unexpected situations".[86] Xi's very own assessment is that the Chinese army – especially its mid-level to upper-middle tiers of command, lack genuine training and prowess in terms of their combat leadership. These inabilities pose a severe obstacle to China's ongoing campaign to revamp its military, to render it more fitting and compatible with the rapidly shifting demands of a globalised era.[87]

Senior military commanders, in the past, have repeatedly noted that the Chinese army remained caught up in "traditional methods" that have yet to be overhauled or improved drastically in preparation for the rise of informational, digital, and cyber-warfare. Operational unit leaders are sceptical over their own personnel's abilities to handle and deploy effectively new technologies. Whilst there certainly is something reassuring about the heightened sense of self-awareness and candour concerning the army's constraints and limitations – coming from its very own commanders, one could also argue that this is a worrying indicator of the defects in the PLA's ongoing reform efforts.

3.4 Is there a civil society in China?

More precisely, to what extent does China possess a "genuine" civil society – space for collective action, agitation, organisation, and contestation around interests, purposes, and values, independent of both the commercial/private sector and the state? Sceptics often posit that with the Chinese state's all-encompassing reach and embedded connections with its civilian populace, bolstered by nascent and digital technologies (what MacKinnon terms "networked authoritarianism"),[88] there exists no civil society in China, for any and all civilian-led activities are necessarily monitored, tacitly condoned, tolerated, or prohibited by the state.

This is a misinformed argument, for three broad reasons. First, it neglects the fact that beyond the politically contentious "baseline" areas over which the Chinese state admittedly maintains a stringent grip, there exists a vast terrain of flourishing, vibrant civilian-led activities, associations, clubs, and spaces that have minimal – if any – state oversight. These include the entertainment and recreational arts sectors, which, despite the Chinese government's promulgation of state-ratified and -endorsed cultural activities and celebrations, have increasingly diversified and evolved towards a greater emphasis upon internationalism and pluralism over the years.[89]

Second, on a more conceptual note, the prying apart of "civil" and "state" may work well in describing the relationship of tension and mutual check-and-balance in the West, when it comes to the civil society's interactions with the government. Yet China possesses a distinctly divergent political culture in this regard, where state and governmental presence in civil society is neither viewed as out-of-the-norm or suspicious, nor interventionist. Most large-scale associations and universities indeed possess Party Secretaries, who nominally check on and report upon the activities and directives of these spaces to the Party – in practice, however, the level of monitoring and oversight remains minimal, especially in spaces that are conventionally accepted to be politically uncontroversial.[90] To equate a civil society with state presence, with a civil society wholly policed and controlled by the state, would be a categorical error.

None of this is to say that civil society organisations in China are as "free" from constraints or legal restrictions as their counterparts in the West. Admittedly, laws governing association incorporation and registration remain more stringent and readily enforced – especially when it comes to international non-governmental organisations, which have faced substantial resistance over recent years when it comes to setting up their presence within China. Yet it would be hasty and premature to conclude that with its strong state, China therefore has no civil society.

Third, indubitably accelerated in part by the influx of high-skill migrants and expatriates, though by-and-large organically driven by the urbanisation and rise of a competitive, proactive middle class, leading cities in China – including Shanghai and Shenzhen – have substantially liberalised in their cultural scenes, overarching ethos and stances on "progressive issues", and openness to cultures that do not conform with the Han majority. This can be seen in the highly progressive values of the new generation of Shanghai millennials, per Cheng Li,[91] who find themselves equally drawn to LGBTQ+ rights, feminist empowerment, and environmental protection as their Western counterparts.

The importance of China's millennials and future generations cannot be overstated. In the following sections, this book shall delve into three specific causes – traditionally associated with "progressive values" in the West, with the objective of establishing two critical tenets: First, there is more that unites and is in common between China's youth, and their counterparts in the West and all across the world, at large. Second, the civil society in China is increasingly vibrant and active – in ways that cannot be straightforwardly curtailed or curbed, even with significant state intervention. Three areas will be explored as a means of elucidating the above two claims: on environmental issues, on issues of sexual liberation and gender equality, and, most fundamentally, the rise of individualism across the board in post-2000s China.

3.4.1 Environmental protection and advocacy

Throughout vast swathes of its decades of rapid economic development, China had been severely affected by heavy pollution and environmental degradation that had resulted from its rapid industrialisation and urbanisation. 20 of the 30 most polluted cities of the world were in China, as of 2008.

Prior to 1980, China had had no environmental NGOs. China's first international NGO was the World Wide Fund for Nature (WWF) China, which was established with the primary objective of protecting giant pandas.[92] As of 2005, the number had increased to over 2,000 officially registered NGOs, alongside a plurality of para-organisations and civil society pressure groups that operated in concert in lobbying and pressing for changes in policies from the government. The leading environmental NGO in China – Friends of Nature – launched its first annual report in 2006, calling for swift remedial action and response to the country's systemic water, air, chemical, and biological pollution. In 2004, 100,000 Chinese college students from 22 provinces partook in environmental activities on Earth Day – testament to how extensively the movement had taken root in public consciousness and amongst the country's youth.

Activists regularly register discontents over rising pollution levels, climate change emissions, and other forms of environmental destruction – through an integrated mixture of offline and online means. Offline means encapsulate the filing of lawsuits against corporations – including SOEs, exposing corruption impacting the environment, protesting infrastructural project, exposing factories' failure to undertake carbon-neutral, and emissions-reducing actions. Online means include, on the other hand, mass campaigns across online fora and social media with the aims of naming and shaming pollutant dischargers and inept local environmental officials.[93]

Over the past decades, environmental activists helped with stopping dam construction on the Nu River in Yunnan, as well as worked with labour activists and unions in bargaining collectively for better and more sustainable labour and industrial practices in factories. A culture of philanthropy, coupled with heightened awareness of sustainability concerns, has promulgated innovative tools and policies ranging from green financing to environmentally conscious community actions (e.g., planting trees, trash recycling, and collection) across major cities and urban hubs in the country.[94] Afforestation efforts across the country have been critical in supporting the country's transition to a greener and more sustainable developmental trajectory, which is – in turn – emphasised as a key governance objective by a number of Chinese political leaders. Indeed, in their account of a "Harmonious Society", President Hu Jintao and Premier Wen Jiabao called for "a harmonious society is one that puts people first", that reflects the needs and values of individuals in accordance with the overarching principle of maintaining a stable and persistent social order and hierarchy.[95] A core component of this, of course, was environmental protection.

More recently, millennial and Gen-Z protesters – such as Zhao Jiaxin and Howey Ou[96] – have spoken up over China's carbon emissions. Whilst the country had pledged to contribute towards an "ecological civilisation", and whilst the country certainly leads the United States on both fronts of reducing emissions and engaging with producing more renewable energy at large, deficiencies remain in the ongoing process of de-carbonisation. Civilians therefore play an instrumental role in pressuring provincial and central governments – though the extent to which the state apparatus is responsive to their demands, of course, is by no means perfect.

A demonstrative exemplar here would be Ma Jun – an investigative journalist-turned-environmentalist/leading academic in environmental sciences in China. Ma Jun began his career as a journalist at the *South China Morning Post*, and specialised in environmental reporting for his career. His *China's Water Crisis* in 1999 ignited a substantial wave of debate – open and behind closed doors – within Chinese civil society. Through his rigorous research and advocacy, he came to direct the Institute of Public and Environmental Affairs – a pioneering public database tracking levels and sites of water pollution in China.

In response to the increasing prevalence and prominence of environmental issues as a subject of concern, it is no surprise that a significant number of Chinese youth are becoming environmentally "woke". Yet the increasingly widespread environmentalism in China is not fundamentally the product of Western influences.[97] Instead, it stems from a complex mixture of cultural thriftiness engrained in Confucianism, an emphasis upon recycling as an act of virtue ("non-wastage"[98]), and extensive state-backed media campaigns portraying climate change as an existential threat to humanity. To the extent that China has an environmentally conscious civil society, its ammunition, its fuel for growth, and its contours cannot be decoupled from the state, which remains a primary patron and backer of the movement, despite their divergences on more specific policy issues.

3.4.2 Sexual liberation and gender equality

Women's rights groups had always played a historically significant role in civil society activism and the spaces that straddled the public and private sectors. As a critical component of Communist ideology, gender equality had long been touted by the Chinese government – especially under Mao Zedong – as a normative principle to be upheld and pursued, both in order to enable the Party to establish political standing and win favours from the country's female population, as well as justify the Party's extensive reach into family life through schemes such as the "One-Child Policy" (though the extent to which the scheme in fact set back and undermined women's rights cannot be overstated – female infanticide was an issue of particular concern, as induced by the policy that had stipulated only one legally permitted birth per family).

At the 1995 World Conference on Women, Party Secretary Jiang Zemin declared that "men-women equality is a basic national policy".[99] Feminist NGOs were amongst the first crop of NGOs that had been set up in China in the 1990s, paving the way for leading feminist alliances, groups, and entities in modern China – including the Anti-Domestic Violence Network. The UN conference also introduced concepts such as domestic violence, rape, and the gendering of policy deconstruction/analysis into Chinese legal parlance. Whilst some of these NGOs are no longer in operation due to a mixture of political pressures from provincial and local governments, and self-censorship tendencies in view of an increasingly tendentious relationship between China and the West, the hope remains amongst select pockets of activists that the demands and interests of women can and should be incorporated into the law in the future.

The feminist movement frequently makes use of critical lawsuits – over cases of discrimination and harassment – as means of expanding the range of female liberties and rights legally enshrined and recognised. In the 2010s, the movement's outcries were buoyed and amplified by feminist bloggers who employed platforms such as WeChat and Weibo to issue political statements. Xixi Luo's online statement in 2018 – in which she revealed that she had ostensibly been sexually harassed by her former PhD supervisor – heralded the beginning of China's very own home-grown #MeToo movement. Of course, as with most other acts of seemingly contentious politics within modern China, such discourses have been viewed and treated with suspicion by elements within the bureaucratic apparatus. A more open, confident, and accommodating China should be willing to bring these demands and concerns into the open, and advance a more egalitarian future for women, men, and those who do not fit neatly into the binary here. Yet the advocacy of such an agenda remains very much work in progress – and requires both strategic acumen from below, and a willingness to accommodate differential and liberal political intuitions from above.

Since the early 2000s, sexual liberation has taken on an additional dimension in China. Not only is the empowerment and emancipation of female sexuality viewed as an integral component of gender progress, but it is also deemed as a necessary and beneficial product of the country's burgeoning trends of consumerism and the middle class. The rise of marketised and commercialised sex (e.g., the advent of sex products, the popularisation of recreational contraception, and the introduction of sexualised entertainment and culture – though the extent to which the latter empowers, as opposed to denigrating women through objectification, remains up for question) has come hand-in-hand with the country's opening-up of markets to Western investment, firms, and products.

Discussions of gender equality should not be – and indeed has not been – limited to solely female empowerment. China's increasingly vocal and visible LGBT+ rights movement plays a critical role in contesting the state's constrictive regulations and regressive legislation over the legal rights and privileges of non-cis heterosexual gender minorities. Same-sex couples are unable to marry or adopt in general, and households fronted by such couples are ineligible for the legal protections afforded to heterosexual couples.[100]

The LGBT+ movement in China offers an illuminating example of how, despite the lack of voluminous or abundant international linkages, local activists can and do creatively leverage discourses, values, and resources indirectly acquired from international movements as a tool for their advocacy and activism.[101] Sichuan offers a particularly insightful case study of how transnational groups, provincial governments, and local NGOs often work in tandem and in conjunction in advancing organic changes to sexual laws, norms, and customs on the ground.

International donors and NGOs cultivated a rather substantial presence in Sichuan in the late 1990s, during the ongoing efforts to combat the emerging HIV/AIDS epidemic. These agents introduced critical knowledge and funding, which vitally nudged the government and general population in the direction of acknowledging the scale and severity of the crisis, as well as the trauma inflicted upon those inflicted by it. The 1990s crisis also facilitated the creation of stable funding channels that regularly redirected funds from international organisations – via the municipal or local governments – to frontline grassroots organisations that had been combating the HIV/AIDS crisis. Many of these organisations later evolved and expanded into NGOs advocating more broad-based improvements and emancipation in LGBT+ rights.

Without the endorsement, or, indeed, support of local officials, such organisations could not have been permitted to exist and operate. The Chinese state is by no means a unitary actor – it must be disaggregated into domestic political structures; structures that have competing interests and clashing values, whose guiding principles vary from region to region. Whilst Sichuan has a relatively vibrant LGBT+ scene, Beijing – the country's capital – remains relatively reticent concerning what the Central administration perceives to be "Western values": values that are to be repudiated for their (ostensible) inimical foreignness to Chinese culture.

All in all, movements advocating sexual liberation and gender empowerment in China do *not* work against their state – they are by no means *anti-state*; instead, they often work in tandem with a combination of local officials and governments, and international organisations, in pressing for legal and political concessions and transformations under the state.

3.4.3 Individualisation and the youth

The Chinese civil society is increasingly *individualised*, with a growing emphasis upon individuals undertaking responsibilities that had previously been assumed by the state and large, overarching associations tasked with social management.[102] The individualisation of China is a natural product of economic privatisations and the increase in premium attached to individualistic "virtues" of perseverance, industriousness, and persistence.

Scholar Yan Yunxiang is of the view that the rise in *individualisation* should not be equated with rising *individualism*.[103] For Yan, individualism connotes the normative and ethical outlook in which the egocentric individual places their own interests, needs, and preferences at the forefront of their decisional and action calculus. In contrast, individualisation constitutes merely the state's treatment of the individual, as opposed to larger collectives – e.g., associations, families, or companies – as the primary unit of social policy. Individualisation entails the assignment of responsibilities, duties, and rights to individuals; whether this would necessarily entail the arising of individualism, however, "varies from one society to another".[104]

The argument proffered here should perhaps be updated in light of recent trends that have cropped up in China over the past decades. With the advent of social media, digital and technological communicative platforms, entertainment shows and "media icons", Chinese youth today are exposed to an unprecedented level of possible choices and personal freedoms.[105] This particularly manifests in the form of choices over one's occupations, as industries are continuously diversified and opened up to foreign investors/firms, and youth-led start-ups and innovation have increasingly thrived on a grassroots level.

A particular exemplar of the latter phenomenon constitutes Shenzhen (cf. Figure 3.3) – a city oft-touted as the "Silicon Valley of China/Asia",[106] where enterprises contributed towards more than 90% of the city's research investment, and over 90% of new patent filings in 2017. Shenzhen has emerged as a global hub of R&D (with research accounting for 4.1% of Shenzhen's total GDP in 2017, nearly double the national average), and a large number of its leading technological firms and companies are spearheaded by highly skilled, educated, professional youth.[107] Shenzhen's total GDP is also larger than Hong Kong's – surpassing the latter in 2018.[108] The ascent of start-up culture and technological entrepreneurship is accompanied by the commensurate surge in individualist-capitalist values in popular discourses – which have attached a higher premium to individuals' personal credentials, experiences, and professional skillsets over the traditionally prized "collective" brands and track records of their firms. It is the individual – rather than the firm – who is celebrated across nascent industries.

FIGURE 3.3 Shenzhen in 1985 vs. in 2015. Shenzhen in 1985 was largely rural and agrarian, with select urban land-plots near the Shenzhen-Hong Kong border. By 2015, 30 years later, Shenzhen had developed into a sprawling metropolis with skyscrapers, advanced infrastructure, and substantial economic and commercial activity. Shenzhen now serves as China's leading tech and innovation hub.

Source: CGTN, (2018) 40 years of opening up: Shenzhen's transformation seen in 10,000 photos, CGTN. https://news.cgtn.com/news/3d3d414d306b6a4d31457a6333566d54/share_p.html

Individualism has also manifested through a heightened attention to individual well-being – in a manner that has added complexity and depth to the rise of the individual: it is not just about the individual as a consumer or as a capitalist. Indeed, many amongst China's more disillusioned, structurally disenfranchised youth have turned to "tang ping" (躺平) (literally translates into "lying down") as an act of defiance (and resistance) against the cutthroat, high-strung, high-pressure work environment and culture – one that values individualised productivity and individualistic success at the expense of well-being and one's family, friends, and social life; one that treats the individual as a "participant in China's economic miracle" and a "capitalistic consumer", as opposed to a well-rounded individual. "Tang ping" denotes the rebuking of unthinking, corporatist culture and the collectivist fetishisation of "success indicators" – e.g., conspicuous consumption of luxury goods and status-based consumption patterns. It reflects an increasingly conspicuous desire in the Chinese psyche for Chinese society to eschew a prodigal, materialist, and hyper-competitive variant of individualism – in favour of a more community-based and holistic development-centred vision of "well-being individualism".[109] In that sense and in their ways, then, Chinese youth today are rebelling against the view that "West is the way".

The above demonstrates two core upshots: first, the celebration and recognition of the individual has been steadily on the rise since Deng Xiaoping's economic reforms; second, the youth have played an increasingly significant role in shaping and moulding the national ethos – whether it be "tang ping" (lying flat)[110] or their support for LGBT+ and sexual liberation movements, China's millennials are at the forefront of the evolution and development of its civil society today – playing a far greater role than their periodical counterparts did in the past.

3.4.4 Constraints and limitations to the Chinese civil society

The Chinese civil society is not without its constraints and limitations. It would be vital for state and citizens alike to grapple and reckon with them – some of them are state-imposed; others arise from a combination of circumstantial and structural constraints.

3.4.4.1 From the reform era to early 2010s

In making sense of why China's civil society is more constrained as compared with its various counterparts in advanced industrial democracies, it behoves the world to parse the intricacies of Communist Party ideology – in particular, the notion of "social management". Scholar Frank Pieke notes that contemporary China is characterised by what he terms *neo-socialism* – a distinctive governmental rationality that emphasises a strong, centralised, and sustained rule under one party, where markets and collective associations have been "selective[ly], partial[ly], and gradual[ly]" liberalised, with substantial degrees of freedom introduced into the composition and implementation of values under these respective corporatist organisations, coupled with a firm grip over the definitive principles and tenets that undergird these entities.[111]

In other words, the Party has evolved – especially during and since the era of Hu Jintao and Wen Jiabao – into a connected, sprawling entity that is devoted towards "managing" the public. Disgraced security tsar Zhou Yongkang had played a pivotal role then in driving social engineering and coordination efforts, as well as absorbing civil society institutions and organisations into the CPC apparatus. Some have argued that the sprawling and explosion of competing interests and values rendered it necessary for the Chinese administration to keep the lid on the pressure cooker – through reining in the excesses of civil society growth; others have posited that the CPC's tightening grip was a part of the augmented project of power centralisation that had put a moratorium on the 90s era of political reforms, with the party adhering to neo-authoritarian tenets[112] of political centralisation and economic liberalisation. In any case, it is apparent that just as its civil society has become increasingly diverse, heterogeneous, and latently potent, the extent of restrictions and regulations placed upon it by the Chinese state has also commensurably increased. At the critical juncture subsequent to the three years of pandemic, whether China's civil society would continue to liberalise – or decline – will depend heavily upon the policies of its current administration.[113]

3.4.4.2 Recent trends

Critics assert that the current administration's adoption of "stronger ideological controls over universities, media, and the Internet; and the passage of national security laws such as the National Security Law, [...] the Foreign NGO Law, [...] and Cybersecurity Law" are both signs of its growing uneasiness towards its booming civil society, and its inherent disposition towards curbing civilian expression and associational freedoms.[114]

To some extent, the objective phenomena described in these criticisms have indeed materialised across certain sectors and spaces. Registration for non-governmental organisations – especially international ones (for whom it is practically very, very difficult and onerous) – has become precipitously arduous, though this is, perhaps, no different from the fate confronting Chinese organisations and companies in the West.[115] There is a palpable sense that strict and avowed compliance with the Party's rule and order has become an increasingly weighted component in determining whether a non-profit organisation could continue to operate.

Independent and vocal grassroots NGOs – especially those who have worked on rights protection and advocacy for disenfranchised groups and minorities – have found themselves subjected to systemic exclusion as new laws effectively prohibited international and foreign NGOs from funding for-profit domestic enterprises – which targeted specifically small- to medium-scale independent NGOs that had previously sought to evade governmental regulations through legally establishing themselves as companies, as opposed to social organisations.[116]

Yet these narratives leave out the bigger picture. The 2016 Charity Law and associated laws opened up significant opportunities for charities to partake in public fundraising, setting up trust, and undertaking government contracts, as well as expanding the legal terms of references for fundraising processes to include online fundraising.[117] The Chinese government has also invested heavily into child welfare, environmental, and anti-discrimination/justice sectors, pledging to set up further centralising authorities and task-forces to coordinate the actions of civil society actors within each area. It is apparent that leading civil society actors have become less autonomous, with a heightened degree of state intervention and oversight over their activities.

Rumours of the "death" of China's civil society are highly exaggerated. From rekindling and "bending" – dynamically – its relationship with local and provincial government officials and, via them, international partners; to consolidating cross-sectoral collaboration and association; to expanding its reach into unchartered waters, the civil society in China has much to give, and much potential yet to be unleashed.

Notes

1 World Bank Open Data (2023) GDP per capita (current US$). Available at: https://data.worldbank.org/indicator/NY.GDP.PCAP.CD
2 World Bank Open Data (2023) GDP per capita, PPP (current international $). Available at: https://data.worldbank.org/indicator/NY.GDP.PCAP.PP.CD
3 Textor, C. (2024) China: Distribution of the workforce across economic sectors 2023 | statista. Available at: https://www.statista.com/statistics/270327/distribution-of-the-workforce-across-economic-sectors-in-china/
4 China Power Team (2024) *Measuring China's manufacturing might*, ChinaPower Project. Available at: https://chinapower.csis.org/tracker/china-manufacturing/; Tong, Z. and Tong, Z. (2024) Exclusive | Made in China 2025: China meets most targets in manufacturing plan, proving US tariffs and sanctions ineffective, *South China Morning Post*, 30 April. Available at: https://www.scmp.com/news/china/science/article/3260307/made-china-2025-china-meets-most-targets-manufacturing-plan-proving-us-tariffs-and-sanctions
5 World Bank Open Data (2023) Employment in services (% of total employment) (modeled ILO estimate) – China. Available at: https://data.worldbank.org/indicator/SL.SRV.EMPL.ZS?locations=CN
6 APCI Greater China Team (2024) *China's 2024 central economic work conference: 6 key takeaways*, APCO. Available at: https://apcoworldwide.com/blog/chinas-2024-central-economic-work-conference-six-key-takeaways/
7 Textor, C. (2024a) China: Public spending ratio 2029 | statista. Available at: https://www.statista.com/statistics/236299/public-spending-ratio-in-china/
8 Lee, A. (2020) Xi Jinping says 'poverty eliminated', but warns of uneven development, *South China Morning Post*. Available at: https://www.scmp.com/economy/china-economy/article/3112554/chinas-xi-jinping-declares-victory-poverty-alleviation-warns

9 Textor, C. (2025) China: Public expenditure on social security and employment in China from 2014 to 2024 | statista, *Statista*. Available at: https://www.statista.com/statistics/455521/china-public-expenditure-on-social-security-and-employment/

Textor C. (2025) Public expenditure in China 2014–2024, *Statista*. Available at: https://www.statista.com/statistics/455466/china-public-expenditure/

10 文小才 (2020) 中国政府消费支出的偏差及矫正, *China Regional Development Network*. Available at: http://www.cre.org.cn/list2/hg/15571.html

11 Zhou, C. (2021) *Global supply chain continues to shift away from China, but it remains the top sourcing location*, SCMP. Available at: https://www.scmp.com/economy/china-economy/article/3131785/global-supply-chain-continues-shift-away-china-it-remains-top

12 Zeng, Z.K. (2021) Chinese supply chains prove resilient to global shocks and pressure, *East Asia Forum*. Available at: https://www.eastasiaforum.org/2021/05/27/chinese-supply-chains-prove-resilient-to-global-shocks-and-pressure/

13 Black, J.S. and Morrison, A.J. (2021) The strategic challenges of decoupling, *Harvard Business Review*. Available at: https://hbr.org/2021/05/the-strategic-challenges-of-decoupling

14 Clarke, J. (2025) What are tariffs and why is Trump using them? *BBC News*. Available at: https://www.bbc.com/news/articles/cn93e12rypgo

15 Wong, K. (2025) 'Good start': China bids to reset ties with Japan amid Trump tariff storm, *South China Morning Post*. Available at: https://www.scmp.com/economy/china-economy/article/3300009/good-start-china-bids-reset-ties-japan-amid-trump-tariff-storm

16 Yu, S.Z. (2021) Why substantial Chinese FDI is flowing into Africa, *LSE Blogs*. Available at: https://blogs.lse.ac.uk/africaatlse/2021/04/02/why-substantial-chinese-fdi-is-flowing-into-africa-foreign-direct-investment/

17 Global Times (2021) ASEAN becomes China's largest trading partner in 2020, with 7% growth, *Global Times*. Available at: https://www.globaltimes.cn/page/202101/1212785.shtml

18 Rosen, D.H. (2021) *Executive summary: The third plenum roadmap*, Asia Society. Available at: https://asiasociety.org/policy-institute/executive-summary-third-plenum-roadmap

19 Yu, J. (2024) China's third plenum marks a sea change in growth model, *Chatham House*. Available at: https://www.chathamhouse.org/2024/07/chinas-third-plenum-marks-sea-change-growth-model

20 Ji, S. (2024) Economist Jin Keyu on why the trade war is still a gift for China, *South China Morning Post*. Available at: https://www.scmp.com/economy/china-economy/article/3278425/economist-jin-keyu-why-trade-war-still-gift-china

21 Every CSR report (2019) China's economic rise: History, trends, challenges, and implications for the United States, *Every CSR Report*. Available at: https://www.everycrsreport.com/reports/RL33534.html

22 Feng, C. and Bermingham, F. (2020) China GDP: Beijing abandons 2020 economic growth target, Premier Li Keqiang confirms at NPC, *South China Morning Post*. Available at: https://www.scmp.com/economy/china-economy/article/3085553/china-gdp-beijing-abandons-economic-growth-target-2020-work

Qiu, S. and Yao, K. (2021) China sets 'low bar' for GDP growth, pledges more jobs, *Reuters*. Available at: https://www.reuters.com/article/us-china-parliament-gdp-idUSKBN2AX03L

23 Zhang, H., Liu, X., and Cao, S. (2021) China to allow couples to have 3 children, step 'leading to fertility-friendly society', *Global Times*. Available at: https://www.globaltimes.cn/page/202105/1225003.shtml

24 Black, J.S. and Morrison, A.J. (2019) Can China avoid a growth crisis? *Harvard Business Review*. Available at: https://hbr.org/2019/09/can-china-avoid-a-growth-crisis
25 Zhou, C. (2021) Global supply chain continues to shift away from China, but it remains the top sourcing location, *South China Morning Post*. Available at: https://www.scmp.com/economy/china-economy/article/3131785/global-supply-chain-continues-shift-away-china-it-remains-top
26 Xinhua (2024) *Xi stresses developing new quality productive forces according to local conditions*, The State Council, The People's Republic of China. Available at: https://english.www.gov.cn/news/202403/05/content_WS65e722bdc6d0868f4e8e4b87.html
27 Yao, A. (2021) China's crackdown on tech and tutoring really directed at inequality, *South China Morning Post*. Available at: https://www.scmp.com/comment/opinion/article/3144390/chinas-crackdown-tech-and-tutoring-really-directed-inequality
28 Tse, E. (2021) What the West needs to know about where modern China is headed, *South China Morning Post*. Available at: https://www.scmp.com/comment/opinion/article/3143186/what-west-needs-know-about-where-modern-china-headed
29 Dollar, D. (2020) These are the three big challenges for China's economy, *Financial Review*. Available at: https://www.afr.com/world/asia/these-are-the-three-big-challenges-for-china-s-economy-20201213-p56n0h
30 Wang, O. and Zhou, X. (2020) China cements Communist Party's role at top of its SOEs, should 'execute the will of the party', *South China Morning Post*. Available at: https://www.scmp.com/economy/china-economy/article/3045053/china-cements-communist-partys-role-top-its-soes-should
31 Guluzade, A. (2019) Why China's state-owned companies still have a key role to play, *World Economic Forum*. Available at: https://www.weforum.org/agenda/2019/05/why-chinas-state-owned-companies-still-have-a-key-role-to-play/
32 Fitch Wire (2024) China's household debt poses moderate risk, but pockets of stress emerging, *Fitch Ratings*. Available at: https://www.fitchratings.com/research/structured-finance/chinas-household-debt-poses-moderate-risk-pockets-of-stress-emerging-18-06-2024
33 Xiao, C. (2024) *How China keeps its debt in order*, Fidelity International. Available at: https://www.fidelityinternational.com/editorial/article/how-china-keeps-its-debt-in-order-e1feea-en5/
34 International Monetary Fund (no date) *Nonfinancial corporate debt, loans and debt securities*, International Monetary Fund. Available at: https://www.imf.org/external/datamapper/NFC_LS@GDD/SWE
35 Al Jazeera (2020) China corporate debt defaults trigger concerns of broader crisis, *Al Jazeera*. Available at: https://www.aljazeera.com/economy/2020/11/13/china-corporate-debt-defaults-trigger-concerns-of-broader-crisis
36 Tan, W. (2018) Trade war begins: US and China exchange $34 billion in tariffs, *CNBC*. Available at: https://www.cnbc.com/2018/07/06/trade-war-worries-us-china-tariffs-to-kick-in-on-friday.html
37 Mahbubani, K. (2022) Is the West triumphant again? *The National Interest*. Available at: https://nationalinterest.org/feature/west-triumphant-again-203396
38 Livesay, B., Petsa, M., and Debusmann, B. (2025) Zelensky told to leave White House after angry spat with Trump and Vance, *BBC News*. Available at: https://www.bbc.com/news/live/c625ex282zzt
39 Fang, M., Lai, W., and Xia, C. (2024) Anti-corruption and political trust: evidence from China, *Preprint*. Available at: https://papers.ssrn.com/sol3/papers

.cfm?abstract_id=4792700; Golden, S. (2014) Power from the people, for the people: The communist party of China and political reform with Chinese characteristics. Available at: https://www.cidob.org/en/publications/power-people-people-communist-party-china-and-political-reform-chinese-characteristics (Accessed: 10 April 2025).

40 China US Focus. Debunking misconceptions about Xi Jinping's anti-corruption campaign. Available at: http://www.chinausfocus.com/political-social-development/debunking-misconceptions-about-xi-jinpings-anti-corruption-campaign/

41 MarketWatch. These numbers show just how much the lives of everyday Chinese have improved in recent decades. Available at: https://www.marketwatch.com/story/these-numbers-show-just-how-much-the-lives-of-everyday-chinese-have-improved-in-recent-decades-2019-10-02

42 Tandfonline (2018) China's special economic zones. Available at: https://www.tandfonline.com/doi/full/10.1080/21681376.2018.1430612

43 NPR (2020) As U.S. views of China grow more negative, Chinese support for their government rises. Available at: https://www.npr.org/2020/09/23/913650298/as-u-s-views-of-china-grow-more-negative-chinese-support-for-their-government-ri

44 Pei, M. (2004) Beijing's social contract starting to fray, *YaleGlobal Online*. Available at: https://archive-yaleglobal.yale.edu/content/beijings-social-contract-starting-fray

45 Huang, Y. (2023) *Rise and fall of EAST: Autocracy, technology*, New Haven: Yale University Press. Available at: https://www.amazon.com/Rise-Fall-EAST-Autocracy-Technology/dp/0300266367

46 Foreign faith in Chinese courts is on the rise (2019). Available at: https://english.court.gov.cn/2019-09/09/c_761751.htm

47 Cross, G. (2021) Reflections on China's legal development, *DotDotNews*. Available at: https://english.dotdotnews.com/a/202106/16/AP60c9831ce4b0c070ccc105a6.html

48 Cross, G. (2021) Reflections on China's legal development, *DotDotNews*. Available at: https://english.dotdotnews.com/a/202106/16/AP60c9831ce4b0c070ccc105a6.html

49 Nair, C. (2018) Migration: A case for stay and build, *YaleGlobal Online*. Available at: Migration: A Case for Stay and Build | YaleGlobal Online.

50 YouTube. Eric X. Li: A tale of two political systems. Available at: https://www.youtube.com/watch?v=s0YjL9rZyR0

51 Baum, R. (1996) *Burying mao: Chinese politics in the age of deng xiaoping*, Princeton University Press. Available at: https://press.princeton.edu/books/paperback/9780691036373/burying-mao

52 Wong, B.Y.S. (2021) *China has an image problem—but knows how to fix it*, Foreign Policy. Available at: https://foreignpolicy.com/2021/04/06/china-image-problem-wolf-warrior-international/

53 Bachelet, M. (2022) *Statement by UN high commissioner for human rights michelle bachelet after official visit to China*, OHCHR. Available at: https://www.ohchr.org/en/statements/2022/05/statement-un-high-commissioner-human-rights-michelle-bachelet-after-official

54 Silver, L., Devlin, K., and Huang, C. (2020) *Unfavorable views of China reach historic highs in many countries*, Pew Research Center. Available at: https://www.pewresearch.org/global/2020/10/06/unfavorable-views-of-china-reach-historic-highs-in-many-countries/

55 Wong, B. (2022) *Making sense of American mass attitudes towards China in 2022*, China US Focus. Available at: https://www.chinausfocus.com/society-culture/making-sense-of-american-mass-attitudes-towards-china-in-2022

56 Crotty, W. (2005) Terrorism in China, in *The Politics of Terror: The U.S. Response to 9/11*. Available at: https://books.google.com/books?id=Mij5aWJnAcQC&pg=PA227&lpg=PA227&dq=william+crotty+terrorism+in+china&source=bl&ots=lwvSKuUg7U&sig=UyBMB2z5n23HtoAa-BoQMPM6LhM&hl=en&sa=X&ei=dqJOT47-KIft0gG4jZm-Ag&ved=0CCEQ6AEwAA#v=onepage&q=william%20crotty%20terrorism%20in%20china&f=false
57 Soloshcheva, M.A. (2017) The Uyghur terrorism, *Iran & the Caucasus*, 21(4), pp. 415–430. Available at: https://www.jstor.org/stable/26548912
58 BBC News (2022) China's economic growth and challenges "Who are the Uyghurs and why is China being accused of genocide?". Available at: https://www.bbc.com/news/world-asia-china-22278037
59 The Economist (2021) Genocide is the wrong word for the horrors of Xinjiang. Available at: https://www.economist.com/leaders/2021/02/13/genocide-is-the-wrong-word-for-the-horrors-of-xinjiang
60 Shan, W. (2021) Xinjiang: What the West doesn't tell you about China's war on terror, *South China Morning Post*. Available at: https://www.scmp.com/comment/opinion/article/3129325/xinjiang-what-west-doesnt-tell-you-about-chinas-war-terror
61 Nair, C. (2021) The world is woke to Western posturing and global white privilege, *South China Morning Post*. Available at: https://www.scmp.com/week-asia/opinion/article/3135049/world-woke-western-posturing-and-global-white-privilege
62 Xu, K. (2021) Mideast states back China's Xinjiang stance, *Global Times*. Available at: https://www.globaltimes.cn/page/202103/1219498.shtml
63 Kuo, K. (2021) Cotton complications in Xinjiang: William Overholt on the case of Esquel, *The China Project*. Available at: https://thechinaproject.com/2021/08/26/cotton-complications-in-xinjiang-william-overholt-on-the-case-of-esquel/
64 Millward, J. (2021) Letter to the Editor, *The Wire China*. Available at: https://www.thewirechina.com/2021/09/01/letter-to-the-editor-september-3-2021/
65 Wong, B. (2024) *China's soft power challenge*, China US Focus. Available at: https://www.chinausfocus.com/society-culture/chinas-soft-power-challenge
66 CGTN (2020) *Decoding China's vision for new era world-class army*, CGTN. Available at: https://news.cgtn.com/news/2020-07-30/Xi-Jinping-envisions-world-class-Chinese-army-in-new-era-SyjxbICP16/index.html
67 Mei, S. and Blasko, D.J. (2024) *Back to the basics: How many people are in the people's liberation army?* War on the Rocks. Available at: https://warontherocks.com/2024/07/back-to-the-basics-how-many-people-are-in-the-peoples-liberation-army/
68 Maizland, F. (2020) *China's modernizing military*, Council on Foreign Relations. Available at: https://www.cfr.org/backgrounder/chinas-modernizing-military
69 Heginbotham, E. *et al.* (2015) *The US-China* military scorecard*: Forces,* goegraphy, *and the* evolving balance *of* power, RAND Corporation. Available at: https://www.rand.org/content/dam/rand/pubs/research_reports/RR300/RR392/RAND_RR392.pdf
70 Thompson, A.P. (2021) *If you build it, they will lose: Competing with China requires new information warfare tools*, CIMSEC. Available at: https://cimsec.org/if-you-build-it-they-will-lose-competing-with-china-requires-new-information-warfare-tools/
71 US Department of State (2020) *China's military aggression in the indo-pacific region*, US Department of State. Available at: https://2017-2021.state.gov/chinas-military-aggression-in-the-indo-pacific-region/index.html

72 Jennings, R. (2021) Year of unusually high US activity noted in South China Sea, *VOA News*. Available at: https://www.voanews.com/east-asia-pacific/year-unusually-high-us-activity-noted-south-china-sea
73 Ng, T. (2018) *China's new light tank for mountainous areas goes into service*, SCMP. Available at: https://www.scmp.com/news/china/military/article/2179892/chinas-new-light-tank-mountainous-areas-goes-service
74 Saunders, P.C., Ding, A.S., Scobell, A., Yang, A.N.D., and Wuthnow, J. (2019) *Chairman Xi Remakes the PLA*, National Defense University Press, pp 2, 5. Available at: https://ndupress.ndu.edu/Portals/68/Documents/Books/Chairman-Xi/Chairman-Xi.pdf
75 Saunders, P.C., Ding, A.S., Scobell, A., Yang, A.N.D., and Wuthnow, J. (2019) *Chairman Xi Remakes the PLA*, National Defense University Press, p. 231. Available at: https://ndupress.ndu.edu/Portals/68/Documents/Books/Chairman-Xi/Chairman-Xi.pdf
76 Gan, N. (2024) *China expels two former defense ministers from Communist Party as military purge deepens*, CNN. Available at: https://edition.cnn.com/2024/06/27/china/china-expels-former-defense-ministers-party-intl-hnk/index.html
77 Maizland, F. (2020) *China's modernizing military*, Council on Foreign Relations. Available at: https://www.cfr.org/backgrounder/chinas-modernizing-military
78 SIPRI (2024) *Global military spending surges amid war, rising tensions and insecurity*, SIPRI. Available at: https://www.sipri.org/media/press-release/2024/global-military-spending-surges-amid-war-rising-tensions-and-insecurity
79 Macrotrends (2025) *China military spending/defense budget*, Macrotrends. Available at: https://www.macrotrends.net/global-metrics/countries/CHN/china/military-spending-defense-budget
80 Maizland, F. (2020) *China's modernizing military*, Council on Foreign Relations. Available at: https://www.cfr.org/backgrounder/chinas-modernizing-military
81 Mainardi, B. (2021) Yes, China has the world's largest navy. That matters less than you might think, *The Diplomat*. Available at: https://thediplomat.com/2021/04/yes-china-has-the-worlds-largest-navy-that-matters-less-than-you-might-think/
82 Mainardi, B. (2021) Yes, China has the world's largest navy. That matters less than you might think, *The Diplomat*. Available at: https://thediplomat.com/2021/04/yes-china-has-the-worlds-largest-navy-that-matters-less-than-you-might-think/
83 Axe, D. (2020) The Chinese navy has a command problem, *Forbes*. Available at: https://www.forbes.com/sites/davidaxe/2020/12/23/the-chinese-navy-has-a-command-problem/?sh=7f5a5fe26268
84 Saunders, P.C., Ding, A.S., Scobell, A., Yang, A.N.D., and Wuthnow, J. (2019) *Chairman Xi Remakes the PLA*, National Defense University Press, Chapter 10. Available at: https://ndupress.ndu.edu/Portals/68/Documents/Books/Chairman-Xi/Chairman-Xi.pdf
85 Chan, M. (2021) *China's military commanders come under attack for outdated training*, SCMP. Available at: https://www.scmp.com/news/china/military/article/3131870/chinas-military-commanders-come-under-attack-outdated-training
86 Blasko, D.J. (2019) *The Chinese military speaks to itself, revealing doubts*, War on the Rocks. Available at: https://warontherocks.com/2019/02/the-chinese-military-speaks-to-itself-revealing-doubts/ – as per 90
87 Blasko, D.J. (2019) *The Chinese military speaks to itself, revealing doubts*, War on the Rocks. Available at: https://warontherocks.com/2019/02/the-chinese-military-speaks-to-itself-revealing-doubts/

88 Mackinnon, R. (2010) *Networked authoritarianism in China and beyond: Implications for global Internet freedom*, Liberation Technology in Authoritarian Regimes. Available at: https://rconversation.blogs.com/MacKinnon_Libtech.pdf
89 LaFarha, (2015) The westernization Of China, *China Daily*. Available at: https://www.chinadaily.com.cn/opinion/2015-06/26/content_21114127.htm
90 Shan, W. and Chen, J. (2021) Chinese youth: Westernised but not pro-democracy, *The China Story*. Available at: https://www.thechinastory.org/chinese-youth-westernised-but-not-pro-democracy/
91 Cheng, L. (2021) *Middle c lass Shanghai*, Brookings Institution Press. Available at: https://www.brookings.edu/book/middle-class-shanghai/
92 WWF, WWF Offices – China, WWF. Available at: https://wwf.panda.org/wwf_offices/china/
93 Xie, L. (2011) China's environmental activism in the age of globalization, *Asian Politics & Policy*, 3, pp. 207–224. https://doi.org/10.1111/j.1943-0787.2011.01256.x
94 Global Greengrants Fund (2005) *China: Proposed dam project suspended – for now*, Greengrants. Available at: https://www.greengrants.org/2005/09/08/china-proposed-dam-project-suspended-for-now/
95 Wu, C. (2005) Interpreting a call for "Harmonious society", *China Daily*. Available at: https://www.chinadaily.com.cn/english/doc/2005-03/08/content_422680.htm
96 Standaert, M. (2019) China's young climate heroes fight apathy – and the party line, *The Guardian*. Available at: https://www.theguardian.com/world/2019/sep/18/china-young-climate-heroes-fight-apathy-party-line
97 Citro, C. (2013) Environmentalism and postmaterialism in China, *Clocks and Clouds*, 3(1). Available at: http://www.inquiriesjournal.com/articles/1606/environmentalism-and-postmaterialism-in-china
98 Birkin, F., Margerison, J., and Monkhouse, L. (2021) Chinese environmental accountability: Ancient beliefs, science and sustainability, *Resources, Environment and Sustainability*, 3. Available at: https://www.sciencedirect.com/science/article/pii/S2666916121000049
99 United Nations (n.d.) Report of the people's Republic of China on the implementation of the beijing declaration and platform for action (1995) and the outcome of the 23rd special session of the general assembly (2000). Available at: https://sustainabledevelopment.un.org/content/documents/13028China_review_en_Beijing20.pdf
100 Hugill & Ip (2019) *Small steps for same-sex couples in China and the region*, Hugill & Ip Solicitors. Available at: https://www.hugillandip.com/2019/11/small-steps-for-same-sex-couples-in-china-and-the-region/
101 Hildebrandt, T. (2012) Development and division: The effect of transnational linkages and local politics on LGBT activism in China, *Journal of Contemporary China*, 21(77), pp. 845–862. https://doi.org/10.1080/10670564.2012.684967
102 Li, Z. and Liang, S. (2019) *Q&A with yan yunxiang about the rise of individualism among Chinese youth in the post-mao era*, USC US-China Institute. Available at: https://china.usc.edu/qa-yan-yunxiang-about-rise-individualism-among-chinese-youth-post-mao-era
103 Yan, Y. (2009) *The individualization of Chinese society*, Routledge. Available at: https://www.routledge.com/The-Individualization-of-Chinese-Society/Yan/p/book/9781847883780
104 Li, Z. and Liang, S. (2019) *Q&A with yan yunxiang about the rise of individualism among Chinese youth in the post-mao era*, USC US-China Institute. Available

at: https://china.usc.edu/qa-yan-yunxiang-about-rise-individualism-among-chinese-youth-post-mao-era
105 Strickland, M. (2012) *Improvised lives: Individualization, youth, and the transition to adulthood in rural China*, UCLA. Available at: https://escholarship.org/uc/item/8t07j035
106 Ge, Y. and Yang, L. (2018) *Facts and figures: Shenzhen vs. Silicon Valley*, CGTN. Available at: https://news.cgtn.com/news/31457a4e356b7a6333566d54/share.html
107 Ge, Y. and Yang, L. (2018) *Facts and figures: Shenzhen vs. Silicon Valley*, CGTN. Available at: https://news.cgtn.com/news/31457a4e356b7a6333566d54/share_p.html
108 Chan, E. Leng, S. (2019) *Hong Kong economy surpassed by neighbour Shenzhen for first time in 2018 as China's hi-tech hub soars*, SCMP. Available at: https://www.scmp.com/economy/china-economy/article/2187949/hong-kong-economy-surpassed-neighbour-shenzhen-first-time-2018
109 Ye, K. (2021) *Weekend long read: 'Lying flat' is the new resistance movement to materialism*, Caixin Global. Available at: https://www.caixinglobal.com/2021-06-05/weekend-long-read-lying-flat-is-the-new-resistance-movement-to-materialism-101723053.html
110 Ji, S., Huifeng, H., and Peach, B. (2021) *What is 'lying flat', and why are Chinese officials standing up to it?* SCMP. Available at: https://www.scmp.com/economy/china-economy/article/3153362/what-lying-flat-and-why-are-chinese-officials-standing-it
111 Pieke, F.N. (2012) The communist party and social management in China, *China Information*, 26(2), pp. 149–165. https://doi.org/10.1177/0920203X12442864
112 Sautman, B. (1990) *Retreat from revolution. Why communist systems deradicalize*, Ann Arbor, MI: University Microfilms International, 669 p.
113 Shieh, S. (2018) *Remaking China's civil society in the Xi Jinping Era*, China File. Available at: https://www.chinafile.com/reporting-opinion/viewpoint/remaking-chinas-civil-society-xi-jinping-era
114 Shieh, S. (2018) *Remaking China's civil society in the Xi Jinping Era*, China File. Available at: https://www.chinafile.com/reporting-opinion/viewpoint/remaking-chinas-civil-society-xi-jinping-era
115 Brooks, C. (2019) *Numbed with fear: Chinese Americans and McCarthyism*, American Experience. Available at: https://www.pbs.org/wgbh/americanexperience/features/mccarthy-numbed-with-fear-chinese-americans/
116 ICNL (2016) *FAQ: China's 2016 charity law*, ICNP. Available at: https://www.icnl.org/wp-content/uploads/China-FAQ-Charity-Law.pdf
117 ICNL (2016) FAQ: China's 2016 charity law, ICNP. Available at: https://www.icnl.org/wp-content/uploads/China-FAQ-Charity-Law.pdf

4

GOVERNANCE IN CHINA

How does the Chinese government govern the country?

The Chinese government – driven and run largely by the Communist Party of China (CPC) – seeks to empower and improve the national strength of China, as well as the ability of the one-party-dominated government to maintain power. The preservation of power, in turn, is viewed largely by the leadership as rooted in its responsibility, commitment, and ability to deliver upon concrete improvements to the well-being of the average Chinese citizen. Most contemporary Chinese leaders are less interested in serving and advancing particular ideological dogma in an ossified manner, though they do not refrain from employing ideology as a means and device in enabling them to govern with efficacy.

Indeed, a central tenet undergirding the contemporary Chinese leadership's thinking over their own country, revolves around the establishment of a "community of shared future for mankind".[1] Per this vision, the 21st century is defined by global challenges that are both interconnected and demanding of international cooperation. President Xi Jinping emphasised in his speech at Geneva in 2017, that it is vital that "we [...] build a world of common prosperity through win-win cooperation", as opposed to zero-sum rivalry. This vision emphasises mutual respect among nations, irrespective of their size or power; it also calls for respecting the sovereignty and territorial integrity of all countries and treating each other as equals.

On a domestic level, embracing this community would behove governments across the world to adopt and consolidate inclusive development that benefits all nations and peoples. This means addressing economic disparities, promoting sustainable development, and ensuring that the fruits of globalisation are shared more equitably by domestic populations. President Xi

DOI: 10.4324/9781003643548-4

advocated, "we should make economic globalisation more open, inclusive, and balanced so that its benefits are shared by all". It is clear that China's foreign policy advocacy and agenda are firmly coherent with and rooted in its domestic policies – fundamentally, China remains a firm beneficiary of globalisation, through trade, investment, and economic liberalisation that has unleashed immense potential in the country's economy. The introduction of market mechanisms and capitalist logic from the 1980s onwards played an instrumental role in enabling the modernisation and evolution of the Chinese economy, as well as the empowerment of Chinese entrepreneurs, investors, and innovators, all critical constituents and components in the contemporary China story.

One of the main criticisms of China by commentators who do not understand it is that it is ostensibly run by a "dictatorship", by a "clique" of nepotists who are selected and hand-picked on grounds of their being loyal *apparatchik* – taking after the later years of the Soviet Union. It follows from this portrayal, then, that China does not have an enduring or tenable form of governance – instead, it operates by the whims and arbitrary decisions of a single person, or a few people with power. This view is a blatant oversimplification, and a deeply flawed and erroneous judgement. This view, whether borne out of ignorance or a ideologically driven desire to reinforce to a wider world a negative view of China, is at the heart of a great deal of current geo-political tensions surrounding China and its relationship with the West in particular. Indeed, this view that has deleterious consequences for all seeking to understand China, in not only cultivating unhelpful misunderstandings, but also precluding the world at large from learning from China where possible.

This section aims to clarify the nature of governance adopted in China.

4.1 Governance system

How does China govern itself? An exhaustive answer to this question would require hundreds, if not thousands, of pages. Only a pithy summary can be provided here – but the gist is this: the Chinese government's governance logic is inherently intertwined with its legitimation discourse. Indeed, the long-standing ruling philosophy of the Communist Party of China (CPC), per Deng Xiaoping, concerns "seeking truth from facts"[2] – to govern pragmatically and efficaciously, is a necessary prerequisite for the government's continued popularity, support from the masses, and overarching stability. Chinese government is pragmatic, experimental, innovative, and fundamentally non-ideological – despite, perhaps, the presence and emphasis upon ideological rhetoric in some of its departments.

The Chinese government's notion of legitimacy, then, can be deconstructed into two core conceptual components: (1) performance legitimacy[3] – a term employed by commentators and academics to capture the distinctive emphasis in modern China upon delivering substantive, concrete positive outcomes that are broadly in line with public expectations and conceptions of the good life (or conceptions of a *majority* amongst the public) and (2) hierarchal legalism[4] – a term introduced here to reflect the complex nature of the Chinese administration, rooted, in turn, in the Confucian emphasis upon hierarchal enforcement and compliance. The administration combines the top-down enforcement of compliance and party discipline with an institutionalised, centralised legal order, with both prongs spearheaded by the CPC. The emphasis upon subservience and acceptance of the established order goes hand-in-hand with the country's distinctive and historically rooted cultural traditions, but also the pressures and demands from the public – for improvements to their quality of life – that officials across all levels must address and resolve.

These two objectives are symbiotic and mutually reinforcing. The durability and tenability of the CPC's rule enable it to carry out swift, largely efficacious policies and executive decisions; on the other hand, the absence of substantial opposition to or deviance from the party ensures that the party, proverbially, "gets things done". In understanding how the Chinese administration governs, therefore, it is imperative that one reflects upon how much of its governance institutions are rooted (or not) in the two doctrines above.

4.1.1 Performance legitimacy

In making sense of "performance legitimacy", two questions must be asked – how does this concept fit within the CPC ideology in *theory*, and how does it play out *in practice*?

The theorisation about performance legitimacy has always been clear – and an underlying strand that has run throughout the governing ideologies of Deng, Jiang, Hu, and Xi. Deng Xiaoping called for a "liberation of thought; pursuit of pragmatism" ("解放思想，实事求是") as he sought to articulate a vision for China that nominally paid tribute to Maoism, whilst reversing the tragic course that China had been placed on in the final years of Mao's rule. Pragmatism was deemed the overarching tenet that defined and motivated the radical reforms that Deng Xiaoping undertook – in delivering goods, welfare, and well-being to the people who needed it the most. In reorienting governance around the livelihood of citizens – as opposed to the obtaining of some grandstanding, historicist vision, Deng[5] offered a triangulating path between the ideological frenzy of Maoist remnants and the zealous cries for reform amongst the progressive members of the party.

Deng Xiaoping's postulates were continued under Jiang Zemin and Hu Jintao – the former added "Moving with the times" ("与时俱进") to the couplet, to reflect the modernising tendencies and processes that unfolded under his watch; the latter continued the ongoing momentum, with the introduction of the highly emphatic slogan "Seek truth from practice" ("求真务实").[6]

What undergirded all three leaders was the emphasis upon delivering practical outcomes and tackling real issues – as opposed to asking theoretical, abstract questions that only served to distract and conceal the practical truth.

As compared with his two most immediate predecessors, Xi Jinping was distinctly more upfront – "Improving people's livelihood and well-being is the primary goal of development", he wrote, as a part of his core theoretical commitments.[7] Xi Jinping Thought – as penned by ideology architect Wang Huning – treats development as a means to an end, of floating *all* boats.

All of this is well in theory. Yet does it hold up in practice? Political scientist Andrew Nathan,[8] in making the argument in 2003 that China might emerge to be a resilient authoritarian state, as opposed to a state that would, like the USSR, collapse and fracture, posited that a variety of institutions and practices adopted by the CPC leadership had enabled it to remain in power. What he perhaps under-estimated, however, was the extent to which these institutions were intentionally and functionally installed with the purpose of genuinely ensuring quality gatekeeping over the actual forms of governance at all levels in the country. By cynically reducing the Chinese government's internal checks and balances to tools sustaining regime "resilience", Nathan neglects the rich, deep literature on the Chinese civilisational ethos of governance – and what governance ought to look like – from prominent academics in China, such as Daniel Bell[9] and Zhang Weiwei's[10] assessment of mechanisms that have enabled the Chinese government to rule successfully. With that said, Nathan should be commended for the detailed and empirically rooted approach by which he examined China's distinctive methods of governance – some of which we shall explore below:

The first mechanism constitutes China's *norm-based succession politics.* Deng Xiaoping presided over a plethora of gentocrats and elders who had made substantial contributions to Chinese politics since the Civil War – these senior statesmen all retired by mid- to late 1990s. Deng Xiaoping himself transferred power over to Jiang Zemin, the first of the three "orderly" and well-planned successions that have taken place since. Whilst Jiang had stayed on to preside over the military – and continues, till this very day, to wield significant influence over affairs in the country, his retirement in the early 2000s denoted a fundamental paradigm shift in CPC succession planning. The Jiang-Hu transition was in turn the first in which senior figures, elderly statesmen, and the military played minimal role, with the majority of the then-selected leadership of the party playing the steering role in supporting Jiang in handing over power to Hu.

In his ascent to the pinnacle of power, Xi was viewed by many as a compromise candidate between multiple antagonistic factions within the party; yet even then, that he was selected, as opposed to a clear representative or spokesperson of a particular faction, was indicative of a pivoting away from detrimental politicking and politicisation of the post of General Secretary.

Critics may remain cynical – but the reality was, China had long been steadily improving the degree of meritocracy in the succession politics at the highest echelons.

The second mechanism featured a shift towards institutionalising *meritocratic considerations playing the predominant role in selection, promotion, and demotion of personnel across all levels.* Whilst the Chinese civilisation had long adopted ideals that promoted the appointment and nomination of highly qualified and skilled bureaucrats to serve in positions of governing influence and relevance, the institutionalisation of such ethos in the past 40 years since reform and opening-up began, has arguably been one of the greatest accomplishments of the CPC.

Over recent decades, the Chinese civil service's admissions process has become notoriously competitive: in 2012, 1.23 million candidates applied for the civil service, with only 1.4% of them accepted into the bureaucracy. By November 2023, the number of applicants hit 2.6 million.[11] Promotions are notoriously difficult – on average, the 900,000 section-head-level civil servants (the most junior rung in the hierarchy) must compete over 40,000 division-head-level probationary posts, with only the most successful candidates amongst these 40,000 eligible for further promotion, to join the 6,000-strong probationary force at the bureau-director level. Amongst all bureau-directors, only 2.6% would make it to the provincial-ministerial level, with a vast majority of civil servants finishing off their careers amongst far more junior ranks.[12]

Now some may argue that such statistics alone is meaningless. The cynic may rightfully object that it is not about the numbers, but the means of selection; if the method of selection is overwhelmingly driven by nepotism and favouritism, rent-seeking and rent-providing, then surely, there could be no meritocracy to speak of, even if it were one million candidates vying for a single post.

Yet those who raise such objections would benefit from closer and more meticulous scrutiny of the rationales and processes by which personnel decisions are made. From the 1980s onwards, the main goal of the CPC leadership – when it came to governance reforms – has been to replace old, revolutionary cadres (gradually losing their capacities to function and govern effectively, in any case) with new, younger cadres with technical expertise. Indeed, most of the current generation of leaders were born after 1949 – they are not "handpicked from those who participated in the Long March", which was a prerequisite condition, for decades since the country's establishment, for senior leadership positions in the party.

In China today, bureaucrats are both rigorously taught and incentivised to care for the citizens they serve, through a range of institutionalised practices that broadly contribute towards and maintain norms of performance-based pay: officials are promoted, dismissed, vetted, and paid on the basis of their ability to deliver upon key governance outcomes. The sacking of officials held accountable for their dereliction of duties is frequent, though by no means ubiquitous at large. Competence is rewarded, whilst ineptitude is penalised. Of course, the operative question – and one that the party must continue to grapple with – concerns what "competence" and "ineptitude" fundamentally mean. The nebulously vague nature of these terms may render them conducive instruments and means by which politicians can engage in self-serving politicking. We may also find excessive the efforts to litigate exhaustively what the measurements and indicators of competence and ineptitude in fact are – to the point where such discussions become prohibitively stifling and generate unwarranted risk-aversion on the part of party cadres. The reality though is that across the board it has not held back progress as it has in other countries

More generally, *the youth are stepping up to positions of political and socioeconomic responsibility.* To illustrate this, note that the membership of the CPC grew by an average of 2.4% per year under Hu Jintao (General Secretary from 2002 to 2012). The party's ranks swell from 68.2 million in 2002 to 82.6 million by 2011, and then to 98.0 million in 2022. A vast majority of these new recruits were fresh, young college grads.[13] Despite the decline in the growth over the past decade, it remains the case that the party has considerably expanded its size since 2000 – see Figure 4.1 for this.[14]

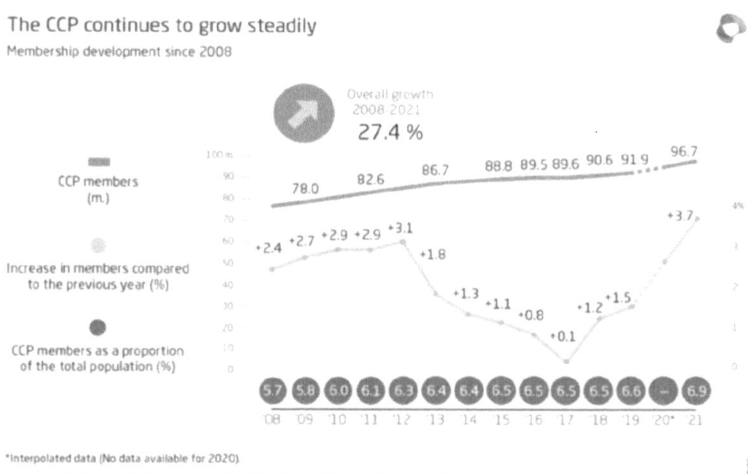

FIGURE 4.1 Communist Party of China membership numbers over time (between 2008 and 2021).

Grunberg, N. (2022) *Who is the CCP? China's Communist Party in infographics, Mercator Institute for China Studies.* Available at: https://merics.org/en/comment/who-ccp-chinas-communist-party-infographics

In the 1990s, the central government introduced the National Civil Service Examination (NCSE) as a standardised and centralised recruitment method that removed the discretionary powers of recruitment from the hands of local and district cadres; recruitment was due to be "open, fair, competitive, and meritocratic", as reinforced through the Civil Service Law. Some have noted that "by committing to a set of clear, enforceable rules that reduce patronage practice by elites", the CPC became attuned to institutionalising "merit-based elite recruitment that fosters a widespread and persistent perception of upward mobility among ordinary citizens".[15]

The third mechanism – and one that uniquely sets China apart from other non-electoral-democratic governments – constituted China's distinctive emphasis upon *functional differentiation and specialisation* amongst its bureaucrats. Bureaucrats were encouraged – since the early 1990s – to specialise in disciplines, preferably from the natural or physical sciences, that were distinct and additional to politics and party theory. Through "tiaos"[16] – vertical systems and lines of authority over various sectors extending down from the ministries of the central government, and through which promotional decisions *could* be made, officials who had previously only reported to their respective *provincial* Governors and General Secretaries were required to report to the "Central Authorities" in Beijing – via the various organs installed under the National Council. The National Council thus presided over a plethora of functionally differentiated and well-defined "verticals" tasked with delivering upon specific policy directives in particular spheres.

4.1.2 Hierarchal legalism

For the better half of the time that has elapsed since its inception, modern China has been searching for a new politico-institutional arrangement to ensure the obtaining of the aforementioned vision of meritocracy. This search for a stable modus operandi became all the more important in the aftermath of two events – the death of Mao Zedong in 1976, which left the country bereft of the personality cult that had stabilised and underpinned its centralised leadership, and the Tiananmen Square Incident in 1989, which saw modern China rocked by a series of large-scale protests culminating at the tragedy in June. As China entered the 1990s, it was desperately in need of a political system that could deliver, above all, stability and order. A set of institutional apparatuses and norms hence emerged – these norms shall be collectively denoted by the term "hierarchal legalism".

There are two components to this ideology. The first comprises the preservation of strict formal *hierarchies*, maintained through the expansive civil service system, and national security apparatus and propaganda organs. The second constitutes the *legalistic* ruling philosophy and laws enshrined under an increasingly networked[17]/connected government.

On the first, the contemporary Chinese government is highly disciplined, undergirded by well-formulated hierarchies that straddle both the geographical (*kuai*) and technocratic-functional (*tiao*) dimensions of governance. Civil servants have been promoted and recognised for their ability to adhere to orders from above, with a critical correctional mechanism that precludes the formation of nepotistic and inept "middlemen" – personnel decisions are undertaken by officials two levels *above* the level in question, which precludes the possibility of horse-trading and locally rooted patronage networks. Additionally, bureaucrats, since the 1990s, have been extensively encouraged (instructed) by the central authorities to partake in mutual commentary and evaluation, with "peer" feedback forming a critical dimension of decisions concerning promotions and transfers.

Even when it came to the central leadership, the hyper-hierarchal element remained clear – the Heads of State Council Ministries (functional equivalent of "Secretaries" in Westminster/American system) are required to report to a combination of the State Council leadership (their nominal superiors, governing the technocratic-functionalist dimensions of national governance) and the Party leadership (their de facto superiors, tasked with overseeing the political-party side of governance). Sitting atop the ladder was the seven-people (once nine-, under Jiang Zemin) Standing Committee, presided over by the General Secretary.

Whilst the level of influence wielded by the General Secretary ebbed and waned throughout time, collectively, the Standing Committee would determine all major policy decisions, directives, and the then-ideology of the party. Each member of the Standing Committee bears a designated portfolio, with apparatus such as the Central Political and Legal Affairs Commission (CPLAC) and Central Commission for Discipline Inspection (CCDI) playing a critical role in assisting senior party leaders in ensuring downstream compliance with their orders over recent years – in response to the historical problem where directives from the Central Administration seldom percolated through to their intended audiences ("政令不出中南海").[18]

As for the *legalistic* component, this book must preface the following by noting that the rule of law has become a precipitously important discursive concept and tool in official party parlance. Party officials have repeatedly called for modernisations to the country's courts, whether it be for the purpose of rendering them more compatible with the needs and demands of international capital (cf. Deng Xiaoping and the early days of Jiang's rule), assisting the state in engaging in prudent, targeted "scientific management" of the country (cf. Hu's "Scientific Development" theory[19]), or, indeed, advancing a vision of "Socialist Rule of Law with Chinese characteristics".[20]

With all that said, how does theory measure up against practice? In making sense of China's legal transformations and reforms, it would be necessary to divide its contemporary legal history into three phases, per legal theorist Carl

Minzner's[21] typology. The first phase constitutes the 1980s to early 2000s; the second phase, the early 2000s to 2012; and the third phase, 2012 and onwards. It would be fundamentally remiss and erroneous to assume that the level and maturity of rule of law have remained the same throughout these periods.

The first phase saw China adopt a distinctively Western or quasi-Western approach to legal reforms. The 1991 Civil Procedure Law radically transformed urban court procedures, calling on courts to "protect the exercise of the litigation rights of the parties, ensure that the people's courts ascertain facts, distinguish right from wrong, apply the law correctly [...]"[22] and to approximate international standards of arbitration and adjudication – especially over civil law cases. China's rapid economic growth and the relative interest of central party authorities in rendering its commercial law more in line with international standards under external pressures (e.g., the country's seeking to join the World Trade Organisation (WTO), which culminated at its eventual accession to the WTO in 2001) were pivotal forces steering this shift. As a result, the number of administrative suits against the government boomed from 0 in 1989 to over 100,000 in 2001; the percentage of successfully mediated civil cases declined steadily from 70% (early 180s) to 30% (early 2000s), as individuals resorted to the court as means of settling their differences.

The second phase saw China pivot away from this ideal of the law established earlier – a heightened emphasis was subsequently placed upon the law's being a coordinative and supplementary tool that facilitated, as opposed to constrained, the state's governance. The "Harmonious Society" (和谐社会) doctrine proposed in 2004 by the Central Administration placed a moratorium on the "Westernisation" of Chinese law. What emerged, then, was a series of reforms that placed greater emphasis upon mediation and resolutions – both within and outside the judicial systems. People's mediation committees administered by local villagers and resident committees played an increasingly significant role in upholding contextually and geographically adapted conceptions of the law; mediation was promulgated within the judiciary, with judges and lawyers alike encouraged to eschew litigation in favour of mediation. "A world without litigation" (天下无讼) was viewed as a pivotal ingredient of a harmonious, non-adversarial society.

Since Xi Jinping took office in 2012, the term "rule of law" has become increasingly prominent and ubiquitously featured in official Chinese state discourse. An official announcement in 2020 declared that "the ultimate goal of China's rule of law is to protect the interests of the people", where "law-based governance [is adopted] for the sake of generations to come and long-term development".[23]

Under Xi, China's advancements in what it views to be rule of law had gone hand-in-hand with Beijing's mass campaigns against corrupt officials and "insubordinate elements" – including individuals in Hong Kong and Macau who had sought to undermine what China viewed as its core interests under "One Country, Two Systems". A tightening of rules of entry and participation into Hong Kong's legislative elections – in view of what Beijing conceives of as active and systemic threats to its rule over Hong Kong, as well as Hong Kong's political order – has transformed Hong Kong's political institutions over the past 25 years.

Xi's China had equally sought to adopt and advocate the Chinese conception of rule of law in its international forays – especially over the flagship Belt and Road Initiative. Past decades have seen the conception of law in state discourse transition from strictly stipulated, absolutist doctrines, to contextually developed and cultivated principles that enabled the party to engage in pragmatic and flexible decision-making as it sought to promote and further its political ends. Predictably, the Western version of "rule of law" diverges rather substantially from the status quo in China – whether this should be normatively worrying or objectionable, however, is a separate question.

4.2 Is there a China Model?

There's the billion dollar question: does China govern by a distinctive "China Model"? Advocates who answer to the affirmative – theorists such as Zhang Weiwei[24] and Daniel Bell[25] – make the argument that the Chinese governance model offers a viable and credible alternative to the Western Westphalian, liberal, democratic order. Zhang argues that a system of elite-selected bureaucrats and public servants – backed by their connections with the people and ability to "feel the pulse" – excels over publicly nominated and selected politicians in governing. Bell makes the culturalist case that China's distinctive politico-cultural history renders the country distinctively suited to a mixed model of governance, with the upper stratum led by meritocratic elites, intermediate layer constituted by experimentation, and bottom layer governed through democratic, village- and municipality-level elections.

These theorists have a point – some of the existing (increasingly mainstream) discourse on China tends to frame China as an authoritarian, inept, illegitimate, and untenable government, suffering from the ailments of the lack of democracy. Such readings may be rhetorically captivating and appealing to a select audience, yet are fundamentally out-of-touch with reality on the ground: as aforementioned, the Chinese public's satisfaction with their government has remained consistently high throughout the opening-up and reform years. Indeed, the support for the Chinese state was best evidenced and epitomised by a rigorous survey conducted by the Harvard Ash Centre, with results published in 2020.[26]

Additionally, there is often a dangerous and erroneous conflation between the lack of formal, electoral democracy, and the ostensible illegitimacy of a government. Yes, Chinese leaders are not selected via democratic elections in which anyone can run and everyone can vote. Yet this does not necessarily render its system of governance illegitimate – especially if it were able to deliver, largely, upon the expectations and needs of the public. The distinctively meritocratic emphasis upon competence and efficiency is by no means a defect – it is, instead and indeed, a virtue that is sorely lacking from many other countries and jurisdictions around the world.

With that said, the existence of a so-called "China Model" should also not be overstated. In particular, the argument that China serves as an exemplar of an alternative system, a wholly separate paradigm from which countries can emulate, could well be overstated. Whilst the global community can certainly learn from China – states at large should imitate its strengths, admire its prowess, and come to terms with many of its successes (and the costs underlying them) – this does not imply that the world should therefore view China as a "model".

To argue that something amounts to a model requires more than suggesting that there can be elements of it from which other countries can learn. It is to posit that there exists completeness, consistency, and replicability in the set of political ideals espoused by the system. This is not the case for China, which continues to struggle in delineating and articulating to the international community a cogent vision or principle set that underpins its governance. Some have suggested that it is pragmatic utilitarianism; others posit that it is meritocratic technocracy – yet if even those who are well-versed with the country's history and politics remain divided over what, *exactly*, the Chinese system *is*, it would appear to be rather premature to conclude that China offers a *model* from which other states can learn.

Nor is China especially keen to export its governance model.[27] It regularly does business with Western electoral democracies; works extensively with developing and fledgling economies – members of the developing world – without demanding that they accede to specific stipulations concerning their political systems. Incidentally, most contemporary Chinese leaders often emphasise that they have no intention to export their governance model – the China Model is neither necessarily suitable for others, nor an ideology that undergirds China's overseas foreign policy. China is uninterested in imposing its modus operandi upon countries for which it may not be applicable – nor, indeed, is it bent on instigating an "axis of authoritarianism".[28]

A vast majority of democracies in the world engage in substantial trade with China; China has not sought to make them any more comparable or alike to itself. Where it has indeed engaged in political interference and promotion of values or goals, it is to advance agenda that directly benefit itself in the domestic setting – i.e., not regime change or regime *type* change. The CPC highlights its distinctive governance model in a defensive manner, in response to often over-hyped criticisms that portray it as fundamentally unjust. It seeks not to vindicate its normative propositions by imposing the same model onto other states, as the United States and the West have, in the Middle East and beyond.[29]

4.3 Transitioning to the present...

China's rise is a rather remarkable phenomenon in many ways – the pace at which its economy has grown, the extent to which the quality of life and average income of its citizens has increased, and, indeed, the political clout and stature it has gained on an international setting, over the past decades, all attest to the country's rather astounding achievements in certain spheres. Yet with its rise has also come unique challenges – challenges ranging from the environmental to the social, from its political institutions to the extent to which its economic growth is, if at all, sustainable, given its demographic circumstances. Whilst the productivity slump and demographic crunch should not be overstated and exaggerated, these have been and remain critical challenges that the nation must confront.

China's developments over the past eight decades should not be viewed narrowly through the prism of a Marxist-Leninist state, but also through the lenses of pragmatism, flexible adaptation, and, perhaps most importantly, the Chinese civilisational ethos. The Chinese people have built up their values and institutional norms over centuries of robust evolution. It is indeed this very self-conception as a confident, comprehensive civilisation that has driven the Chinese state to promulgate and pioneer the Global Civilisational Initiative – an initiative aiming to facilitate dialogue, exchange, and conversation across disparate civilisational systems, all of them sharing and underpinned by a common commitment to human flourishing in ways that are sensitive to their geographical and historical contexts.

Irrespective of its successes or limitations, it behoves the world to take seriously the fact that China's political system does not work in ways that mirror or reflect exactly the West's – and such divergences should be celebrated, as opposed to castigated; should be understood, not dismissed; should be embraced where there exists room for synergy, but critically scrutinised and guarded against where there exist reasonable concerns for others. No country is perfect, and the international community must learn to appreciate the strengths and merits of any political system, whilst being capable of critically appraising and discussing its flaws, especially when speaking about a country that has arisen from an ancient civilisation and presides over 1.4bn people. Only through well-intentioned, informed debate, could improvements to its governance be made. It would be naïve, indeed, to think that China itself is not actively engaged in and aware of such critiques internally.

Notes

1 Zhao, X. (2018) In Pursuit of a Community of Shared Future: China's Global Activism in Perspective, *China Quarterly of International Strategic Studies*, 4(1), pp 23–37. Available at: https://www.worldscientific.com/doi/pdf/10.1142/S2377740018500082?srsltid=AfmBOorlOhe1l0FHvgGix59micQMaOtAISDi6yMfqMLi6vLoRsBlJCDr
2 Huaxia (ed.) (2022) Behind Chinese idioms: Seeking Truth from facts, a lasting wisdom, *Xinhua*. Available at: https://english.news.cn/20220414/4b57b177e6f54f34a3e8ceb58216733d/c.html; International Department, Central Committee of CPC (2018) Constitution of the communist party of china revised and adopted at the 19th National Congress of the Communist Party of China on October 24, 2017. Available at: https://www.idcpc.org.cn/english2023/tjzl/cpcjj/PartyConstitution/
3 Zhu, Y. (2011) "Performance legitimacy" and China's political adaptation strategy, *Journal of Chinese Political Science*, 16, pp. 123–140. Available at: https://doi.org/10.1007/s11366-011-9140-8
4 Note: this is a term coined for the purpose of this report – it draws upon both China's legalistic dimensions (in its distinct emphasis upon the law), as well as the heavily hierarchal nature of China's bureaucracy. See earlier citation re: Baum
5 Nathan, A.J. (2003) China's changing of the Guard: Authoritarian resilience, *Journal of Democracy*, 14(1), pp. 6–17. Available at: https://www.journalofdemocracy.org/articles/chinas-changing-of-the-guard-authoritarian-resilience/ Vogel, E.F. (2013) *Deng Xiaoping and the Transformation of China*, Belknap Press.
6 Howell, J. and Duckett, J. (2019) Reassessing the Hu–Wen Era: A golden age or lost decade for social policy in China? *The China Quarterly*, 237, pp. 1–14. https://doi.org/10.1017/S0305741018001200
7 Headley, T. (2018) A slowing Chinese economy means more instability, *The Diplomat*. Available at: https://thediplomat.com/2018/10/a-slowing-chinese-economy-means-more-instability/
8 Nathan, A.J. (2003) China's changing of the guard: Authoritarian resilience, *Journal of Democracy*, 14(1), pp 6–17. Available at: https://www.journalofdemocracy.org/articles/chinas-changing-of-the-guard-authoritarian-resilience/
9 Bell, D.A. (2015) *The China model: Political* meritocracy *and the* limits *of* democracy, Princeton University Press. Available at: The China Model: Political Meritocracy and the Limits of Democracy on JSTOR.
10 Zhang, W. (2012) *China wave: Rise of a civilizational state*, World Century Publishing Corporation.
11 Luo, Y. and Tian, X. (2023) In China, Competition for Civil Service Jobs Keeps Getting Fiercer, *Sixth Tone*. Available at: https://www.sixthtone.com/news/1014012; Kelter, F. (2023) 'China's youth compete for stable gov't jobs in unstable economic times', *Al Jazeera*, 16 December. Available at: https://www.aljazeera.com/news/2023/12/16/chinas-youth-compete-for-stable-govt-jobs-in-unstable-economic-times.
12 Wang, Y. (2023) 觀察站：一場艱難的升遷之路　為何說中共是「精英政治」, *HK01*. Available at: https://www.hk01.com/article/412588?utm_source=01articlecopy&utm_medium=referral; Understanding the black box of Chinese politics (2022) https://asiasociety.org/policy-institute/decoding-chinese-politics/introduction-black-box-chinese-policy.; Li, C. (2016) *Chinese politics in the Xi Era: Reassessing collective leadership*, Washington, DC: The Brookings Institution Press.

13 Thomas, N. (2020) Members only: Recruitment trends in the Chinese communist party, *Macro Polo.* Available at: https://archivemacropolo.org/analysis/members-only-recruitment-trends-in-the-chinese-communist-party/?rp=m
Xinhua (2023) *CPC sees membership surpass 98 mln*, The State Council, The People's Republic of China. Available at: https://english.www.gov.cn/news/202306/30/content_WS649ecd11c6d0868f4e8dd637.html
14 Grunberg, N. (2022) *Who is the CCP? China's communist party in infographics*, Mercator Institute for China Studies. Available at: https://merics.org/en/comment/who-ccp-chinas-communist-party-infographics
15 Liu, H. (2019) *Upward mobility and authoritarian stability: Merit-based elite recruitment in China*, Columbia University. Available at: https://academiccommons.columbia.edu/doi/10.7916/d8-4sfq-d358/download
16 Wilson Centre (1997) *China Environment Series*, Wilson Centre. Available at: https://www.wilsoncenter.org/publication/china-environment-series-11997
17 MacKinnon, R. (2011) China's "Networked Authoritarianism", *Journal of Democracy*, 22, pp. 32–46. Available at: https://www.journalofdemocracy.org/articles/liberation-technology-chinas-networked-authoritarianism/
18 Li, C. (2012) The battle for China's top nine leadership posts, *Center for Strategic and International Studies, The Washington Quarterly*, 35(1), pp 31–145. Available at: https://csis-website-prod.s3.amazonaws.com/s3fs-public/legacy_files/files/publication/twq12winterli.pdf
19 Fewsmith, J. (2004) *Promoting the scientific development concept*, China Leadership Monitor, No. 11. Available at: https://www.hoover.org/sites/default/files/uploads/documents/clm11_jf.pdf
20 Tiffert, G. (2018) Socialist rule of law with Chinese characteristics: a new genealogy, in H. Fu, J. Gillespie, P. Nicholson, and W.E. Partlett (eds.), *Socialist Law in Socialist East Asia*, Cambridge: Cambridge University Press, pp. 72–96. Available at: https://www.cambridge.org/core/books/abs/socialist-law-in-socialist-east-asia/socialist-rule-of-law-with-chinese-characteristics/53771AD414B644A1AEE7B7421046264C
21 Minzner, C.F. (2011) China's turn against law, *The American Journal of Comparative Law*, *59*(4), pp. 935–984. http://www.jstor.org/stable/23045693
22 Lehman Law (1991), Law of civil procedure of the people's Republic of China Available at: https://www.lehmanlaw.com/resource-centre/laws-and-regulations/civil-proceedings/law-of-civil-procedure-of-the-peoples-republic-of-china-1991.html
23 Xinhua (2020) *Under Xi's leadership, China champions rule of law on journey to modernization*, Ministry of Justice of the People's Republic of China. Available at: http://en.moj.gov.cn/2020-11/19/c_564981.htm
24 Zhang, W. (2021) *What is the unique model behind China's rapid rise?* CGTN. Available at: https://news.cgtn.com/news/2021-06-03/What-is-the-unique-model-behind-China-s-rapid-rise--10NshmTiuPe/index.html
25 Bell, D. (2018) China's political meritocracy versus Western democracy, *The Economist.* Available at: https://www.economist.com/open-future/2018/06/12/chinas-political-meritocracy-versus-western-democracy
26 Cunningham, E., Saich, T., and Turiel, J. (2020) *Understanding CCP resilience: Surveying Chinese public opinion through time*, Harvard Kennedy School ASH Center for Democratic Governance and Innovation. Available at: https://ash.harvard.edu/wp-content/uploads/2024/02/final_policy_brief_7.6.2020.pdf
27 Paul, E. (2021) *What biden's top China theorist gets wrong*, The Lawfare Institute. Available at: https://www.lawfaremedia.org/article/what-bidens-top-china-theorist-gets-wrong

28 Beeson, M. and Xu, S. (2019) China's evolving role in global governance: The AIIB and the limits of an alternative international order, in K. Zeng (ed.), *Handbook of the international political economy of China* (Handbooks of Research on International Political Economy series), Edward Elgar Publishing, pp. 345–360.

29 *Xinjiang – Understanding complexity, Building Peace* (2021) idi International. Available at: https://idi-international.org/wp-content/uploads/2021/05/New-Report.pdf

5

A FORCE FOR GOOD TO THE WORLD?

Benefits, setbacks, and challenges

Much ink has been spilled on China's achievements, but what has China done for the *world* at large? How should China's accomplishments be assessed through the lenses of and contributions towards the world at large?

A substantial proportion of China's population has been lifted out of poverty – indeed, per the World Bank's definition of "extreme poverty"[1] as denoting individuals living on less than $1.90 USD a day, the Chinese government has all but eliminated extreme poverty in the country – with 850 million Chinese lifted out of poverty over the past four decades.[2] These beneficiaries from the end of extreme poverty in China do matter for the rest of the world, insofar as they accounted for over one in ten individuals in 2016[3] – when China achieved what had appeared to be innately impossible only decades ago.

5.1 Benefits

Beyond its domestic successes, the rise of China has also introduced substantial benefits to the world. In making sense of China's impact on the world, two preliminary points must be noted: the first is that many amongst the following benefits are *universal and widespread* – contrary to popular expectations; even countries that are not the intended or direct beneficiaries from China's rise, have found themselves buoyed and aided by the economic rise and achievements of the country; the second is that despite this, not all of the dividends are evenly distributed amongst the international community – there inevitably will be countries that have gained more from China's ascent, than others. Whether such asymmetries are inherent in the nature of the country's

DOI: 10.4324/9781003643548-5

rise, or can be adjusted and transformed through focussed reforms, remains an open question.

5.1.1 A low-cost "factory to and of the world"

China has emerged to become the world's largest manufacturer and an economic powerhouse steering the world's growth over the past decades. With a substantial population and largely affordable and competitive wages (at least, in the first two decades or so since its initial economic opening-up), China has emerged as the default choice for locations for labour-intensive and capital-intensive industries alike: the former, due to the willingness of Chinese workers to work extended shifts for low wages, as well as the abundant supply of readily trained and skilled workers; the latter, with the substantial levels of savings and capital within the Chinese markets.

Admittedly, relatively liberal labour regulations and selective enforcement of regulations concerning labour rights, environmental externalities, and producer quality controls have meant that firms have historically cut corners when it comes to producing in China. Such loose restrictions, coupled with China's significant talent pool and low taxes for exported good, have enabled China to evolve into a preeminent hub for secondary-sector companies – including both domestic firms, and international firms that have been put off by rising costs and difficulty of doing business in the "developed world".

Yet recent years have seen the Chinese state advance long-overdue reforms in ensuring that continued economic growth would not come with immense costs and devastation wrought upon innocent families and civilians. President Xi Jinping has been adamant in steering the country in the direction of "high-quality development" – shifting from merely pursuing growth to the pursuit of "better growth and seeking quality over quantity".[4] China has become one of the most fervent and stringent advocates of environmental laws – especially laws targeting pollution, contamination, and undue and unhinged exploitation of scarce resources. After all, Chinese leaders are well aware of the fact that there is only one planet on which we all live.

China has also undertaken further reforms in rendering its production sector more accessible and amenable to foreign capital – whether it be through lifting restrictions on automobile *production* for foreign firms; stepping up enforcement of intellectual property rights to ensure smooth technological innovation and transfer within the country, or reducing barriers to entry for manufacturers from developing nations.[5] China has been the world's leading exporter and second largest importer for a number of years.[6] When it comes to instrumental goods and products manufactured by China, since 2008, the country has been the world's largest producer of aluminium and steel, as well as of solar panels (86% per year, per the Fraunhofer Institute for Solar Energy Systems[7]).

Some figures would help in grounding the above claims. Historically, China contributed 14% to global economic growth between 1980 and 2000, against 21% from the United States and 7% from Japan.[8] China's contribution towards global trade growth was 4.7% for the same period, as compared with 14% for the United States and 6.9% for Japan. In 2021, Bloomberg had estimated that in the post-COVID era, China's growth would be set to contribute over 1/5 of the total increase in the world's GDP from 2021 to 2026.[9] With five years having passed, the sluggish economic recovery and rising concerns on the part of the private sector certainly have cast a semblance of doubt on such estimations.[10]

As other developing economies emerge to offer comparable, if not cheaper, labour costs as compared with China, some have expressed reservations concerning China's prospects as the "world's factory" – yet such worries are very much overstated. Chinese labour remains significantly cheaper than labour in most advanced, industrial states; additionally, the extensive roster of institutional advantages above suggests that China has much more to offer to prospective producers than just its labour alone.

5.1.2 A substantial consumer market for international businesses and trade

China has provided a critical consumer market for international businesses and trade, having served an instrumental role in driving the world's economic recovery post-2008. The country offers a significant consumer market for international firms and countries alike.

Since China opened its market in 1978, the total volume of export in the world has steadily increased – rising from $2050bn USD in 1980 to $24,900bn USD in 2022.[11] Whilst obviously, not all of such growth could be attributed to Chinese innovation and ingenuity, China's role as a leading global consuming nation cannot be overstated. Per a 2019 analysis conducted by McKinsey, China was the largest export destination for 33 countries, and the largest source of imports for 65.[12] More specifically, China offered a substantial market for resource-intensive and technology sectors through the large number of high-end manufacturing firms concentrated in leading cities such as Shenzhen and Shanghai.

To visualise the organic growth of China's consumer base more effectively, consider the following: China's total consumer spending was $197.2bn USD in 1990, climbing to $6.65trn USD by 2022. Per capita spending has also risen significantly, from $557USD per capita in 1995, to $4,465 in 2022.[13] These trends are indicative of a rapidly expanding, and hitherto largely unsaturated consumer market – they must also be viewed alongside broader statistics concerning China's burgeoning middle class.

Indeed, the Chinese middle class has grown substantially over the past decades. In 2000, China's middle class amounted to approximately 3% of its population. Current estimates put the size of China's middle class at over 700 million people – roughly 50% of the country's population.[14] As even the country's rural areas gradually enter the "*xiaokang*" – e.g., moderate affluence – phase, the Chinese consumer market is anticipated to expand beyond urban centres. Poverty alleviation, with drastic annual reduction in poverty rates, has certainly accelerated the process and amplified the economic benefits brought about by China's demographic dividend.

5.1.3 A vital source of developmental aid, trade, and capital for developing countries

China has been a critical source of developmental aid, trade, and investment to developing countries. Where the West has failed the developing world, China has offered an alternative source of capital with considerably fewer ideological and political strings attached, and a heightened degree of flexibility and freedom that – whilst by no means the product of ostensible altruism – has sought to reconcile and align Chinese interests and the interests of these developing countries. Indeed, in Mao Zedong's own nomenclature, China was to view "Asia-Africa-Latin America" – members of Mao's "Third World" – as allies and friends in their ongoing struggle against members of the imperialist "First World". Whilst the Three Worlds Theory is no longer as germane as it was 50 years ago in explaining China's foreign policy outlook, the underlying ethos remains – to China, political goodwill and reciprocated trust from members of the Asia-Africa-Latin America axis are more important objectives than securing narrow economic gains. From the Belt and Road Initiative to the rise of BRICS+, China has served as a steadfast and sturdy vanguard of the global majority (or proverbial Global South) – a loosely defined set of developing countries that had largely suffered the consequences of economic exploitation and historical injustices at the hands of colonialists from the developed world.[15]

It is hence on this basis that interpretations and appraisals of China's international development/humanitarian aid efforts, trade and economic policies, and capital/investment into overseas territories should be established. On the subject of aid, whilst China's "Official Development Assistance" (ODA) aid was estimated to be anywhere between 6th and 13th out of all major ODA donors in total volume in 2022, with a significant decline between 2019 and 2020 from 6.4 billion USD to 5.0 billion USD – potentially due to COVID-19[16] – China has placed a significant emphasis upon offering indirect aid through loans and development finance. Indeed, between 2000 and 2014, China gave $75bn and lent $275bn aid to other states, as compared with the $424bn offered by America over the same period.[17] What is particularly noteworthy is that on the contrary to popular (mis)conceptions, much of this aid was not offered *to the exclusion of* alternatives: many of China's beneficiaries continued to receive aid and developmental assistance from America and the World Bank.[18]

The model of overseas development adopted by China is worth clarifying through some fact-based analysis. Much talk has been aired concerning China's alleged debt trap – that is, that China would lure countries in through highly competitive loans conditions, only to seize their core infrastructure and vital assets should they fail to repay such loans. This narrative, as pointed out by seasoned political scientists Deborah Brautigam and Meg Rithmire, is innately erroneous.[19] It ignores the level of agency and political capital possessed by leaders of smaller and medium states in relation to China, but also that Beijing's loans and financing conditions are no more stringent than many of those offered by its counterparts in IMF and/or the World Bank. More importantly, China naturally seeks to promulgate an infrastructure-driven approach to developmental finance – which is, whilst plausibly a net outsourcing of its own recipe for success, and thus not necessarily applicable or utile across all contexts, by no means a recipe for "debt trap". The claim that China engages in predatory developmental projects must be carefully examined and tested – and, upon sufficient reflection, duly questioned and rejected.

As for commerce, Chinese trade with developing countries has steadily increased throughout the past decades. In 1986, developing countries purchased about 15% of Chinese exports – predominantly the country's agricultural and light industrial products – and supplied 8% of China's imports.[20] China has steadily increased trading ties with Central/Northern African states – e.g., Chad, Sudan, and Congo – as a means of accessing critical natural resources, e.g., oil and minerals. Total trade between Africa and China was $1.75bn USD in 1992, increasing substantially to $164bn in 2012 and $262bn USD in 2023.[21] Chinese trade has both opened up vast economic opportunities and consumption terrain for African firms, as well as offered African firms and consumers access to goods uniquely offered by China. More fundamentally, trade has been pivotal as a means of uplifting many in Africa from poverty – despite structural barriers that persist to this very day, including corruption and infrastructural deficiencies.

Finally, with ventures such as the AIIB, and BRI, China has substantially increased investment flows into Central Asian, Southeast Asian, and African countries, providing much-needed stimulus and seed funding for domestic infrastructural projects.

As of the mid-2010s, China had become the second largest source of outward FDI; indeed, in 2022, Chinese outward FDI reached 163.1bn USD, narrowly edging Japan's 161.5bn USD, though still significantly behind the US' 373bn USD.[22] The Chinese Eximbank has provided governments in developing countries with low-rate loans and associations with existing

Chinese companies, which supplied both capital and skills for the development or reconstruction of local infrastructure and offshore stations that met the interests of both China and its international partners. For concessional loans, the bank has historically supplied no-interest-rate and low-interest-rate loans to developing countries, with terms of up to 20 years and grace periods of 7 years. Such loans come with relatively low interest rates and minimal regulations – the upside of which is that countries find it substantially easier to access these loans than European counterparts; the downside of which is that the quality control – at times – could well be lacking.[23]

5.1.4 A key, constructive player in responsible global governance – especially on issues pertaining to international security and public health

China's ability to influence and shape the decision-making processes of multilateral institutions has indisputably increased over the past decades. Yet what is often neglected is the positive benefits on fronts of stabilisation, diversification, and increased egalitarianism within such institutions that China has induced. In reflecting upon the constructive role played by China in moulding dynamics in these structures, it is imperative that three different perspectives be considered: first, on questions of progressive reforms to multilateral institutions; second, on questions of how China has delivered or helped these structures deliver on critical issues, such as international security and public health; and finally, on how China has succeeded in fostering alternative, albeit not necessarily detached, institutions through which both developed and developing countries alike can benefit.[24]

When it comes to established multilateral institutions such as the WTO, the IMF, the World Bank, and the Paris agreement, China has largely lived up to its commitments and pledges, though has come under attacks in certain quarters for its alleged inability to take on the greater responsibilities associated typically with developed countries.[25] Yet such a characterisation neglects the extent to which China has sought to advance reforms and restructuring within these organisations in a way that favours countries that are historically left out of an American-led order – many of these states can be found in Europe, specifically smaller- and medium-sized nations within the European Union that have been long-neglected by the Anglo-American axis of power in these institutions. In 2016, Chinese Finance Minister Lou Jiwei stressed the need for structural reforms in IMF and World Bank to spur global economic growth[26] – such reforms ought to promulgate the transfer of more development resources to low-income countries in poverty reduction and ownership-centric development; additionally, China had repeatedly called on the World Bank to step up cooperation with middle-income and mid-sized economies (two distinct sub-groups) across, respectively, Latin America and Southeast

Asia, and Mediterranean and Eastern Europe, in advancing much-needed domestic structural reforms.[27]

On matters of global importance ranging from security and counterterrorism and public health, China has played an instrumental role as a collaborator and partner to the United States and Europe. China had stepped up – in the aftermath of the 9/11 tragedy – to become one of America's most reliable and committed partners in preventing and tackling terrorism – from supplying political and economic backing to US-led/advocated international peacekeeping efforts in the United Nations, to offering material support to counter-insurgency units in South and Central Asia. China has also worked closely with America in pressing for more transparency and accountability in Pakistan's nuclear technology, and in liaising between the West and North Korea on the latter's nuclear missiles programme. The Bush administration acknowledged China's contributions towards counter-terrorist efforts at numerous Six-Party Talks on North Korea's nuclear weapons (2003–2007). More recently, China and the US have stepped up to greater cooperation and efforts in counteracting the threat from lone-wolf and organised terrorism, with the former manifesting through improvised explosive devices and the latter through entities such as the now-near-decimated Islamic State (ISIS).[28]

Chinese commitment to global health has substantially increased over the past decade, with frameworks for collaboration with African (cf. FOCAC) and Latin-American (cf. via BRICS) states consistently incorporating health cooperation and exchange in their remit. The 2017 Joint Communique of The Belt and Road Health Cooperation and Health Silk Road set out substantive means through which China sought to work with other countries along the Belt and Road, in tackling pressing challenges to global public health.[29] Further back in time, China had stepped up its transparency and openness in sharing substantial volumes of data – in the aftermath of the SARS outbreak in 2003. Despite recent upheaval and politicisation of the ongoing efforts in combating COVID-19, China remains a reliable source of medical and health technology and information that would only be of increasing importance as the world's overpopulated planet seeks to navigate the biohazards associated with the modern age.

China's conception of multilateral and international engagement has by no means been limited to only established institutions. China has been a key advocate of collaboration and synergy within international entities such as the G-20 (Group of Twenty – featuring EU and 19 other countries) and BRICS (Brazil, Russia, India, China, and South Africa). China has sought to work with other members of G20 in opposing trade protectionism, advancing low-carbon economic reforms that address issues arising from global climate change, and to offer a new, reformed global financial order that is more equitable and accessible for parties that have historically been excluded from the Washington Consensus – including, of course, European states that have yet to reap the gains (in full) from their European Union membership.[30] It is worth noting that from the Chinese perspective, its increased engagement with such institutions was never conducted with the intention of supplanting them – indeed, the whole point of its offering economic concessions and benefits to prospective allies, is to consolidate its presence and ability to leverage upon these institutions, as opposed to dismantling them. This point should be relatively apparent given the above.

5.1.5 A critical engine of technological and scientific research worldwide

China's technological growth has been propelled by four trends in its history – a significant population and source of human capital, a job market that has operated on largely meritocratic grounds post-liberalisation, a substantial inflow of diaspora scientists returning from overseas universities and tech giants, and extensive investment into science by the administration.[31] Consequently, the four decades post-Deng Xiaoping have seen China evolve to become a hub for technological research and innovation across the world.

Multinational corporations have been encouraged by the Chinese government to create R&D centres in China, which roped in domestic Chinese talents in producing patented products and cutting-edge research. In 2010, China had 1,200 such R&D centres, with 400 out of the 500 Fortune 500 companies having established such centres in the country.[32]

Now, a perennial question remains as such – to what extent do the products of scientific research conducted in China "spill over" in enriching the world at large? Valid questions can indeed be asked over the extent to which Chinese research findings are accessible and utilisable by the world: what benefits the Chinese population may not benefit the rest of the world, as some sceptics posit.

In response, the international community would benefit from looking at some hard numbers. Whilst the science and engineering (S/E) workforce in America remains significantly ahead of China's, the reverse can be observed for the number of bachelor's and doctoral S/E degrees awarded by China and the US: since the early 1990s, China has awarded substantially more S/E bachelor's degrees to undergraduates than the US, and in the mid-2000s, China overtook the US in terms of the number of S/E doctoral degrees awarded. Combining the two sets of data yields the following observation: throughout large swathes of the past four decades, China has been a net exporter of scientific and technological talents to the rest of the world. Whilst recently introduced programmmes such as the "*Qianren Jihua*" have sought to recruit top-tier talents in returning to China, such progammes are – by and large – in the fledgling stages; many Chinese scientists and engineers enjoy working abroad, even notwithstanding the souring relations between China and certain countries, as well as the bellicose rhetoric with which members of the Asian diaspora have been targeted throughout past decades.

More generally, China has been a critical hub of technological and scientific knowledge – publicly disseminated through journal articles. China had been the fastest-growing country in terms of article productivity, with an annual growth rate in *quantity* of articles by 15%, and a continued increase in average citation numbers – indicative of the *quality* of research – between 1990 and 2011.[33] More recently, in the 2010s, the research and science/development sectors in China have continued to consolidate their competitive edge over other leading states in the world – in industries such as artificial intelligence (AI) and nanotechnology, Beijing is racking up an increasingly impressive and apparent lead over its Western counterparts.[34] Chinese research in spheres ranging from aerodynamic sciences to pharmaceuticals, from engineering to bio-technology, has played an invaluable role in expanding the knowledge base across the world – especially for nations that have conventionally been locked out of academic and epistemic structures in both research inputs and outputs. Looking ahead, China is likely to make substantial contributions in fields such as artificial intelligence (AI) and environmental technology. Both China and the rest of the world alike would benefit from further collaboration and synergy.

5.2 Challenges

Yet China's contributions to the world have also been hindered by its fair share of setbacks and risks accompanying its rise, which must be taken seriously by China and the rest of the world alike. Some amongst these surfaced in the past and have been resolved subsequently; others remain unresolved and could well threaten to not only undo China's progress and the goodwill it has accumulated, but also the advances and improvements made by the world at large over the past 40 years.

Set aside the question of present-day challenges and risks for now (we shall return to them later); the following comprises problems that had arisen over the past 40 years, and that have nevertheless received at least a significant volume of attention and redress on the part of the Chinese state and society at large. This is not to say that these problems have been fully resolved – but they must be differentiated from the nascent, up-and-coming challenges that this book shall address later.

5.2.1 Socioeconomic inequalities and divisions

Alongside a significant number of opportunities, the post-Mao Zedong era of economic reforms also brought along a plethora of socioeconomic problems to China – amongst which, no less, is the exacerbation of the long-standing rural-country divide, and the amplification of socioeconomic inequalities at large. World Bank estimates suggest that China's Gini Coefficient peaked at 43.7 in 2010, declining continuously since then to approximately 35.7 as of 2021 (Figure 5.1).[35]

Whilst the country had made substantial progress in eliminating absolute poverty, it remained the case – throughout most of the 1990s through to the early 2010s – that there existed vast disparities between individuals residing in lofty, hyper-modernised Central Business Districts in major coastal cities, and those who inhabited the underdeveloped inland countryside. Whilst we must take stock of the progress and improvements made by China over the years in eliminating poverty, it is equally imperative that we are cognisant of the predicaments and challenges it has overcome in the past. The following section addresses some of the problems and solutions presented by the Chinese state in response to the prevalent inequalities throughout the earlier days of its era of economic reforms. Some of these problems may no longer apply as descriptions to present-day China – understanding them remains critical.

The primary and foremost cause of inequalities in post-1980s China consisted of the heavy concentration of developmental policies and capital in urban areas and major cities. Throughout the 1980s and 1990s, state investments predominantly prioritised urban areas, favouring redirecting capital into infrastructure and production in clustered urban regions – which housed approximately one-quarter of the country's population. Deng Xiaoping's adage, "Let

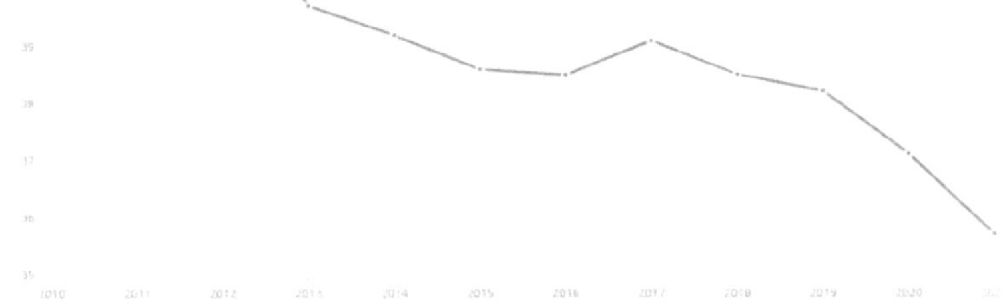

FIGURE 5.1 Gini coefficients of China between 2010 and 2021.

Source: World Bank Group, Gini Index – China 2020 – 2021, World Bank. https://data.worldbank.org/indicator/SI.POV.GINI?end=2021&locations=CN&start=2010

some people get rich first", was taken to be a directive that authorised a heavily urban-centric developmental approach, with heavy-industry and agricultural development disproportionately skewed towards cities with more fertile land and concentrated capital for rapid industrialisation. The disparities in access to infrastructure, the network effects and economies of scale uniquely associated with highly concentrated and saturated production economies in cities, as well as the relatively advanced quality of life in cities, all contributed towards a disparate disjunction between cities and countryside, with most factors of production and downstream economic gains accruing to the former. The absence of a fully functional, legally regulated land market in the rural countryside (which prohibited farmers from capitalising upon lands they had held), as well as the strict Hukou systems that effectively bound individuals to their birthplaces, cumulatively caused further deterioration in the early 2000s.[36] This was in turn self-reinforcing – firms, businesses, and investors were attracted disproportionately to the cities, where consumer markets were readily available and willing to expend; capital flight from the countryside, especially Central China, further deprived residents of rural areas of their capacity to climb the "social ladder".

A study suggested that over 10% of China's total inequality, as of 2014, could be attributed to the urban–rural gap.[37] Urban–rural disparities can be considered a primary undergirding cause for aggregate inequalities, for two reasons: first, they had long been entrenched since the early days of the People's Republic, with the countryside suffering considerably more under the mass atrocities and turmoil of the Great Leap Forward[38] and the Cultural Revolution;[39] second, there existed substantial path-dependency in the lives of rural migrants, who – due to their places of birth – found it incredibly difficult to seek job opportunities that could lift themselves up into the class above bare subsistence. The primary sector – especially under mechanisation of labour and the expansion of conglomerates – was neither lucrative nor viable as a means of social uplifting, even under the market reforms introduced by Deng. The urban–rural divide also amplified the effects of other causes of inequalities, such as the inland/costal divide, and education/human capital disparities across regions in China.

A second, and precipitously significant factor, comprised the inland-coastal inequalities that permeated China in the 1990s and early 2000s. A 1999 paper suggested that whilst the contribution of rural–urban inequality remained dominant amongst all causes of China's inequality, the inland-coastal contribution had become increasingly important throughout the early to mid-1990s. Income in coastal provinces more than tripled between 1989 and 2004, whilst the income in inland provinces merely doubled.

The inland-coastal dichotomy itself was the product of asymmetrical distribution of actual power that favoured cities and provinces with historically entrenched economic wherewithal and long-standing political capital – e.g.,

Guangdong (the most populous province in China), Shanghai (with its legacy and background as one of the most international and business-friendly cities in the country), and Fujian (another coastal province). Such disparities were exacerbated by reform-era policies that favoured cities that could readily engage in trade via shipping routes – amongst other forms of economic activities to which coastal regions were distinctly suited. The inland-coastal divide, alongside the aforementioned Hukou system, once again contributed towards the clustering of economic growth in highly developed and sophisticated coastal cities, as opposed to the inland regions.

A subsidiary factor constituted the education level-induced disparities in the country. The Chinese public place a distinct and substantial emphasis upon academic credentials and qualifications – as an indicator or proxy for ability, and, beyond that, credibility. Disparities in access to education not only undermined the ability of the poor and disenfranchised to accrue the necessary knowledge and accreditation, but it also prevented them from developing the quintessential networks and connections to escape their socioeconomic circumstances. Disparities in education levels compounded urban–rural and inland-coastal divides, in prying multinational conglomerates and foreign investors away from the countryside and to the cities, where the citizens were and remain more likely to be better-educated on average.

On a broader note, a highly unequal and divided China would threaten to place an acute bottleneck on the engines of growth in the country – frustrating both foreign companies' efforts in their search for a stable, reliable, and continuously expanding consumer market, and the Chinese administration's vision that with more of China urbanised and modernised as prospective "money for taking", there would be greater incentives on the part of wavering states to engage China in bilateral trade and civil society exchanges. A more egalitarian China would benefit all in the world – it would also pave the way for a more politically stable and consolidated government, with minimal domestic insurgency and sociopolitical instability.

Indeed, Beijing had undertaken active efforts – since the early 2000s – to correct course on the matter. From subsidising education and industrial development in the countryside and inland areas, to facilitating smoother and easier rural-to-urban migration and remittance of income via relaxed Hukou restrictions, to redirecting capital to medium-sized and small cities,[40] the Chinese administration has undertaken active steps to quell inequality – though the extent to which it will succeed, remains to be seen.

5.2.2 Environmental pollution

China's rise has also produced substantial costs for the country's environment – both in terms of environmental degradation and with respect to China's greenhouse gas emissions. Whilst the former's consequences have remained largely contained within the borders of the country (with the exception of acid rain and marine life depletion), the latter has had apparent spillover consequences – though it must be noted that such costs must be compared with and situated in the context of the voluptuous historical emissions by countries in the West. In any case, China's environmental decline had been a highly salient and urgent issue in the country throughout the late 1980s, 1990s, 2000s, continuing into the early days of Xi's tenure – only then were measures aimed at tackling the environmental crisis (as later discussed) finally rolled out.

China's environmental quality rapidly deteriorated under its heavy industrialisation. Per the Chinese Ministry of Health, by 2007, industrial pollution had rendered cancer China's leading cause of death; ambient air pollution alone killed hundreds of thousands, impairing the productivity of even more citizens. 500 million people[41] in China lacked access to safe and clean drinking water, as a result of contamination by factories who released – illegally, in violation of ill-enforced laws – toxic and biohazardous waste into rivers and streams. The sulphur dioxide and nitrogen oxides generated through industrial activities (including, the burning of coal) had produced copious volume of acid rain, which had spread beyond the borders of China into Korea and Japan. An unpublished internal report by the Chinese Academy of Environmental Planning in 2003 suggested that up to 300,000 people died each year from air pollution, mostly due to cardiovascular and pulmonary diseases.[42]

It must be recognised that China has made substantial attempts to tackle air pollution over the past decade. Average Particulate Matter (PM) 2.5 concentrations decreased by a third between 2013 and 2017 across 74 cities. Beijing recorded a record-low PM2.5 score in August 2019 and is no longer amongst the top 200 most polluted cities in the world.[43] The Chinese government had introduced aggressive afforestation measures and promulgated a rapid transition to electric vehicles, which led to a substantial decline in the emissions of exhaust gases and other pollutants in the production process of diesel cars.

China nevertheless remains afflicted with an incredibly urgent waste problem. China's largest dump – the Jiangcungou landfill in Shaanxi Province – reached saturation in 2019, 25 years ahead of schedule. In 2017, China collected over 215 million tonnes of household waste in urban areas, up from the 152 million in 2007.[44] The actual figures would be much higher if rural waste were included – indeed, China produced 300 million tonnes in total in 2012, across rural and urban areas combined. Attempts to regulate electronic waste have been criticised for the difficulty of enforcement and policing those who deviated from the norms. Whilst China had previously pledged to recycle 35% of waste in major cities by the end of 2020,[45] the jury is still out over whether such pledges and policy commitments have in fact succeeded.

Finally, on the question of greenhouse gas emissions. China had historically relied predominantly upon coal as the primary source of energy. Bouts of surges in coal demand since 2001 attest to the fact that it would be incredibly difficult for the country to wane off the fuel, despite the fact that peak production of coal is anticipated to occur anytime between 2016 and 2029.[46] Furthermore, China has indeed been the world's largest emitter of CO_2 since 2006 – in 2019, China is estimated to have emitted over a quarter of the world's greenhouse gases, followed by 11% by the USA, and 6.6% by India. Such numbers should nevertheless not be taken as indicative when it comes to the level and degree of emissions – after all, China's per capita emissions remain substantially lower than the US – the per capita emission in 2019 was 10.1 tonnes, as compared with the US', which was 17.6 tonnes per capita. China is by no means the sole or major producer of greenhouse gases in the world's history, and discussions of its environmental track record ought to reflect this fact.

The Chinese government recently declared that it would aim to reach peak emissions before 2030, and carbon neutrality by 2060. The ambitiousness of these goals is apparent – yet, should China indeed succeed, it could well serve as an exemplar and precedent for others to follow.

5.2.3 Corruption and political inefficiencies

Corruption has long been and remains amongst the most odious problems prevalent in China since the country's establishment in 1949. Corruption permeates all levels of administration, ranging from the local and provincial to the national and central administration. Commentators have attributed China's corruption to the "organisational involution" – the habitus cultivated amongst a new crop of nouveau riche and newly promoted cadres,[47] triggered by the enormous dividends derived through the country's economic liberalisation. Throughout the late 1980s to the early 2010s, corruption had remained at the top of the list of priorities and items of concern for the general public.

Setting aside normative qualms, on a purely consequentialist level, corruption has been to the detriment of the ruling party. In 2007, Minxin Pei estimated that the economic toll of corruption amounted to at least 3% of China's national GDP.[48] In late 2006, almost 25% of surveyed business executives rated their local officials' integrity as "bad", with 12% remarking that they were "very bad". Officials regularly engaged in bribery, kickbacks, theft, and squandering or siphoning off public funds – as means of entrenching their political control, building long-standing rent-based networks, and lining their own pockets.

Corruption in China plays out in predominantly two forms – incidental and embedded. Incidental corruption denotes instances of corruption that involve blatantly and apparently criminal behaviours, such as bribery, scam, extortion, theft, and forced expropriation of land. On the other hand, embedded corruption was far harder to detect, manifesting through pork barrel politics, policies, and planning decisions that favoured (covertly) particular interest groups and parties, and the offering of (dis)favourable business conditions to aspirant businesspersons. Straddling both kinds of corruption were behaviours that existed in the "twilight zone" of the law – e.g., forced evictions caused by party cadres' (legally ambiguous) purchasing of siphoned-off housing as a means of bribing senior housing officials.[49]

Not all corruption was "equal" in their damage. Some forms of corruption were more deleterious than others. Corruption studies expert Yuen Yuen Ang noted that "the right kind of corruption" had been somewhat helpful in spurring China's growth, from incentivising party officials to accept the transition to a market economy, and – on a more granular level – engage in activities that maximised economic gains for *all*. The practice of corruption required there to be *something* to embezzle, to steal, to *profit off* – thus a modicum of corruption, Ang argued, was quasi-necessary in facilitating China's smooth transition into a post-Mao Zedong economic model. An over-zealous castigation of corruption could well cause us to overlook its necessity – especially in a rapidly liberalising and reforming country that had freshly emerged from decades of sustained political turbulence.[50]

Yet corruption, by and large, posed substantial problems for China. Corruption had become increasingly concentrated in state-controlled sectors, especially towards the early 2000s. Substantial costs arose from corruption – directly and indirectly impairing economic growth, usually through the gross inefficiencies of money spent towards bribery, as opposed to productivity-boosting policies and plans. Behaviours exhibited by corrupt officials, such as illegal land exproporiation, seizure of civilian assets and property, and blatant transgression or defiance of anti-embezzlement regulations, had – in the past – vastly undermined public buy-in and support for local and provincial officials.

The uncertainties induced by corruption impeded growth in foreign investment, as well as exacerbating the undue influence of party cadres and administrative officials over the economic structures and fields of competition under their jurisdictions. Capital flight left sectors and economic spaces bereft of capital, as corrupt officials often transferred their gains to offshore accounts in Hong Kong and beyond. Illegal embezzlement and transfer of cash also abetted criminal elements – e.g., gangs and triads, who benefited off being able to bribe police and judiciary officers.

Since Xi's rise, however, corruption has been tackled head-on, with a heavy emphasis upon transforming and regulating the lifestyles and practices of party members – with focus centred around enforced thriftiness and frugality, minimisation of fraternisation and socialisation, and crackdowns on conspicuous consumption. Officials have been instructed to shift from an extravagant, profligate lifestyle, towards one in which they eschew luxury. Xi has also spearheaded and overseen crucial drives combating systemically rooted corruption on grassroots levels, in forms of both prosecuting and dismissing corrupt officials, and augmenting the remit and powers of investigative committees and taskforces charged with overseeing disciplinary matters within the party.[51]

5.3 China's rise – Our assessment

In sum, this book submits that China's rise should be read through the framework of *unbounded opportunities* and *bounded costs*. The costs to the world arising from China's ascent are apparent – whether they stem from innate weaknesses in the Chinese political system, contingent flaws and mistakes made along the way as China evolved and grew, or the precarious power equilibrium that characterises how the nation interacts with other states as it rises. These costs are also relatively *clear* and *containable* – both in terms of resolutions that address their roots, as well as ameliorative measures that reduce substantially the level of uncertainties and risks posed by their existence. In short, the downsides can be predicted, managed, and curtailed – the probability of a "black swan" arising out of China's rise is by no means zero, but is certainly comparatively trivial. From environmental pollution to corruption and political intransigence, the Chinese administration itself has every incentive to curb these problems – on these fronts, the incentives of China, and the world at large, are most certainly aligned.

In contrast, China's rise offers the world *unlimited potential*, whether it be in engaging with China as the prospectively largest consumer market in the world; in drawing upon Chinese talents and innovation in plugging much-needed gaps in terms of goods and produce; in tackling shared challenges ranging from climate change, public health disasters, to international terrorism. Chinese migrants, academics, and technicians play a pivotal role in driving forward innovation across the world. They also serve as valuable, important voices to platform and feature in an increasingly globalised world, as national and cultural boundaries blur and dissolve.

This is not to say the challenges and risks brought about by China's rise ought to be neglected – indeed, far from it. If China and the world are to collaborate, are to work together, it behoves all parties – to resolve the differences and deleterious effects that its rise has and continues to generate. To ignore these pitfalls, or to dismiss them as unwarranted – even where they are well-substantiated and evidenced – would be counterproductive in our pursuit of a better, shared future.

Notes

1 Frykholm, A. (2016) *Ending extreme poverty*, World Bank Group. Available at: https://www.worldbank.org/en/news/feature/2016/06/08/ending-extreme-poverty
2 World Bank (2024) *The world bank in China*, World Bank Group. Available at: https://www.worldbank.org/en/country/china/overview
3 2016 World Population Data Sheet www.worldpopdata.org. Available at: https://www.prb.org/wp-content/uploads/2016/08/prb-wpds2016-web-2016.pdf
4 Xinhua (2024) *What to know about China's high-quality development*, The State Council Information Office, The People's Republic of China. Available at: http://english.scio.gov.cn/m/in-depth/2024-03/18/content_117066836.htm
5 Grosse, R., Gamso, J., and Nelson, R.C. (2021) China's rise, world order, and the implications for international business, *Management International Review*, 61, pp. 1–26. https://doi.org/10.1007/s11575-020-00433-8
6 Akram, S. (2024) World's top exporters and importers, *World Options*. Available at: https://uk.worldoptions.com/news/worlds-top-exporters-and-importers
7 Jackman, J. (2025) The 9 largest solar panel manufacturers in the world, *Sunsave*. Available at: https://www.sunsave.energy/solar-panels-advice/solar-energy/largest-manufacturers
8 Link directs to main page; Vamvakidis, A. and Arora, V.B. (2001) The impact of U.S. Economic growthon the rest of the world: How much does it matter?, *International Monetary Fund*, 2001(119). https://doi.org/10.5089/9781451854176.001; China Embassy (2021) *China's contribution to world economy*. Available at: http://np.china-embassy.gov.cn/eng/78085/bd/200410/t20041027_1998103.html.
9 Tanzi, A. (2021) China's growth set to drive world economy in post-pandemic years, *Bloomberg*. Available at: https://www.bloomberg.com/news/articles/2021-04-06/china-s-growth-set-to-drive-world-economy-in-post-pandemic-years?embedded-checkout=true&leadSource=uverify%20wall
10 Posen, A.S. (2023) The end of China's economic miracle, *Foreign Affairs*. Available at: https://www.foreignaffairs.com/china/end-china-economic-miracle-beijing-washington
11 Sabanoglu, T. (2023) Trends in global export value of trade in goods from 1950 to 2022, *Statista*. Available at: https://www.statista.com/statistics/264682/worldwide-export-volume-in-the-trade-since-1950/
12 Woetzel, L., Seong, J., Leung, N., Ngai, J., Manyika, J., Madgavkar, A., Lund, S., and Mironenko, A. (2019) *China and the world: Inside the dynamics of a changing relationship*, McKinsey and Company. Available at: https://www.mckinsey.com/featured-insights/china/china-and-the-world-inside-the-dynamics-of-a-changing-relationship
13 Macrotrends, China Consumer Spending 1960–2025. Available at: https://www.macrotrends.net/global-metrics/countries/CHN/china/consumer-spending
14 China Power Team (2021) How well-off is China's middle class? *China Power*. Available at: https://chinapower.csis.org/china-middle-class/
15 CGTN (2024) *How China advances future development of the Global South*, CGTN. Available at: https://news.cgtn.com/news/2024-10-24/How-China-advances-future-development-of-the-Global-South-1xXPxSroqNa/p.html
16 Kitano, N. and Miyabayashi, Y. (2023) China's foreign aid as a proxy of ODA: preliminary estimate 2001–2022, *Journal of Contemporary East Asia Studies*, 12(1), pp. 264–293. https://doi.org/10.1080/24761028.2024.2316532

17 AidData (2021) AidData's Global Chinese development finance dataset, Version 2.0. Available at: https://www.aiddata.org/data/aiddatas-global-chinese-development-finance-dataset-version-2-0
18 Olander, E. (2021) China – Africa: Top 10 issues going into 2021, *The Africa Report*. Available at: https://www.theafricareport.com/57044/china-africa-top-10-issues-going-into-2021/
19 Brautigam, D. and Rithmire, M. (2021) The Chinese 'debt trap' is a myth, *The Atlantic*. Available at: https://www.theatlantic.com/international/archive/2021/02/china-debt-trap-diplomacy/617953/
20 Kastner, S.L. (2016) Buying influence? Assessing the political effects of China's international trade, *The Journal of Conflict Resolution*, 60(6), pp. 980–1007. Available at: http://www.jstor.org/stable/24755936
21 China Africa Research Initiative (2024) China-Africa bilateral trade data overview. Available at: https://www.sais-cari.org/data-china-africa-trade
22 Chu, W. (2023) *China's going out programme: Optimised outcomes*, HKTDC. Available at: https://research.hktdc.com/en/article/MTQ5NTg4MDgzMg
23 Massa, I. (2011) *Export finance activities by the Chinese government*, Directorate-General For External Policies of the Union, European Parliament. Available at: https://www.europarl.europa.eu/RegData/etudes/note/join/2011/433862/EXPO-INTA_NT(2011)433862_EN.pdf
24 Olson, S. and Prestowitz, C. (2011) *The evolving role of China in international institutions*, The Economic Strategy Institute. Available at: https://www.uscc.gov/sites/default/files/Research/TheEvolvingRoleofChinainInternationalInstitutions.pdf
25 Dollar, D. (2020) *Reluctant player: China's approach to international economic institutions*, Brookings. Available at: https://www.brookings.edu/articles/reluctant-player-chinas-approach-to-international-economic-institutions/
26 SCMP Editorial (2016) *China's calls for reform at the World Bank, IMF and ADB cannot be ignored any longer*, SCMP. Available at: https://www.scmp.com/comment/insight-opinion/article/2018461/chinas-calls-reform-world-bank-imf-and-adb-cannot-be-ignored
27 Lou, J. (2015) *Governors statement No. 29*, Boards of Governors of the World Bank Group and the International Monetary Fund. Available at: https://www.imf.org/external/am/2015/speeches/pr29e.pdf\
28 Park, Y. U.S.-China counter-terrorism co-operation and its perspective on human rights, Asia Focus 56, Asia Program. Available at: https://www.iris-france.org/wp-content/uploads/2017/12/Asia-focus-56.pdf
29 Husain, L. and Bloom, G. (2020) Understanding China's growing involvement in global health and managing processes of change, *Global Health*, 16, p. 39 https://doi.org/10.1186/s12992-020-00569-0
30 Li, M. (2011) Rising from Within: China's search for a multilateral world and its implications for Sino-US relations, *Global Governance*, 17(3), 331–351. Available at: http://www.jstor.org/stable/23033751
31 Xie, Y., Zhang, C., and Lai, Q. (2014) China's rise as a major contributor to science and technology, *Proceedings of the National Academy of Sciences U.S.A.*, 111(26), pp. 9437–9442. https://doi.org/10.1073/pnas.1407709111
32 Springut, M., Schlaikjer, S., and Chen, D. *China's program for science and technology modernization*, The U.S.-China Economic And Security Review Commission. Available at: https://web.archive.org/web/20130102190020/http:/www.uscc.gov/researchpapers/2011/USCC_REPORT_China's_Program_forScience_and_Technology_Modernization.pdf

33 Xie, Y., Zhang, C., and Lai, Q. (2014) China's rise as a major contributor to science and technology, *Proceedings of the National Academy of Sciences U.S.A.*, 111(26), pp. 9437–9442.
34 Marr, B. (2021) China poised to dominate the Artificial Intelligence (AI) market, *Forbes*. Available at: https://www.forbes.com/sites/bernardmarr/2021/03/15/china-poised-to-dominate-the-artificial-intelligence-ai-market/
35 World Bank Group, Gini Index – China 1990 – 2021, World Bank. Available at: https://data.worldbank.org/indicator/SI.POV.GINI?locations=CN
36 Zhai, F., Hertel, T., and Wang, Z. (2006) Labor market distortions, rural-urban inequality and the opening of China's economy, *Economic Modeling*, 23, pp. 76–109. Available at: https://docs.lib.purdue.edu/cgi/viewcontent.cgi?article=1027&context=gtapwp
37 Xie, Y. and Zhou, X. (2014) Income inequality in today's China, *Proceedings of the National Academy of Sciences U.S.A.*, 111(19), pp. 6928–6933. https://doi.org/10.1073/pnas.1403158111.
38 Peng, X. (1987) Demographic consequences of the great leap forward in China's provinces, *Population and Development Review*, 13(4), pp. 639–670. https://doi.org/10.2307/1973026
39 Shan, W. (2019) *Out of the Gobi*, Wiley 1st Edition. Available at: https://www.amazon.com/Out-Gobi-Story-China-America/dp/1119529492; Brown, K. (2013) City versus Countryside in Mao's China: Negotiating the divide, *Asian Affairs*, 44(2). https://doi.org/10.1080/03068374.2013.795677
40 Wu, N. (2014) Income inequality in China and the urban-rural divide, *The Journalist's Resource*. Available at: https://journalistsresource.org/economics/income-inequality-todays-china/; Zhang, Z.Y. (2019) *China is relaxing hukou restrictions in small and medium-sized cities*, China Briefing. Available at: https://www.china-briefing.com/news/china-relaxing-hukou-restrictions-small-medium-sized-cities/
41 Kao, E. (2018) *Air pollution is killing 1 million people and costing Chinese economy 267 billion yuan a year, research from CUHK shows*, SCMP. Available at: https://www.scmp.com/news/china/science/article/2166542/air-pollution-killing-1-million-people-and-costing-chinese
42 Kan, H. (2009) Environment and health in china: Challenges and opportunities, *Environ Health Perspect*, 117(12), pp. A530–A531. doi: 10.1289/ehp.0901615.
43 IQAir (2018) *Air quality in Beijing*, IQAir. Available at: https://www.iqair.com/china/beijing
44 Jin, E. (2019) A rubbish story: China's mega-dump full 25 years ahead of schedule, *BBC*. Available at: https://www.bbc.com/news/world-asia-50429119
45 Huang, H. (2019) *China's radical new rules to recycle rubbish*, SCMP. Available at: https://multimedia.scmp.com/infographics/news/china/article/3038540/china-waste-sorting/index.html
46 Aden, N.T., Fridley, D.G., and Zheng, N. (2008) Outlook and challenges for Chinese coal. https://doi.org/10.2172/1050632
47 Lu, X. (2001) Cadres and corruption: The organizational involution of the Chinese communist party, *JSTOR*. Available at: https://www.jstor.org/stable/3182311
48 Pei, M. (2007) *Corruption threatens China's future*, Carnegie Endowment for International Peace. Available at: https://www.policyarchive.org/handle/10207/6370
49 Dyer, G. (2010) Housing boom fuels corruption in China, *Financial Times*. Available at: https://www.ft.com/content/8642412e-7aee-11df-8935-00144feabdc0

50 Ang, Y.Y. (2020) *Unbundling corruption: Why it matters and how to do it*, OECD Development Matters. Available at: https://oecd-development-matters.org/2020/06/25/unbundling-corruption-why-it-matters-and-how-to-do-it/
51 barboza, D. (2023) Yuen Yuen Ang on the evolution of corruption in China, *The Wire China*. Available at: https://www.thewirechina.com/2020/05/31/yuen-yuen-ang-on-the-evolution-of-corruption-in-china/

6

CHINA AND THE WORLD

On its international image and relations

China's growth has been accompanied by a corresponding increase in the frequency and depth of its affiliation, interaction, and engagement with the world at large. A robust understanding of Chinese politics cannot be decoupled from how the country views itself in relation to the international community, as well as how countries across the world perceive and approach China.

With that said, one of the most common mistakes undergirding attempts to make sense of China is to treat the country as an insular, disjointed, and isolated power that resembles "rogue nations" – nations that have been long siphoned off from Western trade networks due to political or ideological interests. This could not be further from the truth – per the latest complete survey conducted by the Lowy Institute a few years back, 128 of the 190 countries in the world were trading more with China than they do with the United States, as of 2018. China counts amongst the most active participants in international, multilateral institutions including the United Nations, the International Monetary Fund, and the World Bank. China and the rest of the world cannot be separated – nor should they be – from one another.

The country remains integrally interconnected and integrated into the world at large – a fact that not only benefits billions around the world but also the country's very own citizens. Indeed, the 2021 CPC and the World Political Parties Summit, held after the 100th anniversary of the Communist Party of China, was attended by over 500 heads of states and party leaders from over 100 countries – testament to the appeal and prominence of China as an international leader.[1,2] To assert that China is a "pariah" or "excluded from" the rest of the world would be a claim that runs contrary to the surging popularity and receptiveness towards China amongst developing countries

DOI: 10.4324/9781003643548-6

– especially in light of the blatant hypocrisy and double standards exhibited by the West over Israel's genocidal actions in Gaza, as well as the flip-flopping vacillation of Donald J Trump when it comes to the war in Ukraine. In short, it is high time for Western commentators to recognise and address the innate biases underpinning their reading and interpretation of China's relations with its neighbours and the world beyond.[3]

6.1 China's relations and images in respective regions

The following sections seek not to be an exhaustive and comprehensive survey of China's relationships with all possible geographical regions and communities in the world. Instead, the objective is to elucidate relationships of particular significance – whether they be from an economic, geopolitical, strategic, or military perspective – to China's ascent as a global power. We will delve into both the substantive components of the relationships, as well as China's perceptions and reception by key stakeholders in these regions, as a means of providing the international community with the necessary facts to appraise the successes and failures of China's foreign policy government. To the extent that certain regions have been omitted, this is not because of their irrelevance at large – but because of their relatively marginal importance in relation to the cause of the task at hand.

With that said, some context would be needed in order to enable our true comprehension of how Beijing pursues its diplomatic interests and foreign policy postures.

To understand this historical context is crucial to our appreciating the recent tonal shifts and transformations in Chinese diplomacy – towards what some have dubbed "wolf warrior diplomacy":[4] a term that carries negative connotations and overtones of admonishment directed towards diplomats who are perceived to be acting and speaking out-of-line in an excessively belligerent manner. No such references are made to American and European diplomats, many of whom over the last 20 years have sough to frighten and bully other nations, including their leaders, across the world who do not share their world view. Whilst such antics and trenchant rhetoric have drawn criticism and reservation from many prominent Chinese intellectuals and foreign policy analysts,[5] we should not overlook the rationale and historical motivation undergirding this conscious shift in tone and approach: as the attitudes of the Chinese domestic masses shifted, so, too, did the repertoire and approaches adopted by its diplomats.

Yet what had perhaps been omitted by vociferous voices extolling China's rise and ascent, is the importance of restraint that had historically informed Chinese grand strategy. From the early 2000s onwards, the Chinese Ministry of Foreign Affairs had come under increasing public pressure and partial criticism for being "too soft" on foreign rebuking and allegations.[6] The concern was that whilst Chinese economic and military strength continued to grow, its state was not behaving with the confidence and assertiveness that would be expected of a power on the cusp of "being great". Former leader Deng Xiaoping's adage "Lay low and bide your time" (韜光養晦)[7] appeared to no longer apply, as – with the advent of online forums and nationalistic discussion sites – Chinese netizens demanded a more vocal and confident China on the international stage.

The trenchant and assertive rhetoric with which Chinese diplomats declared and defended their country's ostensible interests yielded mixed results when it came to bolstering the country's perceived credibility, especially amongst countries who were already sceptical of Beijing's strategic intentions. Indeed, in June 2021, President Xi Jinping himself called upon China to have a more "trustworthy, lovable and respectable" image – a most understandable and fundamentally pragmatic vision for a country of such substantial economic and strategic heft.[8]

With that said, we should never underestimate the shrewdness, intellectual robustness, and responsiveness of Chinese diplomatic leaders. This should be appreciated in the context that many Western observers, and even diplomats from countries outside the West, make the mistake of allowing their prejudices and bias to hamper their collaboration with others. The years 2023–2024 have seen China embark upon a proactive charm offensive – aiming to mollify the concerns of foreign investors whilst playing up the possibility for China to cooperate and work constructively with foreign partners. The softening in rhetorical overtures and the shift towards highlighting positive-sum room for synergy and advancement of mutual interests have gone a long way in enabling Beijing to reposition itself on the international stage in the aftermath of the post-COVID reopening.[9]

6.1.1 ASEAN

China's role in ASEAN and Southeast Asia – in general – has substantially and steadily increased over the years. Whilst the United States remains predominant across a large number of regions around the world, its slipping grip in ASEAN – as compared with China's rising influence – is highly evident. In accordance with a measurement devised by the Atlantic Council,[10] China's influence capacity – i.e., a number that broadly indicates how influential a state is (in terms of both volume of ties and extent of asymmetrical dependence between countries) over another state – in Southeast Asia first overtook of the United States in the late 2000s, and has steadily grown over the past decade.

China's increasing influence and presence in the region can be attributed to two primary factors:

First, whether it be through the ASEAN–China Free Trade Area – established in the early 2000s, or the more recent signing of the Regional Comprehensive Economic Partnership (RCEP), ASEAN states have become increasingly *economically intertwined and interdependent with* China, with Chinese investment and infrastructural loans increasing in both intensity and quantity across a plethora of states in the region. China has emerged as the largest trade partner to ASEAN for large swathes of the past decade.

Second, China has stepped up to play a *larger mediating and arbitrating role* in the region through lending its presence and political weight to conflict resolution – perhaps best epitomised by the country's approach to the ongoing Myanmar crisis, in which it has continuously worked with ASEAN states in coordinating the implementation of ASEAN's advocated proposals – e.g., ASEAN's five-point consensus.[11]

Trade between ASEAN and China has more than doubled since 2010, from 235.5bn USD to 507.9bn USD in 2019.[12] This figure has since then surged further to 911.7bn in 2023,[13] no less benefiting from the supply chain shuffle, realignment, and de-risking that had contributed towards the rise of Southeast Asian countries as a site for joint ventures between local companies, and their Chinese and American counterparts, respectively.[14]

In 2013, Xi Jinping marked his visits to Indonesia and Malaysia with calls for "a closer ASEAN–China Community with a Shared Future".[15] The Maritime Silk Road and Belt and Road Initiative, first mentioned and discussed in September 2013 by Xi Jinping in Kazakhstan, very quickly stepped up to a critical role in bridging the gap between civil societies and firms, inducing into Southeast Asia a large volume of new ideas, institutions, and diplomatic-cum-political norms.[16] Chinese academics have termed China's expanding influence in Southeast Asia as a critical component of the "revival" of the "Golden Age" of the diplomacy China practised during the Tang dynasty, which saw the silk road offer an alternative and prescient model of intercontinental trade diplomacy, prior to the emergence of *Pax Americana*.

China has accrued considerable influence (measured by the plurality of domestic/national-level relational power) in three ASEAN states – Cambodia, Laos, and Myanmar.[17] At their core, these states' relationships with China remain economically dynamic and symbiotic. Both Cambodia and Laos have grown into China's sturdiest and most consistent partners in the region – they have each respectively played a critical role in blocking ASEAN from criticising China's militarisation of the South China Seas, as well as voicing support in favour of China's policies towards Hong Kong. Cambodian leaders, in particular, have long seen Beijing as a source of stable and sustainable political backing, which in turn enables them to withstand domestic challenges and opposition, as well as international sanctions and exclusions by the West-led bloc.[18]

On that note, the upshot is clear – under Donald Trump's first term, America appeared to pivot increasingly towards the Middle East and away from the Asia-Pacific in economic and political investments; China had rapidly and tactically sought to fill the vacuum. Not only has China since emerged to be a critical stakeholder in regional issues ranging from maritime disputes to territorial conflicts, but it is also a leading supplier of economic developmental aid, loans, investment to smaller and medium-sized states, who often find themselves locked out of multilateral institutions under the Washington Consensus.

Whether Chinese efforts have paid off in bolstering the country's appeal amongst ASEAN citizens, however, remains a contentious topic. The 2020 Survey Report released by ISEAS in January 2020 (pre-COVID-19 pandemic) reflected lacklustre support ratings for China and America alike in Southeast Asia. 60% of respondents in the region had little to no confidence that "China would 'do the right thing' to contribute to global peace, security, prosperity, and governance" – only 17% had confidence in China. 1.5% viewed China as a benevolent power, whilst 38% endorsed the view that "China is a revisionist power" – down from 45% in 2019.[19]

The 2024 Survey Report marked a significant shift. Out of nearly 2,000 respondents from the 10 ASEAN nations, 50.5% now prefer China, compared to 49.5% for the US. This marks a stark change from 2023, when only 38.9% favoured China, while 61.1% chose the US. Notably, Indonesia, the region's largest economy, has increasingly leaned toward China, with 73.2% favouring China in 2024, up from 44.3% in 2022 and 53.7% in 2023. The poll included informed respondents from diverse sectors such as academia, business, and government, indicating a broad-based shift in regional sentiment.

Despite the growing inclination towards China, this shift should not be mistaken for a wholesale endorsement of China over the US. ASEAN nations prioritise their own self-interests and may align with either power based on what best serves their domestic objectives. For instance, 83.3% of respondents in the Philippines and 79% in Vietnam still favour the US, largely due to ongoing territorial disputes with China and the US's strategic involvement in the region. Furthermore, the US' declining support in Islamic-majority ASEAN countries could be due to its stance on the Israel conflict, whilst China's relative neutrality in the same conflict has possibly improved its image.

Furthermore, the return of Donald Trump and the rise of a virulent form of "America First" foreign policy will certainly continually shape ASEAN attitudes. Trump's "America First" approach previously caused unease in the region. More comprehensive surveys are needed to fully understand these dynamics and their implications for future US–ASEAN relations. As Singaporean Defence Minister Ng Eng Hen bluntly put it on the sidelines of the Munich Security Conference 2025, Asia's image of the United States has "changed from liberator to great disruptor to a landlord seeking rent".[20] Much of the previously extant goodwill and trust in the US has now been replaced by a sizeable dosage of scepticism, concern, and plain distrust. The latter is also true of the views of millions around the world about how major Western media report on China and other global events. The reporting on Gaza was probably the tipping point.

With that said, what has emerged to be relatively uncontroversial is that across ASEAN, many amongst both the policy elite and the citizenry are convinced that ASEAN should continue with its policy of broad neutrality – with calls for greater emphasis upon cultivating the organisation's capacity to fend off pressure from Beijing and Washington alike. An increasingly fraught US–China relationship would do very little good to ASEAN, whose member states have benefited largely off the trade spill-overs and operating the supply chains for the vibrant bilateral trade between the two leading economies. The ASEAN–China relationship is likely to become precipitously significant and tight, as US–China and US–ASEAN relations alike undergo substantial and increasing turbulence.

6.1.2 India

The relationship between China and India is as old as the hills and mountain peaks which separate the two countries, as both share a 1,200 km border. It is a civilisational relationship marked by ancient trade routes and age old exchanges between religious teachers and philosophers. Both also experienced to different degrees, conquest, colonisation, and splintering of territories.

The modern history of China and India is, in the minds of many of their respective citizens, perhaps most widely understood by the relationship and events since the creation of the People's Republic of China in 1949 and the independence of India from British rule in 1947.

The war in 1962 probably still defines the modern era relationship between the two.[21] Since then both nations have, to their credit, relied on diplomatic channels to resolve differences primarily around border issues. There have been several skirmishes, the latest and most sensitive being the clashes in 2020 in the disputed border area of Galwan Valley in Ladakh. Some of the disputes hark back to territorial issues arising from regions that the Chinese accuse the British India Government of annexing from China. Both sides and independent scholars have different interpretations of the events that marked this period going back to the start of the 20th century when India was a British colony and the touchy issue of Tibet.

Despite fear-mongering by mainstream media about a war triggered by border issues, both China and India have recognised the need to improve relations and not escalate matters. From the Chinese point of view, India is potentially one of the largest markets in the world and potentially a critically important trading and economic partner. For India, there is recognition that China can play a key role in its development given the importance of its industrial supply chains in the global economy and the opportunity for trade, especially when it comes to issues related to food security, technology and access to resources.

What is important to bear in mind is that India, with a population of 1.5 billion – compared to China's 1.3 billion – occupies a land mass that is one third that of China. Both countries need each other and politically wise leaders on both sides have allowed common sense to prevail over the years. More importantly it is also well understood that it will be a boon to regional and even global peace.

In this regard, it is not an exaggeration to say, given that both countries, together with neighbours Pakistan and Bangladesh account for about 3.5 billion people, more than 40% of the global population, that the relationship whilst fraught at times, is perhaps amongst the three most consequential relationships for global peace and prosperity.

These population numbers across the four countries are, in a perverse way, also the root cause of geopolitical tensions that drive the ever-evolving relationship between both nations.

China sees the need to have good relations with both Pakistan and Bangladesh to further its economic interests and in that process help both countries develop. This is especially true of Pakistan which is rich in resources and potentially a food basket too and a market for Chinese goods and services. Thus, it is investing in infrastructure in these countries as part of The One Belt One Road Initiative (OBOR).

This is opposed by India, which views Pakistan as a terrorist state and thus sees China's intentions as malicious, insincere, and dangerous.

Another area of contention is their different views on the role BRICS plays in a multi-polar world. The Chinese see BRICS and their support for it as essential for the creation of a multi-polar world to counter the stated goals of the West, led by the US, to contain China and deny it its place in the modern world.

India, however, views BRICS, given its appreciation of China's ascent over the last 20 years and its prowess in many areas, as an association in which it is a critical partner. It thus does not want BRICS to be an association in which China takes the lead or leverages it to pursue its strategic goals. In this regard India seeks to project itself as being neutral but at the same time staying close to its Western allies and aligned to their bid to contain China.

At the people-to-people level, it is interesting to note that most Chinese have a keen interest and even positive appreciation of Indian and Hindu traditions as they have a sound understanding that India is the birth place of the great religions of the world, such as Hinduism and Buddhism.

The view in India, largely influenced by a media that, perhaps because it is "free", has in recent years become rapidly anti-China. This is very obvious mainly on television news channels, though a similar phenomenon is not the case in China.

Recent events such as the meeting between President Xi Jinping and Prime Minister Narendra Modi on the sidelines of the BRICS Summit in Kazan, Russia, in October 2024, send a positive signal for the future. The meeting followed an agreement between both leaders to disengage from hostilities and resolve issues through dialogue.

The hope now is that relations will be normalised, direct passenger flights will be resumed, visa restrictions will be lifted, and bans on Chinese companies will be removed. The desire is to normalise economic ties and allow for greater interaction to build trust and goodwill.

It is commonly understood that business leaders in India have been at the forefront of urging the Indian Government to improve relations, remove restrictions because they believe these are hurting India's industrial and manufacturing sectors.

The good news is that the delicate dance between the elephant and the dragon has been initiated, and the first steps suggest that both sides are in favour of staying on the dance floor.

As China is the more influential global player at this stage with a larger economic footprint, strategic moves on the international front to support India would be a game changer. An example would be supporting India's admission to the Security Council of the UN, given that it is the most populous nation in the world.

6.1.3 Japan

The relationship between China and Japan can be best described by one word: "Nanjing". The Chinese have never allowed its people to forget what happened in Nanjing and do not believe the Japanese have apologised for the war crimes committed in 1937/1938.

This, along with the view that Japan continues to be one of the strongest allies of America in the Asia-Pacific region, together with Australia, means that trust has been difficult to build to re-purpose the relationship for the 21st century.

Yet Japanese businesses and investments have thrived in China and, in fact, contributed to the opening up of China going back at least 30 years.

In many ways, given the "Nanjing" factor, the Chinese believe that the onus is on Japan to make a significant conciliatory move. To this date, and in the eyes of China, Japan has not done that. At the same time, the Chinese have appeared to be willing to let ambiguity about the nature of the apology prevail and allow sleeping dogs to lie. Provocative actions by Japan's leaders especially paying homage to war dead at the Yasukuni Shrine, is viewed as a provocation as it is deemed as honouring war criminals. This then leads to a cycle of tit for tat with China retaliating including resuming claims about islands the Japanese consider belong to them. These include the Senkaku Islands, known to the Chinese as the Diaoyu Islands. Here too, as in the case of China's relations with India, both countries have not escalated issues and peace has prevailed.

Amidst these decade old tensions, there is hope with trade and tourism as two important pathways.

Chinese consume large amounts of Japanese goods and Chinese make up the second largest group of tourists in Japan after Koreans. Japanese businesses have also benefited enormously from access to the world's largest market.

In November 2024, both countries held a summit in Peru with President Xi Jinping and Prime Minister Shigeru Ishiba, agreeing to the need for a "strategically mutually beneficial relationship".

Japan's great allegiance to the US remains a barrier to improving relationships, even though China understands Japan is caught between a rock and a hard place.

For China, Asian stability cannot be shaped by – or rely so much – on the US, to the point where Asian countries must bend over backwards to keep irrational US leaders like President Donald Trump happy.

The Chinese view is that regional issues must be settled and negotiated between regional actors and not shaped by an unreliable non-regional player such as the US. Going forward, the crux of stability in North Asia will, in many ways, be the relationship between China and Japan, which is fundamental to other issues such as the Korean peninsula. After all, these two economic and technology powerhouses of Asia can lead the transformation of the region if they come together as allies.

Regional experts widely believe that historical antagonism should no longer be enough to prevent a rapprochement, and both nations will need to take entrenching steps to reverse the status quo. To do so, each has to accept that the other has legitimate concerns. Beijing will need to give up its anger over the Second World War. It must also offer some kind of guarantee in exchange for Japan loosening its agreement with the US. And Tokyo must accept that its strong American ties hinder its ability to act as an honest broker in East Asia and prevent its rise as a central and independent player in the region. It must understand that, to Beijing, a neighbour, Tokyo's relationship with Washington, a distant ally, appears to be a threat.

The unpredictability of the Americans in recent years, along with the return of the Trump administration, is pushing both countries closer. The hope is that both will realise that a strong new relationship not muddled by US relations will be in the interests of their economies and the region as a whole.

6.1.4 North America

China's relations with North American states encompass, more specifically, its relationships with two countries – the United States and Canada. As the world's two largest economies, the US and China are economically, politically, and technologically intertwined, with synergy and collaboration between the two states pivotal in tackling many of the most pressing problems in the world today. Since President Richard Nixon's seminal visit to China in 1972, and as a direct result of China's economic reforms and opening-up, the two countries have emerged as the top trading partners of each other – till recent years. China had been the largest trading partner of the US until 2019 – when it slipped to third place given the escalating trade tensions.[22]

In recent years, bilateral relations between China and the US have experienced substantial strain, as a result of President Donald Trump's precipitous isolationism and bellicosity towards China, as well as swift – albeit largely restrained – riposte from select segments of the Chinese diplomatic cadres and population. From his telephone conversation with Tsai Ing-wen (Taiwan) in December 2016, to his initiation of the US–China Trade War, and – most recently – the attempts of his White House in politicising and weaponising the COVID-19 outbreak, Donald Trump had contributed substantially towards the deterioration of bilateral communications and amicability between the two states. On the other hand, nationalist pressures from within Chinese borders had compelled Beijing to adopt a more trenchant and defensive stance internationally, lashing out at what it perceives to be undue and unfair American interference with its domestic and internal affairs – it is thus a combination of these factors that has cast a severe shadow over the highly significant, albeit volatile, relationship.

More attention must be paid to the role played by Taiwan as a site and catalyst of Sino-American confrontations. Historically, leaderships in Beijing and Taiwan alike have largely abided by – with moderate contextual and rhetorical deviations – the principle that there remained One China, and that both Mainland China and Taiwan alike had merely been manifestations of different interpretations of the same country.[23] This view, paired with the tacit recognition from both sides of the Taiwan Strait that a military conflict would be deeply undesirable for the people on the Mainland and Taiwan alike, had paved the way for a largely tenable *modus vivendi* in which the Taiwanese people enjoyed high levels of political autonomy and increasingly greater economic affluence and prosperity through tightening trade relations and bilateral engagements with China.

Symmetrically and complementarily, Washington had largely accepted this arrangement throughout the first 16 years of the 21st century, with "strategic ambiguity" coming to typify its approach and stance over the Taiwan Straits. America would duly recognise that Taiwan was a part of China, yet would equally continually commit substantial volumes of military and strategic aid towards the island. As a commentary piece in the *Royal United Services Institute* advocated, "strategic ambiguity trumps strategic clarity on Taiwan".[24] These are sentiments that are shared by many, more pragmatic voices across both sides of the straits, who are reticent over the prospects of either an invasion from Beijing, or military skirmishes and confrontation between China and America at large, in the region.

Despite rhetorical gestures to the contrary, as well as the ignominious visit by House of Representatives Speaker Nancy Pelosi to Taiwan in September 2022, it appears that neither Biden's Washington nor Xi's Beijing has substantial resolve or interest – at least as of 2025 – to severely disrupt this largely tenable status quo. Indeed, the immediate past leader of Taiwan, Tsai Ing-wen had also measuredly toned down and reined in speech that might be construed as pointing towards secessionism. Yet some in the West nevertheless sought to exploit the Ukraine war to suggest that Taiwan would ostensibly be next, a narrative that had been played up by the more ideologically entrenched and vocal incumbent leader of Taiwan, William Lai Ching-te – once again a remarkable sign of how every opportunity would be seized upon to demonise China in international discourse.

China–Canada relations have also deteriorated considerably over recent years, with heightening tensions over altercations and incidents, including the arrest of Meng Wanzhou (Huawei)[25] by the Canadian government (on suspicion of violating US sanctions laws against Iran), the detainment of Michael Kovrig and Michael Spavor[26] by state security forces in China, and Canada's outspoken commentary on Beijing's approach to Hong Kong over the 2019 anti-extradition protests, 2020 National Security Law, and the ongoing trials of "pro-democracy" politicians deemed by Beijing. It is well worth noting that despite Canada's increasingly vocal stance and opprobrium towards China on issues pertaining to human rights, the two states remain deeply economically interconnected – with Sino-Canadian trade totalling 119.5 billion Canadian dollars as of 2023.[27]

In seeking to make sense of China's reception in North America, note the following critical caveat – the attitudes of the public/masses towards China must and ought to be disentangled from those of the political elite: whilst the latter have exhibited distinctively more hostile sentiments towards China, as a result of a mixture of electoral incentives and ideological differences, the American and Canadian publics harbour broadly less antagonistic sentiments towards the country – though the elite-public gap has indeed somewhat narrowed over recent years.[28] The recent migration of millions of Americans to the Chinese social media platform Xiaohongshu in response to the potential shutting down of TikTok is a great indication of the desire of people to move beyond the politics and engage with people around the world to learn about their different lifestyles, culture and traditions.

Some numbers would be helpful in quantifying the above phenomena. Negative views of China amongst Americans reached a record high in 2020, with 73% of respondents holding unfavourable views towards the country – according to a Pew Research Center survey. The trade war kick-started a rapid deterioration in American attitudes towards China, only for the drop to be catalysed by the perception that China was ostensibly responsible for the COVID-19 pandemic. Gallup surveys have also found that by 2020, a strong majority of respondents (67%) espousing negative views of China.

Popular perceptions of China amongst Americans have seemingly trended towards the burgeoning bipartisan consensus amongst the country's parliamentarians. The elites' views in foreign policy and think-tank spaces have considerably soured since ten years ago[29] – in the aftermath of what they touted as authoritarian encroachment and elimination of checks and balances within China (though the extent to which this view holds true, of course, is questionable, given the previous sections of analysis). When it comes to the masses, in a 2020 Chicago Council survey, however, that China's rise as a world power was deemed the third most critical threat to the United States – just below the COVID-19 pandemic and rise of domestic, violent extremism.[30] These are worrying results from the perspective of China's quest for heightened soft power and respect abroad.

China's reputation has – equally, been somewhat tarnished in Canada by a combination of escalating geopolitical threats, resentment towards China over the COVID-19 pandemic, and extensive (albeit potentially inaccurate) portrayals of the country's hardening stance on domestic issues, including Hong Kong, Xinjiang, and Taiwan.[31] In 2023, data released by the Angus Reid Institute found that a majority of Canadians believed their government should view Beijing as either a threat to its interests (40%) or an enemy (22%). Only Russia solicited a more hostile response amongst all surveyed countries.[32] It is ironic to note that since then and in the short space of two years the US has become the greatest threat to Canada with the Trump administration seeking to impose damaging tariffs and even threatening annexation.

Whether these perceptions point to a substantive case for decoupling, however, remains to be seen. The concerns harboured by citizens in Canada and the United States over China are neither as unresolvable nor as intractable, as some may posit them to be. What is needed from China is a clearer and more approachable exemplification and staking-out of its position – as well as assuaging of the concerns of states over its foreign policy. This – in theory – does not require China to forego its fundamental interests or compromise its core baselines.

The fulcrum of the somewhat gloomy prognosis over the future of China-North America relations lies not with the "signal", or the "substance" – e.g., the economic and political fundamentals undergirding how these states' interdependence and interconnectivity in fact operate. Instead, the crux of the matter rests with perceptions. The more the United States and Canada lash out explicitly and vociferously over China's alleged problems, the less likely it is for these states to find or broker compromises – this, in turn, would only be a recipe for disaster, as all parties involve inadvertently dial up their rhetoric and vitriol, in order to preserve their credibility at large. This is how a vicious cycle of escalation, tensions, and conflicts could well potentially arise – to the detriment of all stakeholders involved.

Much ink has been spilled over the substantive contents and nature of the US–Canada–China relationship – and it would be futile to seek to encapsulate all that is relevant within a few pages; nor would that do it justice. With that said, it is imperative to note the common patterns that undergird both US–China and Canada–China relationships:

Significant economic interconnectivity and interdependence remain a dominant factor at work. As much as talk of an ostensible new Cold War is tempting, China and the US, and China and Canada, remain hugely economically interdependent – this description applies specifically to Canada, in relation to China (the former is economically dependent upon the latter), as well as the US–China bilateral relationship. China was Canada's third largest trade partner (behind only the US and European Union) in 2019.[33] North America and China remain deeply embedded in each other's supply chains, technological research and dissemination networks, as well as core trade-based industries. Despite recent decoupling and impediments induced by political and security considerations, China remains a vital economic partner and engine of growth for North America.

The world at large would benefit from China and the US taking joint political responsibilities in relation to global leadership. China and the US' collaboration is instrumental in ensuring effective, expedient, and timely responses to some of the most imminent and substantial problems confronting the world today – ranging from global warming and climate change (over which the sharing of renewable energy and resources is pivotal), to epidemics and international security threats (e.g., terrorism). It is inevitably the case that the US, Canada, and China do not see eye to eye on questions of *implementation* – though the extent to which they diverge over their substantive interests should not be unduly exaggerated. Fundamentally, all three countries would benefit from a cleaner, more stable, and cohesive global community where states are mindful of each other's territorial integrity and sovereignty. This is a vision that caters not only to Chinese interests, but to the needs and demands of the American and Canadian peoples.

What is crucially important here is that differences over geopolitical and strategic contentions must be managed and need not manifest as sites of active conflict. China's rise as a power inevitably comes with a roster of challenges for the rest of the world, as aforementioned. Amongst them constitutes the values and principles that underpin its government, as well as its 1.4bn strong population. It is hence of utmost importance that China and the US resolve their disagreements over China's and the US' domestic and foreign policies, through constructive dialogue that compartmentalises and silos off issues into manageable chunks – as opposed to engaging with one another in homogenised, lump-sum blocs that can neither be resolved through fruitful negotiation, nor discussed in an effective and efficient manner.

6.1.5 Europe

Europe and China enjoy a significant level of mutual interdependence and synergy that concurrently comes with a fair share of fundamental disagreements in values and governing practices. The EU–China relationship constitutes one of the, if not the most preeminent trade relationships in the world. Since China's accession to the World Trade Organisation in December 2001,[34] the EU's goods exports to China have grown – on average – by over 10% per year, and service exports by over 15% a year. This has yielded substantial benefits for EU producers – specifically in markets such as the automobile and telecommunications industries. As of 2023, China was the EU's second largest trading partner after the US, with the first place alternating consistently between China and the US over the several preceding years.[35] In 2021, prior to the downturn in Sino-European relations,[36] the EU and China had been the largest trade partners of one another, with bilateral trade amounting to 586bn Euros in 2020 – an increase by nearly 50% relative to the amount in 2010 (397bn Euros).[37] The EU runs an overall trade deficit with China – despite its net surplus at large, which is enabled largely by the EU's exports to third parties that have in turn seen rising exports in relation to China.

The EU's and China's FDI in one another has also increased over the years, with both parties' investors and capital playing a critical role in promulgating economic growth domestically. Between 2008 and 2017, the stock of EU FDI in China increased from 54 billion euro in 2008 to 178 billion euro in 2017.[38] The stock of Chinese FDI into the EU increased by a factor of 50 during the same period – increasing from $840 million in 2008 to $42 billion in 2017.[39]

With that said, the pace at which European FDI in China has decelerated substantially over recent years, with the primary impediments resting with the minimal investor protection laws and substantial inequality in market access, as well as growing concerns over geopolitical and policy risks. Joint venture requirements have involved transfers of intellectual property from EU firms to Chinese counterparts, thereby undermining the appeal of investing in China.

Whilst Chinese policymakers had historically viewed the economic and commercial components of its relationship with the EU as separable from ideological or political differences, it appears that this view is decreasingly shared by their counterparts in the EU. More recently, the EU–China Comprehensive Agreement on Investment (CAI) hit an abrupt and untimely snag, as a majority of MEPs in the European Parliament (599 to 30, with 58 abstentions) voted to freeze discussion of the agreement.[40] MEPs cited concerns ranging from China's increasing belligerence in rhetoric and foreign policy positions, the country's human and labour rights records, and – more contemporarily – the heated exchanges over Hong Kong and Xinjiang.

Statements by select European politicians portrayed Hong Kong as a city that had rapidly dissipated political and civil freedoms under encroachment from Beijing, whilst Beijing viewed the EU opprobrium with a combination of cynicism and defiance – in the eyes of the Chinese government, its decisions and actions within Hong Kong were well within its remit of restoring stability to a polity that had been rocked by substantial turmoil including acts that would be categorised as terrorism in the West.[41] Select Hong Kong politicians and activists that have left the city have in turn taken to lobbying European states – amongst others – in uniting in condemning and pushing back against China. Yet it would be inconceivable to think that such lobbying efforts alone had sufficed in undermining the CAI – more systemic misconceptions and long-standing ideologically driven grievances were indeed at work, e.g., the fundamental inability on the part of Europe to accept that there could exist a plurality of equally valid political systems being one.

If passed, the agreement would have introduced greater accountability and transparency, as well as securitisation of confidentiality, to EU investment and firms' operations in China – thereby paving the way for substantially greater economic integration and collaborative ventures between Europe and China.[42] The costs (opportunity or actual) induced by the suspension could well be substantial – especially in light of the recession triggered by the ongoing pandemic.

Hence for actors to posit that the disagreements between the EU and China can be reduced into a question of economic interest divergence – alone – is over-simplistic and unreflective of what is at stake in the relationship. Flashpoints ranging from Huawei's presence and security in the region, to China's practices concerning intellectual property and technology transfer from EU companies, to the increasing vitriol in bilateral exchanges, have indubitably cast a shadow over the future of EU–China relations.[43]

With that said, the fundamentals of the EU–China partnership remain intact and pivotal, in several, critical ways:

Economic synergy and synthesis. Both the EU and China alike would benefit from a commitment to work "constructively and expeditiously towards the resolution of a number of market access and regulatory issues", per the press release from the EU over the EU–China Summit.[44] In this "complex and vital partnership", it is imperative that the EU and China identify areas over which cooperation and further entrenchment of ties would be to mutual economic benefit – including, of course, expanding market access, regulating behaviours and practices of corporations, sharing and pooling research and development, and lowering the barriers for effective investment. China and the EU alike have much to gain from one another – China, from the dynamic, incorporated, and holistically robust consumer markets and capital in the EU; the EU, from the rapidly growing wealth pool and capital-intensive production sectors in China – as well as the productivity surplus that is likely to emerge under the country's heavy investment into cutting-edge technology.

Coordination of responses towards global challenges. The EU has called upon China "to assume greater responsibility in dealing with global challenges through the rules-based international system, promoting international peace and security, and adhering to international standards to support sustainable development, especially in Africa".[45] Similarly, *Global Times* has identified the fact that the EU–US partnership is afflicted by "conflict of interests" – and argued that the EU's joining the "US-led rivalry against China"[46] could induce substantial costs upon the EU – hindering its ability to collaborate effectively with China on matters ranging from climate change, denuclearisation, to public health crises.

Maintenance of regional and global geopolitical security and stability. China and the EU have worked closely across a plethora of geopolitical challenges – ranging from terrorism and pirates in East Africa to tensions and civil strife in Eastern Europe. The mutual acceptance of de-militarising and diffusion of geopolitical tensions – particularly those over Central Asia and in relation to China – would further the interests of both China and EU countries. In order to maintain genuine geopolitical security for all stakeholders – especially those in Eurasia – it is critical that EU member states and China alike set aside ideological differences in demarcating areas of mutual non-interference, and areas over which convergence and interactions – from a geopolitical perspective – could well be inevitable. Tensions cannot be wholly diffused, but they can be contained at least somewhat effectively. It is pivotal that disagreements over China's (rather limited) overseas military presence and NATO/EU's geopolitical interests be resolved through dialogue and conversation, as opposed to heated and intransigent disagreements.

The three points outlined here critically affirm the adage that the signal must be separated from the noise. The signals concerning bilateral relations remain largely positive – China and the EU alike would benefit from deepened and broadened ties, though the noise – the optics and perceptions, that is – certainly amounts to a bleaker and more raucous picture. It is imperative that both parties bridge their differences in vision, ideology, and commitments, through open and unreserved dialogue, but also an acknowledgment of the validity of each other's core interests and concerns. Only then, could bilateral relations be repaired expeditiously, to the benefit of all stakeholders involved.

6.1.6 Africa

Sino-African relations can be captured by five key characteristics:

First, Africa has historically enjoyed a highly prominent status *within official CPC ideology* – on a conceptual-cum-theoretical level, it features prominently as a core pillar to China's tripartite "Asian–African–Latin American friends" (亞非拉朋友)[47] framework, which is in turn a core constituent of Mao Zedong's Three Worlds theory. Africa is viewed as a critical exemplar of China's "developing countries"-oriented diplomacy – which is why cultivating political goodwill and sociocultural reciprocity in Africa is of paramount importance to Chinese leaders, even at the expense of economic revenue, if necessary.

Second, both China and African states alike have benefited substantially from the *deepening of bilateral economic ties.* Trade between China and Africa increased by 700% during the 1990s, with China currently being Africa's largest trading partner. Jiang Zemin's "Go out" policy (adopted in the 1990s) demarcated the initiation of China's development-centric foreign aid and trade policy, with a subsequent explosion in the volume of Chinese capital and trade with Africa. Whilst Chinese manufacturers supply the African market with goods for which they possess excess stocks, as well as high-quality consumer products that are relatively scarce in Africa, African states supply China with vital raw materials and natural resources – including oil, wood, and minerals.

Third, Africa serves as a *critical cornerstone to China's international development programmes* – as epitomised by China's BRI and the Exim Bank (a government bank under direct leadership of the State Council). As of August 2022, 52 African states had signed onto an agreement or understanding with the Belt and Road Initiative, per Chinese official announcements.[48] A vast majority of Africa remains relatively underdeveloped in terms of its infrastructure, with a substantial need for rails, roads, and energy. Chinese loans and investment are not only accessible, but also comparatively expedient and come with fewer internal strings attached, as juxtaposed against counterparts from the European Union or the United States.

Fourth, China also serves as a *growing military partner* to African states – when it comes to tackling cross-border and joint military-security threats. In July 2017, China established its first overseas military base in Djibouti, as a primary base for peacekeeping missions in the region. China is an avid contributor towards peacekeeping forces at the United Nations, and maintains a large presence of military corps in Africa, with two primary purposes – brokering peace and mediating in conflict zones, and cracking down on infra-continental crimes and terrorist activities. China has also leant critical support to governments in the continent through supplying drones and military technology.[49]

Fifth, as compared with its Western counterparts, China is by far a more proactive player in promulgating *health diplomacy* in Africa. Health care development and medical aid have been at the forefront of Chinese developmental campaigns in the region. In March 2020, Beijing announced plans to construct an African Centre for Disease Prevention and Control research facility in Nairobi, building upon its past track record of supporting and funding Africa's anti-Ebola efforts in 2014.[50] During the ongoing COVID-19 pandemic, Beijing has seized actively upon President Donald Trump's retreat from international leadership, as an opening through which it has disseminated mutually advantageous and vital medical aid amongst African countries. By May 2021, China had delivered 22 million doses of vaccines to Africa; in contrast, it was only in June 2021 that then-President Joe Biden pledged that the United States would deliver 10 million vaccines to Africa.[51]

How have China's efforts in the region impacted – or strengthened – its reputation? The results are mixed. In 2016, the pan-African survey research Afrobarometer found that 63% of surveyed citizens – from 36 countries – generally had positive feelings towards China's assistance.[52] China's popularity had largely remained at the same levels in 2020 (when the survey was again conducted), albeit with fluctuations and ebbs/flows amongst certain states. The 16-country average – on whether China was viewed as the best model for development – increased slightly from 22% in 2014/2015, to 23% in 2019/2020. The upshot is that over the second half of the 2010s, whilst China had not considerably expanded its net volume of positive reception in Africa at large, it was capable of largely maintaining its levels of support throughout the past five years – as well as tapping into nascent regions for newly gained support.

With that said, the preliminary release of a new opinion survey conducted by Afrobarometer in 2023 could well prove to be cause for concern. Both the US and China encountered declining popularity in Africa, with the percentages of individuals who viewed US and Chinese influence as positive both at 49%.[53]

An area worth mentioning here is the Sahel region – the region wedged between the Sahara Desert to its north and the Sudanian savanna to the south.[54] Many of the states here are highly conflict-prone and conflict-ridden. China has been pivotal in offering security and development support to these states, as well as operating peace and security operations in the region at large. China's growing involvement and presence has vastly improved locals' perceptions of the country – in Burkina Faso, China's development model's popularity increased substantially, from 20% in 2014/2015 to 39% in 2019/2020. Similarly, an overwhelming majority (80%) of Guinean citizens perceive China's economic and political influence to be positive.

With that said, there exist reasons to think that China's reception is not unidimensionally positive – there exist reservations and concerns on the part of some populations. Indeed, as of 2020, the perception that China's influence on their country was positive had declined from 65% to 60% across 16 countries, concurrent with reputational gains by Russia and UN organisations more broadly. Amongst those who were conscious of Chinese assistance programmes, a significant number were worried about loan repayment; a majority felt that their governments had borrowed too much from China.[55]

It is imperative that China addresses these concerns – not only as a means of consolidating its economic presence in the region, but also to ensure that it can rekindle ties with countries with cooling perceptions of the country. Otherwise, China could well find its involvements in Africa inhibited by negative or cynical optics.

6.1.7 Middle East

China and the Middle East have seen rapidly evolving and amalgamated ties over recent years. The years of denouement and termination of the Cold War saw Beijing swiftly establish ties with states in the region, with all states in the Middle East having established economic and diplomatic relations with China by 1992. China benefited largely from petrochemicals in the Gulf as a means of fuelling its energy supply and economic growth; Middle Eastern states, on the other hand, saw substantial prospective gains to be made through the vastly untapped and unexplored markets in China, as well as the prospects for capital synergy and synthesis through joint ventures.[56] Hence the early 2000s and 1990s saw China and the Middle East foment a largely economic-in-kind, though broadly open-ended relationship that paved the way for subsequent collaboration.

From 2008 onwards, Chinese policy in the region took a distinctly and sharply political turn, as Beijing dispatched – monumentally – three naval vessels to partake in counter-piracy operations in the Gulf of Eden, in 2008. China continued developing and harnessing its regional security presence throughout the Arab Spring and ensuing civil wars (e.g., the 2011 Libyan Civil War, and, more recently, the Yemeni civil war), to engage in extensive evacuation operations for Chinese citizens located in the region. China also contributed a substantial number of troops to the United Nations peacekeeping missions in the region.

The commencement of the BRI in 2013 saw the Middle East transformed into a geopolitical-strategic partner for China, with the region designated a "neighbour" region by Beijing at the Third Plenary Session.[57] Wang Jisi – China's leading foreign policy expert – called upon the country to "march westward";[58] "As Washington rebalances to Asia [...] the relationship between the United States and China has become increasingly contentious and zero-sum", Wang argued.[59] As Eyck Freymann argued in *Foreign Policy*, "if China's goal is to achieve influence without entanglement in the Middle East, the BRI is succeeding brilliantly".[60]

China's support in the region straddles the Sunni-Shiite divide. Whilst Iran and Shiite paramilitary groups in Iraq and Syria have openly embraced the infrastructural investment and economic support from China, their sentiments are largely shared by states ranging from Saudi Arabia, the UAE, to Kuwait – who have, in turn, hired Huawei to construct their 5G telecom infrastructure, in face of American pressure. The Middle East has become one of China's staunchest and most consistent partners in its health diplomacy efforts, acting as a regional distributor – as well as recipient – of Chinese aid. Even Israel has remained largely defiant in face of American pressures towards it to limit its commercial interactions with China.

There are several key characteristics worth noting when it comes to the China–Middle Eastern relationship:

A heavy emphasis upon *resource extraction and supply* – from the Middle East to China. China depends heavily upon the Middle East as a source of oil – it is the largest buyer of the region's oil, and is plausibly the sole external power with strong resource and energy ties with every major country in the region. The Middle East acts as a critical repository of energy for China – and China is acutely aware of this fact, which has promulgated it to reciprocate with substantial concessionary loans and capital inflows.

The Middle East views China as a *strategic counterweight and balance* against American presence and hegemony in the region. Chinese economic aid and investment often come with far fewer ideological and political strings attached, with no attempt on China's part to weigh in over the geopolitical disputes in the region. This renders China highly divergent from the United States, which has been embroiled in the conflicts and tensions constitutive of the region over the past decades.

China views the Middle East as a part of its externally projecting, wide-reaching economic diplomatic project – the Belt and Road Initiative. This, in turn, implies that states in the region are likely to be counted upon as vital allies and civil society partners, as well as suppliers of technology, research, innovation, and capital that China needs in order to expand into both North Africa and Central Asia. The Middle East operates as a figurative outpost for Chinese interest – not in the sense of exporting Chinese ideology, but largely with respect to regulating and policing China's interests across the two continents straddled by the Middle East.

Finally, China is stepping up to playing an increasingly prominent role as a *neutral* and *sovereignty-affirmative mediator in regional disputes*. For instance, in response to the crisis in regime succession in Afghanistan, China has offered to play a facilitative role in liaising between and mediating the negotiations and discussions between the Taliban administration and the previous administration of Afghanistan. China has also pledged to play a proactive role in supporting the country's reconstruction in the aftermath of the civil strife that has afflicted it for over two decades.[61] Additionally, whether it be in mediating between Israel and Palestine over the ongoing war in Gaza, or in facilitating the rekindling of diplomatic relations between Saudi Arabia and Iran, it is evident that China is stepping up to play the role of a good-faith broker in a highly geopolitically fraught part of the world.

What of the perceptions of China in the region? In face-to-face surveys conducted nationwide during 2018–2019, at least half of the respondents to an Arab Barometer survey in nine out of 12 countries in the Middle East and Northern Africa region expressed a desire to enhance their economic connections with China. This sentiment was particularly strong in Jordan, where 70% of participants supported closer economic ties, followed by Libya with 63%, and Sudan with 62%. Conversely, in the surveyed nations, Algeria and Egypt showed the least enthusiasm for bolstering economic relations with China, with only 36% and 30% of respondents, respectively, favouring such a move.[62]

More recently, as a result of the COVID-19 pandemic, China's reputation in the region has indeed suffered setbacks. Whilst 48% of the surveyed by a 2021 study reported that their perception of China had remained the same throughout the outbreak, 30.4% reported that it became "slightly more negative" and 15.2% reported that it became "much more negative". Only 7% reported that their perception of China had improved during the pandemic. 85% reported that they saw China as "very/somewhat responsible" for the outbreak. With that said, a majority (62%) of the respondents also felt that Arab states should work with China to combat COVID-19, especially in the pooling of vaccines and medical resources. Moreover, nearly 80% of those surveyed noted that they viewed China as wielding a positive economic influence on the region, through the delivery of developmental aid and injection of investment into the region.[63]

The upshot is clear: whilst Middle Eastern states' denizens welcome China for its economic presence and contributions to the region, there remains a fundamental angst and scepticism towards the country, which have indubitably been exacerbated by the perception that China was ostensibly responsible for the COVID-19 outbreak. Repairing relations and its image in the region requires addressing this perceptual issue head-on.

6.1.8 Latin America

States in the Latin American region possess both economic and symbolic significance for China. It features some of the world's most rapidly growing and populous economies – e.g., Brazil; it also encapsulates some of China's most long-standing international allies, including Cuba, Venezuela, and Argentina.

Economically, China's trade with Latin America has rapidly increased over recent years. The first decade of the 21st century saw China-Latin American trade increase by 13-fold, from $10bn USD to $130bn USD.[64] The value of trade surged to $483bn USD by 2022, reflecting an impressive increase by over 40 times in the total volume of trade over the first two decades of the 21st century.[65] 92% of Latin American exports in 2010 to China were commodities; reciprocally, 85% of Chinese investment went to extractive industries, as well as 60% of Chinese loans. In 2019, Chinese companies invested $12.8bn in Latin America, up 17% from 2018, with particular focus and emphasis upon regional infrastructure – e.g., ports, dams, roads etc.[66] It is apparent that Latin America serves as a vital source of commodities and extraction-based goods and products for China, though in recent years, its secondary role as a consumer market for Chinese exporters has also grown substantially.

Politically, China has been heralded as offering an alternative source of patronage and support to Europe and the United States by Latin American nations that have sought support from the international community for infrastructural development and economic injections. The establishment of the BRICS group – perhaps formally demarcated by the inaugural BRICS summit in 2009 – has closed significantly the distance between China and Brazil, with the latter pivoting to China under President Jair Bolsonaro's presidency. China also lent support to President Nicolás Maduro during the presidential crisis of 2019, standing by the country's sovereign government as it faced challenges from the West-backed candidate of Juan Guaidó. As a general rule-of-thumb, China seeks not to couple its economic presence in the region with heavy-handed political interference, though it has indeed retaliated against the crop of nine countries (e.g., Paraguay and Honduras) in the region that have refused to recognise the legitimacy of Beijing as the official Chinese government – and that have opted instead to maintain relations with Taiwan, as the "true China".[67]

Chinese involvement in the region scaled up considerably throughout the course of the COVID-19 pandemic. China is Latin America's main vaccine provider[68] – offering countries in the region expedient and relatively economical access to vital resources in combating the ongoing pandemic. The US has sought to – though may well struggle – match China's efforts in distributing vaccines, masks, and medical apparatus to Latin America. Only 6 million US-supplied doses will go to South and Central America, as compared with the over 75.8 million (as of May 2021) that China had already delivered.[69]

Chinese interactions with the region can be encapsulated through the following propositions:

1. (1) China has precipitously *displaced* America as the primary provider of economic support and trade in Latin America; its quest for strategic displacement is unlikely to materialise via militaristic competition or the

vying for geopolitical dominance. Instead, China seeks to cultivate economic ties and reciprocal goodwill in the region by bankrolling infrastructural enhancements and reforms, as well as structural overhauls of the financial markets and systems in the respective countries. All in all, China is bent less on achieving military dominance over the region, than economic influence – with the ultimate objective of enriching both Latin American states and China, thereby establishing more enduring partnership relations and ties.[70]

2. (2) Chinese foreign policy in the region cannot be decoupled from its *internal and domestic policy priorities* – e.g., the reunification between Mainland China and Taiwan under "One China". China has made recognition and acceptance of the Communist Party of China-led administration as the sole representative of China a necessary condition in the establishment of diplomatic and political ties with states. Indeed, over the past five years, the Dominican Republic, El Salvador, and Panama have switched their recognition from Taiwan to China, offering China invaluable votes at the United Nations and support for Chinese appointments to critical multinational institutions.[71]
3. (3) Latin America remains *highly discursively and rhetorically significant* as a core element of China's worldview and aspirations of empowering traditionally and historically disenfranchised states that have been excluded from the world's stage. Indeed, a core prong of Chinese foreign policy – since the days of Mao Zedong and Zhou Enlai – has comprised the empowerment of Latin American and African nationalist movements and the liberation of colonised peoples from white settler colonialism.[72] Whether such rhetoric is genuinely upheld by or adhered to China is a different question, though it is apparent that Latin America clearly occupies a preeminent position within China's value hierarchies and foreign policy priorities.

How has China been received in the region, then? The 2012 Americas Barometer suggested that China was perceived favourably across Latin America – that it was viewed as an influence that is both mildly strong and mildly positive in the countries within the region.[73] A majority or plurality of Latin American states' populations – surveyed in a 2019 Pew Research poll – harboured a favourable view towards China. Indeed, in countries such as Mexico and Brazil, younger generations held distinctly more favourable views of China.[74] China clearly enjoys a high level of popularity in the region, though the extent to which this could be attributed to its genuine popularity – as opposed to the innate scepticism espoused by national populations in the region towards the United States and the West at large – remains a question that has yet to be answered.

6.1.9 The "Five Eyes" of English-speaking Countries

The Five Eyes refers to an intelligence alliance comprising Australia, Canada, New Zealand, the United Kingdom, and the United States. These states have signed onto the UKUSA Agreement – a treaty for joint cooperation over signals intelligence. The Five Eyes' origins could be traced to the Cold War, though formalisation and institutional recognition of its activities only kicked in – gradually and progressively – throughout the early 2000s.

The Five Eyes alliance has – in the past – voiced its concerns and reservations over China's foreign and domestic policies, including the country's disqualifying of elected legislators in Hong Kong in November 2020, as well as the specific case of Meng Wanzhou – a Huawei executive who was arrested by Canadian authorities for alleged charges of fraud and conspiracy in the United States (see above). Chinese critics have castigated the Five Eyes alliance as emblematic of a nascent "Eight-Nation Alliance"[75] – bent on undermining China's rise and ascent through supercilious containment efforts.

Despite the rhetoric from a small, select minority of parliamentarians and politicians, the Five Eyes is by no means a homogenous entity – nor is it a politically unified superstructure with shared values and interests. Indeed, as the New Zealand Foreign Minister Nania Mahuta argued in a statement in April 2021, New Zealand would not let the Five Eyes alliance dictate its bilateral relationship with China, as well as the country's resolve to preclude undue escalation in tensions through the expansion in remit for the intelligence grouping. Mahuta and Prime Minister Jacinda Ardern's remarks were widely viewed as signs of New Zealand's adamant wishes to maintain constructive, collegiate economic and political ties with China, as opposed to partaking in the precipitously anti-China campaign initiated by the other members of the alliance.

China's foreign ministry has repeatedly criticised the Five Eyes – then-spokeswoman Hua Chunying declared, "the Five Eyes have taken coordinated steps to gang up on China", in response to Australia and New Zealand's joint statement on Xinjiang. The Alliance also discussed the prospects of – though never came to a material consensus over – cooperating beyond intelligence sharing, including on critical technology, Hong Kong, and the COVID-19 pandemic.[76]

It is vital that the international community recognise that the Five Eyes alliance is not – by any meaningful or substantial measure – a full-fledged economic or political alliance. Nor is it intended to be, given the disparate and disjointed trade, financial, and ideological positions of the alliance's members. China should – and likely does, to an extent – recognise this critical fact. Whilst China has repeatedly lashed out and retaliated against the alliance in public, such speech should not be interpreted as indicative or expressive of the country's genuine resolve to attack or undermine members of the alliance

– insofar it reflects China's growing uneasiness and annoyance towards what Beijing perceives to be foreign interference. The Five Eyes alliance is but a rhetorical synecdoche in Chinese state/official discourse – a stand-in for the hawkish, bellicose elements in the West at large.

6.2 How should the world engage with China? – Towards a tentative outline of working principles

How should the world engage with China? Here, this book shall conclude its substantive sections with a charter of working principles that would enable countries to engage with China in a constructive and mutually respectful manner. These principles are by no means exhaustive, yet should hopefully provide a functional roadmap towards more dynamic relations between states and China. With these tenets, the hope is that China can be approached neither as an enemy, nor as an unconditional ally. Countries must not be naïve about Chinese intentions – but nor should they over-exaggerate the dangers and risks associated with the Chinese government, and thereby ignore the vast spectrum of possibilities and opportunities affiliated with symbiotic collaboration with the country.

6.2.1 A Renewed Charter of Working Principles

The following encapsulates some of this book's more structured recommendations and prescriptions concerning how the world at large ought to engage with China:

6.2.1.1 Constructive collaboration and symbiotic engagement over critical global challenges

The world is confronted by challenges of both global scale and importance. In seeking to make sense of China's rise – and to respond to its evolving needs, behaviours, and preferences, it is critical that the world seeks to work with China to combat and tackle these shared challenges – for which collective action and cooperation are not optional, but necessary. There are at least three areas for which this is the case – in facilitating public health management, combating climate change, and maintaining economic and financial stability worldwide.

On *public health*, there exist two core dimensions on which cooperation is necessary. First, in pooling and sharing resources, intelligence, data, and research pivotal to resolving global health challenges – whether they be pandemics, epidemics, or atypical and rare diseases. Chinese funding and support have proven to be critical to the WHO's continued successes – especially on fronts related to monitoring and tracking the risks of influenza pandemics, and cooperation over the provision of medical supplies and humanitarian aid amidst ongoing conflicts around the world.[77] To the extent that the WHO is indeed afflicted by bureaucratic inefficiencies and intransigence, the solution should rest with the development of bilateral health cooperative arrangements between China and other states, which could helpfully supplement the WHO's efforts in places where the organisation is currently most lacking.[78]

Second, even on issues pertaining to China's domestic and internal health policies – e.g., investigating the transmission mechanisms and origins of COVID-19 – it is all the more important that countries work with China on grounds on which it feels respected and treated as an equal. Elsewise, information- and data-collecting missions would fail; pushes for greater accountability and transparency would also fail. As the above highlights, the Chinese government is hyper-rationalistic and instrumentalist – it recognises and embraces the room for the pursuit of joint, shared interests. International stakeholders must demonstrate how its interests converge with those of the global community at large – as opposed to brandishing inflammatory rhetoric that undermines the credibility and efficacy of calls for cooperation.

On *the environment*, there is much that the world could gain from working with and learning from China. The April 2021 joint statement between the United States and China highlights both parties' resolve to combat the existential risks posed by climate change, through the sharing of research and development (R&D) capital and coordination in deployment of green technologies and renewable energies.[79] More generally, as a signatory to the Paris Agreement, China has undertaken substantial pledges concerning carbon neutrality – China has declared its commitment to reaching peak emissions before 2030, and achieving carbon neutrality by 2060.[80] China should not be alienated from international efforts at halting or ameliorating the transformations to the climate – indeed, and perhaps more urgently, China must be offered a viable path to contributing towards cooperative schemes, in a manner that captures and reflects the country's interests, whilst ensuring that it lives up to considerations of fairness by which it should be bound.

On the front of renewable energy development, states should seek to cooperate with China in maximising output of affordable and cost-effective green energy. The United States' recent ban of solar panel material, as well as its twice-withdrawal from the Paris Agreement, is a worrying sign that vitriolic ideological squabbles and disputes have in turn undermined its ability to produce solar panels – in turn a pivotal component of energy transition efforts worldwide.[81] States should seize upon the comparative advantages of China – its relatively low manufacturing costs, economies of scale, and concentration of capital (backed by the state) – as opportunities for a relatively transitional cost-free shift towards greener, safer, and more sustainable energy sources in the long run.

Finally, China remains a vital engine of *global economic growth*. A slowing Chinese economy is in few parties' interests – especially in light of the interconnectivity spurred by globalisation, and the innate difficulties embodied in decoupling. From financial markets to trade supply chains, most – if not all – countries in the world require China's continued economic success in order to ensure that they remain economically functional; their businesses operational; their investments practicable. In turn, through its pioneering advances in digi-finance and crypto-finance, China has stepped up to playing a leading role in global finance, both as a source of innovative systems and policies, as well as a contributor of liquidity and capital. Whilst China's role certainly cannot compare directly against that of the United States – as of yet – the instrumentality of the system to global financial markets would only increase, in the aftermath of the pandemic and entailed recession, over the upcoming years.

6.2.1.2 Critical, dynamic, and constructive engagement with the aims of facilitating gradual reforms across the world – in China and elsewhere

As the above has demonstrated, China is not without its own concerns, challenges, and problems to tackle – just as any other rapidly developing, broadly mature society or country. It is also indisputable that much remains to be desired in areas ranging from labour rights to economic transparency and accountability, from China's overarching developmental directions and potentially over-ambitious economic statecraft to its domestic population policy. None of this can be redressed through isolationism and containment – and the calls for closing China off against international collaboration and exchange are both perilous and unconducive towards the country's growth.

Yet the international community must also be mindful of the distinctive governance logic that underpins the Chinese system – where Chinese leaders do not take kindly to perceived infringements upon national sovereignty, especially given the country's past brush-ins and experiences of colonial invaders and imperialist conquest at large. Countries around the world must engage critically and dynamically with China – with the aims of facilitating gradual, domestic reforms that are neither ideologically predisposed towards values that do not conform with the Chinese ethos, nor risky and precarious in a way that jeopardises the overall stability of the country.[82]

In practice, this requires international counterparts to China to pay heed to and acknowledge – at least in public and in external speech – the validity of China's sensitive baseline demands and needs. Other states should also acknowledge that on issues of internal sovereignty and domestic affairs, the Chinese government's will and intentions should be respected. In exchange for these concessions, countries should and can press for more carefully calibrated reforms to China's overseas presence – ranging from economic policies, aid policies, to how it operates multilateral institutions such as the AIIB and the Belt and Road Initiative.

Gradualism is not only an option, but a necessity when it comes to China. The stauncher and harder the international community presses China, the less likely it is that moderates and reformists within the country would have the manoeuvring room to convince their counterparts of the merits of liberalisation, devolution, and heightened accountability and transparency – none of which are distinctly "Western" in kind.[83] Nor should such critiques be couched in terms of "democracy-driven" ideology – each and every country has its own governing ideology, and to unduly hone in on particular ideological preoccupations, is neither practical in terms of motivating reforms, nor normatively justified.

A corollary of this is that in dealing with China, compartmentalisation is key – firewalling areas of cooperation off from areas of competition is vital, with the aim of minimising the space in which direct confrontation and conflict are viewed to be, or in fact, necessary. For instance, cooperating over climate change, public health crises, and international security should be kept distinct and disparate from competition along economic fronts. Even within the shared sphere of economics, China and the world at large should continually deepen their financial synergy and capital consolidation, even whilst competition proceeds along alternative dimensions – e.g., trade and commerce. It is imperative that countries eschew a zero-sum, all-or-nothing mindset when it comes to China. Only through listening, responding, and accommodating could all parties – in their relationships with China – reap maximal rewards.

One caveat: as argued by analyst An Gang:[84]

> the US claimed that its approach to China will be "competitive when it should be, collaborative when it can be and adversarial when it must be". In other words, the US doesn't want conflicts and disagreements to affect cooperation with China on issues that concern the US This is fundamentally arrogant: The US seeks to both suppress the development of China and restrict China's reactions – and that's never going to happen.

The world at large must remain vigilant and wary against the possibility that such compartmentalisation will not be taken kindly – necessarily – by the Chinese populace and government. The perception that the West is seeking to proverbially "have the cake and eat it" is perhaps not wholly accurate – yet could well derail efforts at de-escalating and containing the simmering tensions. If perceptions of the West are mishandled, relations between China and the world at large are likely to be further strained – which would be to no one's benefit.

A core motif has persisted throughout the public statements issued by Chinese diplomats – that is, their fundamental aversion to what they perceive to be signs of hypocrisy and inconsistency. Foreign Ministry spokespersons have repeatedly insisted that other states should "drop double standards on human rights".[85] If criticisms by the global community are seen by the Chinese bureaucracy as unilaterally and unequivocally targeting only China – this would do very little in spurring China to change, adapt, evolve, or reform. Instead, what would most likely emerge – and this is indeed a phenomenon that is evidenced by recent events – is a risible, assertive brand of defensive nationalism, that renders the country recalcitrant and immutable towards any and all forms of external critique.

6.2.1.3 Cultivating cross-national, perspectival empathy – Seeing the world through China's lenses

The final point on which this book will end is that the world at large would benefit from developing perspectival empathy – an ability to view global events and changes through the lenses of China. A fundamental hamartia that afflicts many countries' interactions with China – is a relative deficiency in the "Chinese perspective". States often interpolate, or overlay, their readings of China with their own subjective preferences, values, and understandings of global affairs.

Yet China, as a historically rich and politically complex entity, cannot and should not be reduced to Western stereotypes alone. To parse China's behaviours, preferences, and stances on critical issues through ostensible "universal values" – may render one's worldview more parsimonious; may indeed render states' foreign policy towards China more aligned and in-line with their domestic policy. Doing so, however, would do very little in ensuring that states can grapple with and predict – with accuracy and expediency – China's next moves and national policies.

Understanding China requires acknowledging the distinctive predisposition and orientation of its policymakers, appreciating the hierarchy and structures of selection and promotion, and making sense of its current problems and setbacks in view of the country's substantial achievements over the years. Such empathy must extend beyond linguistic or superficial resonance – in doing so, states would find themselves more attuned to the signals and messages expressed by China, but also more accustomed to the unique idiosyncrasies involved in cultivating deeper, interpersonal ties with Chinese diplomats, bureaucrats, and politicians.

None of this is to say that the international community must therefore accede to any and all of China's demands. Empathy does not imply concession; concession does not imply foregoing one's national interests. If anything, empathising with the Chinese perspective would enable the international community to better articulate their demands, worries, and suggestions in a manner that is amenable to Chinese interests – that can be readily interpreted and understood by China, not as hostile gestures, but as an invitation to dialogue, compromise, and discussion.

The rising tensions between China and its neighbouring countries, as well as the world at large, need not be inevitable. Ameliorating and containing these problems, however, requires an active and conscious effort on the part of all stakeholders. Only through frank and rigorous conversations – unhindered by ideological biases and presuppositions – could the world navigate fruitfully and strategically China's rise, and embrace it as a welcome agent of constructive change to the global order.

Notes

1 Ghosh, I. (2020) *How China overtook the U.S. as the world's major trading partner?* Visual Capitalist. Available at: https://www.visualcapitalist.com/china-u-s-worlds-trading-partner/; Rajah, R. and Albayrak, A. (2025) *China versus America on global trade*, Lowy Institute. Available at: https://interactives.lowyinstitute.org/features/china-versus-america-on-global-trade/

2 IDCPC (2021) China insight special issue on CPC and world political parties summit. Available at: https://www.idcpc.gov.cn/english2023/dzwk/zgkx/202307/P020230717028654090872.pdf

3 Nair, C. (2024) Israel-Gaza war: How the world can restore humanity and lead process for lasting peace in Middle East, *South China Morning Post*. Available at: https://www.scmp.com/week-asia/opinion/article/3264030/israel-gaza-war-how-world-can-restore-humanity-and-lead-process-lasting-peace-middle-east
Nair, C. (2023) Anti-China rhetoric is off the charts in western media, *The Diplomat*. Available at: https://thediplomat.com/2023/02/anti-china-rhetoric-is-off-the-charts-in-western-media/

4 Dian, X. and Liu, Y. (2023) The rise and fall of China's wolf warrior diplomacy, *The Diplomat*. Available at: https://thediplomat.com/2023/09/the-rise-and-fall-of-chinas-wolf-warrior-diplomacy/

5 Wong, C. (2020) Too soon, too loud: Chinese foreign policy advisers tell 'Wolf Warrior' diplomats to tone it down, *South China Morning Post*. Available at: https://www.scmp.com/news/china/diplomacy/article/3084274/too-soon-too-loud-chinese-foreign-policy-advisers-tell-wolf

6 Jerdén, B. (2014) The assertive China narrative: Why it is wrong and how so many still bought into it, *The Chinese Journal of International Politics*, 7(1), pp 47–88. Available at: https://academic.oup.com/cjip/article/7/1/47/574393

7 Deng, F. (2024)鄧小平說的韜光養晦並未過時 , HK01. Available at: https://www.hk01.com/%E4%B8%AD%E5%9C%8B%E8%A7%80%E5%AF%9F/1031820/%E9%84%A7%E5%B0%8F%E5%B9%B3%E8%AA%AA%E7%9A%84%E9%9F%9C%E5%85%89%E9%A4%8A%E6%99%A6%E4%B8%A6%E6%9C%AA%E9%81%8E%E6%99%82

8 McDonell, S. (2021) Xi Jinping calls for more 'loveable' image for China in bid to make friends, *BBC*. Available at: https://www.bbc.com/news/world-asia-china-57327177

9 Wong, B. (2024) *In the year of global elections, China must pragmatically re-engage the West*, China-US Focus. Available at: https://www.chinausfocus.com/peace-security/in-the-year-of-global-elections-china-must-pragmatically-re-engage-the-west?gad_source=1&gclid=Cj0KCQjw3bm3BhDJARIsAKnHoVXw5W52uwXcQRzPtkhA6S_OzePtAAYRZinirWtr9x0uvrcXpCqIyo8aAvFDEALw_wcB

10 Moyer, J.D., Meisel, C.J., Matthews, A.S., Bohl, D.K., and Burrows, M.J. (2021) *China-US competition measuring global influence*, Atlantic Council, ISBN-13: 978-1-61977-173-4. Available at: https://www.atlanticcouncil.org/wp-content/uploads/2021/06/China-US-Competition-Report-2021.pdf
11 Tani, S. (2021) *ASEAN meets with China as progress on Myanmar consensus stalls*, Nikkei Asia. Available at: https://asia.nikkei.com/Spotlight/Myanmar-Coup/ASEAN-meets-with-China-as-progress-on-Myanmar-consensus-stalls
12 ASEAN-China Economic Relations (2025) Association of South East Asian Nations. Available at: https://asean.org/our-communities/economic-community/integration-with-global-economy/asean-china-economic-relation/
13 HSBC China (2024) Opening doors in the ASEAN-China corridor. Available at: https://www.business.hsbc.com.cn/en-gb/insights/accessing-capital/opening-doors-in-the-asean-china-corridor
14 Wong, B.Y.S. (2024) Opinion: ASEAN playbook shows how small states can navigate big power rivalry, *South China Morning Post*. Available at: https://www.scmp.com/comment/opinion/article/3248660/us-china-tensions-asean-playbook-shows-how-small-states-can-navigate-big-power-rivalry
15 Bibhudatta, A. (2023) China's relationship with ASEAN: An explainer, *orfonline.org*. Available at: https://www.orfonline.org/research/china-relationship-asean-explainer/
16 Callahan, W.A. (2016) China's 'Asia dream': The belt road initiative and the new regional order, *Asian Journal of Comparative Politics*. Available at: https://www.academia.edu/25631014/Chinas_Asia_Dream_The_Belt_Road_Initiative_and_the_new_regional_order?email_work_card=thumbnail
17 Burrows, M. *et al.* (2021) *China-US competition*, Atlantic Council. Available at: https://www.atlanticcouncil.org/wp-content/uploads/2021/06/China-US-Competition-Report-2021.pdf
18 Rim, S. (2025) *Cambodia and China: Is the 'Ironclad Friendship' starting to rust?*, The China-Global South Project. Available at: https://chinaglobalsouth.com/analysis/cambodia-and-china-is-the-ironclad-friendship-starting-to-rust/
Lim, C. (2023) *2023/101 'Reviewing China's elite-centric approach in its relations with Cambodia' by Chhay Lim*, ISEASYusof Ishak Institute. Available at: https://www.iseas.edu.sg/articles-commentaries/iseas-perspective/2023-101-reviewing-chinas-elite-centric-approach-in-its-relations-with-cambodia-by-chhay-lim/
19 Cook, M. (2020) Unfavourable views: Southeast Asia's perceptions of China and the US worsen amid covid-19, *ThinkChina*. Available at: https://www.thinkchina.sg/unfavourable-views-southeast-asias-perceptions-china-and-us-worsen-amid-covid-19
20 Ang, M. (2025) *Ng Eng Hen: Image of us in Asia has changed from liberator to disruptor to landlord seeking rent, Mothership.SG – News from Singapore*, Asia and Around the World. Available at: https://mothership.sg/2025/02/ng-eng-hen-us-image-asia/
21 Ramachandran, S. (2022) *The long shadow of the 1962 war and the China-India border dispute*, Jamestown. Available at: https://jamestown.org/program/the-long-shadow-of-the-1962-war-and-the-china-india-border-dispute/
22 Kiernan, P. *et al.* (2019) *Tariff fight knocks off China as Top U.S. Trading partner*, WSJ. Available at: https://www.wsj.com/articles/china-lost-spot-as-top-u-s-trading-partner-in-first-half-11564749251
23 Hass, R. *et al.* (2023) *Understanding the one China policy*, Brookings. Available at: https://www.brookings.edu/articles/understanding-the-one-china-policy/
24 Sussex, M. and Clarke, M. (2021) *Why 'strategic ambiguity' trumps 'strategic clarity' on Taiwan*, Royal United Services Institute. Available at: https://rusi

.org/explore-our-research/publications/commentary/why-strategic-ambiguity-trumps-strategic-clarity-taiwan
25 Wong, N. and Wingrove, J. (2018) Arrest of Huawei executive tests Canada's already strained ties with China | Financial Post, *Financial Post.* Available at: https://financialpost.com/news/economy/huawei-arrest-tests-china-canada-ties-as-trudeau-weighs-5g-risk
26 Chiu, J. and MacCharles, T. (2018) Ex-diplomat who worked on Trudeau's Hong Kong visit detained in China | the star, *Toronto Star.* Available at: https://www.thestar.com/news/canada/2018/12/11/former-canadian-diplomat-detained-in-china-amid-rising-tensions-reports-say.html
27 Statista (2024) Canada's merchandise trade balance with China 2023 | statista. Available at: https://www.statista.com/statistics/469811/canada-merchandise-trade-balance-with-china/
28 Kim, P. (2021) *U.S. perceptions of China in the pandemic era and implications for U.S. policy*, Carnegie Endowment for International Peace. Available at: https://carnegieendowment.org/2021/01/21/u.s.-perceptions-of-china-in-pandemic-era-and-implications-for-u.s.-policy-pub-83684
29 Dina Smeltz, I.H.D. (2018) *2018 Chicago council survey*, Chicago Council on Global Affairs. Available at: https://www.thechicagocouncil.org/research/public-opinion-survey/2018-chicago-council-survey
30 Dina Smeltz, I.H.D. (2020) *2020 Chicago council survey*, Chicago Council on Global Affairs. Available at: https://www.thechicagocouncil.org/research/public-opinion-survey/2020-chicago-council-survey
31 Bolongaro, K. (2021) *Negative views of China harden in Canada on arbitrary detentions*, Bloomberg. Available at: https://www.bloomberg.com/news/articles/2021-03-16/negative-views-of-china-harden-in-canada-on-arbitrary-detentions
32 Korzinski, D. (2023) *Friends and foes: Most Canadians say Ottawa should approach China as a 'threat' or 'enemy'*, Canadian Opinion Research. Available at: https://angusreid.org/canada-us-china-friends-foes-favourability-of-nations/
33 Canada, G.A. (2021) *Government of Canada*, GAC. Available at: https://www.international.gc.ca/trade-commerce/economist-economiste/analysis-analyse/china-canada-2020-commerce-chine.aspx?lang=eng
34 Gao, T., Dominguez-Jimenez, M. and Dadush, U. (2019) Bruegel. Available at: https://www.bruegel.org/sites/default/files/wp-content/uploads/2019/11/WP-2019-09-China-finalincl-edit.pdf
35 Trade and Economic Security (2024) *EU trade relations with China*, Trade and Economic Security. Available at: https://policy.trade.ec.europa.eu/eu-trade-relationships-country-and-region/countries-and-regions/china_en
36 Made, J. van der (2021) *European Parliament votes to freeze EU-China investment deal*, RFI. Available at: https://www.rfi.fr/en/business/20210520-european-parliament-votes-to-freeze-eu-china-investment-deal-cai-human-rights-sanctions-xinjiang-hong-kong
37 Statistics Explained (2025) EU. Available at: https://ec.europa.eu/eurostat/statistics-explained/index.php?title=China-EU_-_international_trade_in_goods_statistics
38 European Parliament (2021) EU-China relations in challenging times. Available at: https://www.europarl.europa.eu/RegData/etudes/BRIE/2021/698751/EPRS_BRI(2021)698751_EN.pdf
39 Le Corre, P. (2018) *On Chinese investment and influence in Europe*, Carnegie Endowment for International Peace. Available at: https://carnegieendowment.org/posts/2018/05/on-chinese-investment-and-influence-in-europe?lang=en

40 Wong, B. (2021) *Repairing the EU-China relationship requires pragmatism and flexibility*, China US Focus. Available at: https://www.chinausfocus.com/foreign-policy/repairing-the-eu-china-relationship-requires-pragmatism-and-flexibility
41 Hynes, P. (2022) Exclusive: The revolution industry and how the Hong Kong police were targeted, *Fridayeveryday*. Available at: https://www.fridayeveryday.com/exclusive-the-revolution-industry-and-how-the-hong-kong-police-were-targeted/
42 Fallon, T. (2021) The strategic implications of the China-EU investment deal, *The Diplomat*. Available at: https://thediplomat.com/2021/01/the-strategic-implications-of-the-china-eu-investment-deal/
43 Wong, B.Y.S. (2021) *China has an image problem—but knows how to fix it*, Foreign Policy. Available at: https://foreignpolicy.com/2021/04/06/china-image-problem-wolf-warrior-international/
44 European Commission – European Commission (2020) *EU-China summit: Defending EU interests and values in a complex and vital partnership*, European Commission – European Commission. Available at: https://ec.europa.eu/commission/presscorner/detail/en/ip_20_1159
45 European Commission – European Commission (2020) *EU-China summit: Defending EU interests and values in a complex and vital partnership*, European Commission – European Commission. Available at: https://ec.europa.eu/commission/presscorner/detail/en/ip_20_1159
46 Global Times (2021) Conflict of interests hard to hide in EU-US summit. Available at: https://www.globaltimes.cn/page/202106/1226244.shtml
47 李久林：毛澤東關於亞非拉的戰略思想--理論-人民網 (2013) *CPC News, China*. Available at: http://theory.people.com.cn/BIG5/n/2013/1009/c83867-23138945.html
48 Nedopil, C. (2025) *Countries of the belt and road initiative (BRI)*, Green Finance & Development Center. Available at: https://greenfdc.org/countries-of-the-belt-and-road-initiative-bri/
49 Popescu, N. and Bitzinger, R. (eds.) (2017) *Defence Industries in Russia and China*, EU Institute for Security Studies. Available at: https://www.iss.europa.eu/sites/default/files/EUISSFiles/Report_38_Defence-industries-in-Russia-and-China.pdf
50 Procopio, M. (2022) *China's Health Diplomacy in Africa: Pitfalls behind the leading role*, ISPI. Available at: https://www.ispionline.it/en/pubblicazione/chinas-health-diplomacy-africa-pitfalls-behind-leading-role-25694
51 Lovelace Jr, B. (2021) *U.S. to split 55 million Covid vaccine doses between Latin America, Asia and Africa*, CNBC. Available at: https://www.cnbc.com/2021/06/21/covid-vaccine-us-to-split-55-million-doses-between-latin-america-asia-and-africa-.html
52 Chingwete, A. *et al.* (2016) *China's growing presence in Africa wins largely positive popular reviews*, Africa Portal. Available at: https://www.africaportal.org/publications/chinas-growing-presence-in-africa-wins-largely-positive-popular-reviews/
53 Staden, C. van (2023a) *New Afrobarometer polling shows both China and the U.S. losing popularity in Africa*, The China-Global South Project. Available at: https://chinaglobalsouth.com/analysis/new-afrobarometer-polling-shows-both-china-and-the-u-s-losing-popularity-in-africa/
54 Dan Suleiman, M. (2017) Sahel region, Africa, *The Conversation*. Available at: https://theconversation.com/sahel-region-africa-72569
55 Soule, F. and Selormey, E.E. (2020) How popular is China in Africa? New survey sheds light on what ordinary people think, *The Conversation*. Available at: https://

theconversation.com/how-popular-is-china-in-africa-new-survey-sheds-light-on-what-ordinary-people-think-149552
56 Lyall, N. (2019) China in the Middle East: Past, present, and future, *The Diplomat*. Available at: https://thediplomat.com/2019/02/china-in-the-middle-east-past-present-and-future/
57 Lyall, N. (2019) China in the Middle East: Past, present, and future, *The Diplomat*. Available at: https://thediplomat.com/2019/02/china-in-the-middle-east-past-present-and-future/
58 Freymann, E. (2021) *Influence without entanglement in the Middle East*, Foreign Policy. Available at: https://foreignpolicy.com/2021/02/25/influence-without-entanglement-in-the-middle-east/
59 Michael, E. O'Hanlon, P.B.S., Telhami, S., and Czin, J.A. (2016) *March west: China's response to the U.S. rebalancing*, Brookings. Available at: https://www.brookings.edu/blog/up-front/2013/01/31/march-west-chinas-response-to-the-u-s-rebalancing/
60 Freymann, E. (2021a) *Influence without entanglement in the Middle East*, Foreign Policy. Available at: https://foreignpolicy.com/2021/02/25/influence-without-entanglement-in-the-middle-east/
61 Wong, C. and Ng, T. (2021) 'Us chaos': China vows to help Afghanistan and insists America pays too, *South China Morning Post*. Available at: https://www.scmp.com/news/china/diplomacy/article/3146986/china-calls-us-be-investigated-civilian-deaths-afghanistan (Accessed: March 19, 2025).
62 Robbins, M. (2021) *Fragile popularity: Arab attitudes towards China*, Arab Barometer. Available at: https://www.arabbarometer.org/2021/12/fragile-popularity-arab-attitudes-towards-china/
63 McGinn, J. (2021) *Arab perceptions of China during the COVID-19 pandemic: Insights from the UAE*, Middle East Centre. Available at: https://blogs.lse.ac.uk/mec/2021/05/19/arab-perceptions-of-china-during-the-covid-19-pandemic-insights-from-the-uae/
64 Koleski, K. (2011) *Backgrounder: China in Latin America*, U.S.-China Economic and Security Review Commission. Available at: https://www.uscc.gov/sites/default/files/Research/Backgrounder_China_in_Latin_America.pdf
65 Rios, K. and Barrios, R. (2023) China's engagement with Latin America and the Caribbean, *Congress.Gov*. Available at: https://crsreports.congress.gov/product/pdf/IF/IF12660/1/
66 Nugent, C. and Campell, C. (2021) China's effort to become Latin America's most important ally, *Time*. Available at: https://time.com/5936037/us-china-latin-america-influence/
67 Nugent, C. and Campell, C. (2021) China's effort to become Latin America's most important ally, *Time*. Available at: https://time.com/5936037/us-china-latin-america-influence/.
68 Stuenkel, O. (2021) Vaccine diplomacy boosts China's standing in Latin America, *Foreign Policy*. Available at: https://foreignpolicy.com/2021/06/11/vaccine-diplomacy-boosts-china-in-latin-america/
69 Harris, B. *et al.* (2021) Chinese jabs dominate Latin American vaccination campaigns, *Subscribe to Read*. Available at: https://www.ft.com/content/511d3cee-b388-4eb5-a667-e693349ad564
70 Nugent/London, C. and Campell/Beijing, C. (2021a) China's effort to become Latin America's most important ally, *Time*. Available at: https://time.com/5936037/us-china-latin-america-influence/
71 Nugent/London, C. and Campell/Beijing, C. (2021a) China's effort to become Latin America's most important ally, *Time*. Available at: https://time.com/5936037/us-china-latin-america-influence/

72 *Support for the countries and peoples of Latin America in their struggle to safeguard national independence and state sovereignty* (no date) 中华人民共和国外交部. Available at: https://www.mfa.gov.cn/mfa_eng/zy/wjls/3604_665547/202405/t20240531_11367544.html; Sun, J.Y. (2023) Decolonisation, the cold war, and Afro-Asian solidarity: China, Kenya, and Zambia at a crossroads, 1949–1964, in *Kenya's and Zambia's Relations with China 1949–2019*. Boydell & Brewer (Eastern Africa Series), pp. 22–45.

73 Velasquez, N. and Armony, A. (2016) *A honeymoon with China? Public perceptions in Latin America and Brazil*, IPEA Br. Available at: https://repositorio.ipea.gov.br/bitstream/11058/6539/1/TdM_v2_n2_Honeymoon.pdf

74 Silver, L. (2019) *People around the globe are divided in their opinions of China*, Pew Research Center. Available at: https://www.pewresearch.org/fact-tank/2019/12/05/people-around-the-globe-are-divided-in-their-opinions-of-china/

75 Cui, F. (2020) 'Five eyes' could be poked blind if China's sovereignty and security harmed, warns Chinese FM spokesperson, *Global Times*. Available at: https://www.globaltimes.cn/content/1207378.shtml

76 Needham, K. (2021) New Zealand says 'uncomfortable' with expanding five eyes | reuters, *Reuters*. Edited by M. Perry. Available at: https://www.reuters.com/world/china/new-zealand-says-uncomfortable-with-expanding-five-eyes-2021-04-19/

77 World Health Organization (no date) *Global health response and cooperation*, World Health Organization. Available at: https://www.who.int/china/our-work/global-health-response-and-cooperation

78 World Health Organization (no date) *Responding to the humanitarian crises in Yemen*, World Health Organization. Available at: https://www.who.int/china/activities/responding-to-the-humanitarian-crises-in-yemen

79 U.S. Department of State (2021) *U.S.-China joint statement addressing the climate crisis*. U.S. Department of State. Available at: https://2021-2025.state.gov/u-s-china-joint-statement-addressing-the-climate-crisis/

80 Xu Klein, J. (2020) China nudges up its commitment to reduce carbon dioxide emissions, *South China Morning Post*. Available at: https://www.scmp.com/business/article/3113737/china-pledges-cut-carbon-footprint-65-cent-2030

81 South China Morning Post (2021) US bans imports from Chinese solar panel firm over Xinjiang Forced labour claims, *South China Morning Post*. Available at: https://www.scmp.com/economy/china-economy/article/3138513/us-bans-imports-solar-panel-material-chinese-company-over

82 Wong, B. (2021a) *China and the West see each very differently and that is the problem*, Nikkei Asia. Available at: https://asia.nikkei.com/Opinion/China-and-the-West-see-each-very-differently-and-that-is-the-problem

83 Wong, B. (2021c) *This is why I will never abandon Hong Kong*, Nikkei Asia. Available at: https://asia.nikkei.com/Opinion/This-is-why-I-will-never-abandon-Hong-Kong

84 Gang, A. (2021) *A list too far*, China US Focus. Available at: https://www.chinausfocus.com/foreign-policy/a-list-too-far

85 The State Council Information Office of the People's Republic of China (2021) *China urges us to drop double standards on human rights*. Available at: http://english.scio.gov.cn/pressroom/2021-03/26/content_77349158.htm

7
CONCLUSION

7.1 China's rise: Legitimacy and challenges

China's rise is – in many ways – a remarkable phenomenon in its rapidity, extent, and comprehensiveness. Yet its trajectory, in the grand scheme of history, is highly analogous and similar to the trajectories of many past power – indeed, the United States and the United Kingdom included.[1] It is tempting to see China's story as extraordinary – yet doing so would obscure both the extent to which it has in fact learnt from other states' successes and slip-ups, and the very fact that China's story can and should be replicated by other states.

A more accurate understanding of China's contemporary history would require us to situate its developments in a wider historical context – in which the country has sought, and largely succeeded (economically) in pursuing the revival of its historical pre-eminence as a global power. Whilst the Chinese state today does not seek to export its governance model and principles, it serves as a valuable exemplar and test case for countries seeking to pursue a similar developmental trajectory – one spearheaded and propelled by a potent and competent administration with a heavy grip over national politics and economic developments underpinned by a commitment to lift hundreds of millions out of poverty.

Over the past four decades of economic reforms and opening-up, China has lifted hundreds of millions out of poverty, recovered its historically well-endowed status as a leading global economy (albeit not as a hegemon), and brought about substantial improvements to the quality of life of many of its citizens, including many of its once impoverished ethnic minority communities. Its astronomical ascent and steadfast developmental path has much to do

DOI: 10.4324/9781003643548-7

with the country's emphasis upon infrastructural investment, ability to seize upon its comparative advantage of low wages, competitive workforce, and expansive depository of resources, and willingness to embed itself within the wider supply chains that constitute the global economy. China is as much a beneficiary of globalisation as it is of its top-heavy, yet dynamically responsive government.

The results of the substantive military, political, and economic reforms undertaken by the Communist Party of China (CPC) are apparent and significant. China's military has transitioned from a large, unwieldy, and inefficient army in the early 1980s into a streamlined, effective, and highly disciplined force by the early 2020s. Economically, the country is now the world's largest in terms of total GDP (by purchasing power). Politically, China is amongst the leading contributors and most substantial powers in international organisations such as the United Nations, World Bank, and the International Monetary Fund, as well as establishing sustainable, viable parallel structures that complement – yet do not undermine, necessarily – existing initiatives and structures.

None of this is to say that China is without its flaws, and the Chinese authorities would be the first to agree. Many structural issues exist – some have persisted stubbornly from the pre-reform era; others are relatively nascent phenomena that resulted from the marketisation and economic liberalisation of the country. These issues range from structurally rooted corruption (albeit they have indeed been cracked down upon under the current administration), human rights concerns – especially in terms of civil and political liberties – to the country's deep-rooted nationalism. Throw into the mix worries over its ageing demographics, long-struggling state-owned enterprise sector, and localised corruption, notwithstanding the substantial attention and attempts at redress over the past decade by the government, and it is clear that the path ahead is by no means straightforward. With that said, in many ways, these problems are not all that different from that in other nations such as America.

It would be naïve to think that China need not seek self-improvement and reforms when in reality the Chinese government and its leaders are in the main trained specifically to drive continuous improvement. It would be dangerous, indeed, to ignore the constructive criticisms that many view to be intrinsically important and conducive in facilitating the country's organic improvements. Yet it has been through progressive transformations – ranging from reductions to pollution, streamlining and improving transparency in governance, enshrining stable succession norms, to developing a truly tenable and inclusive "Double Circulation" economy – that the country has advanced the interests of all, as opposed to the select few.

The international community would benefit vastly from recognising two core tenets concerning China's developmental pathways – the first is that the interests of both the country and the international community alike are best served through frank, forthcoming, and egalitarian dialogue and conversations between national leaders and civil societies, as opposed to demonisation, castigation, and selective outrage; the second is that it will take time for China to grow and mature as a power – that nationalistic and jingoistic narratives projected by state apparatus may not always be reflective and truly indicative of the country's real progress, but nor should they be discarded as mere propaganda, for there exists much truth in their portrayal and reflection of China's overcoming of struggles of its own.

All of this is to say that there exist challenges and opportunities in how the international community has opted to engage China over recent years. On one hand, the economic bonds and links, multilateral political institutions, and open exchanges between civilians, academics, and youth between China and the rest of the world, have proven to be pivotal in uplifting the quality of life for a large proportion of China's population. Opportunities have grown out of – and will continually enrich China's international presence and collaboration with other states. In acknowledging that the government is not all there is to China – and that this is a country with immense heterogeneity, robustness, pluralism, and, fundamentally, cultural variety – we are hence at least a step closer to grappling with how we can engage and work with the 1.4 billion constituents of this civilisational power. It cannot be ignored or simply demonised out of imagined fears or genuine concerns.

On the other hand, there remain, too, vast challenges when it comes to China's relations with the rest of the world – especially those stemming from conflicting economic interests, clashing ideologies and value frameworks, as well as deterministic narratives that portray China and the West as ostensibly being on an inevitable path to confrontation. These narratives are disingenuous and erroneous, and would only serve to sow unnecessarily seeds of division between China and the rest of the world. It need not be a zero-sum or negative-sum game – all parties involved should be cognisant of this fact. Yet whilst these narratives proliferate and prevail in the time being, there is little that can be directly done to tame the unwarranted and paranoid antagonism directed towards China amongst many purported "observers" of its domestic affairs.

We live in hope. This book has hopefully offered a useful conduit through which those interested in China's rise, growth, and developments can make sense of the distinct means through which China governs itself. The Chinese government is steered by a deeply rooted and historically grounded devotion towards its people – one could even term this as a point of foundational fixation. The ruling elite of China are interested in, in equal parts, the performance legitimacy of their administration, as well as the extent to which hierarchal legalistic norms are adhered to by the population, and upheld swiftly through official institutions. These two core tenets in turn underpin the perceived legitimacy of the regime, as well as its significant popularity amongst the masses.

7.2 Understanding China: International cooperation

The above chapters have sought to elucidate many of the issues and features of China's past, present, and future. It is well worth noting that the above cannot, and should not, be taken – in any meaningful sense – as an exhaustive account of all there is to China, one of the most enigmatic and dynamic countries in the world today. Instead, the intention of this book is to offer a comprehensive, balanced, and reasonably in-depth analysis of China – that hopefully succeeds in unpacking the merits and demerits of its ascent, how it governs, its interactions with the rest of the world, and the strengths and opportunities that characterise its present state. We cannot cover everything in but a few hundreds of pages – indeed, much of the above can and ought to be augmented and examined in more depth.

This book closes with the following remarks and recommendations. Irrespective of where one stands on China – how one perceives, judges, or seeks to interact with China – it is of paramount importance that there exists sufficient understanding of China and what it has to offer. This process is by no means straightforward. At present, discourses over China are often heavily skewed by geopolitical and strategic calculus.

On one hand, a more balanced view of China does not mean acceding to the official narratives embraced by parties aligned with or against China – indeed, it would require us to do away with partisan and ideological preoccupations as much as is possible, in order to gain a truly reflective and accurate glimpse into China today. On the other hand, in search for balance and nuance, it is important not to conflate this task with one that shuts out sources, viewpoints, and opinions simply because of pre-existing biases concerning their ostensible credibility – or lack thereof. Official state media, unofficial media, investigative journalists, civil society research by think tanks and academics, speeches, dialogues, open debates, these should all be drawn upon and leveraged as critical means of accessing the bigger, full picture concerning the country. This can be the starting point of understanding China and building a new era of cooperation.

This book has hitherto largely refrained from adopting an excessively prescriptivist approach – for it is written with the conviction and belief that individuals, ranging from researchers, thinkers, to policy advocates and politicians alike, would benefit from making up their own mind on China and how to deal with China, after perusing the facts presented here. With that said, we hope to conclude with a few brief thoughts on how the future forward between China and the rest of the world ought to be navigated. We hope that the following could offer practical solutions largely amenable to all parties – regardless of their specific national and political commitments.

First, seek *common understanding*. A deeper and more salubrious understanding of this vast, ancient civilisation is a necessary, but insufficient, condition for mutually amenable cooperation and collaboration. China benefits vastly from working with, not against, the international community – whether it be in cultivating its domestic legitimacy, in enshrining governance outcomes, or, indeed, in establishing its international presence and role as a leading global power. The world, too, benefits from a China that is more embedded and interconnected within the global political arena – a China that sees its interests aligned with, and not inimical to, the interests of the international order. None of these envisioned outcomes could be achieved without a serious search for common understanding and the resolution of shared disagreements and conflicts between countries. Even if a common understanding of issues and convergence in stance cannot be fully achieved, it is of the utmost importance that all parties involved agree upon certain core facts and rules of engagement – and initiate a departure from the "us vs them" geo-politics of recent years – concerning the path ahead for China and the world at large.

Second, *pursue collaboration and cooperation wherever possible*, but do so in a way that is mindful of the interests and baselines of all parties. China and the international community alike will inevitably possess non-aligned, even conflicting, interests in certain areas, yet such divergences need not be all there is to China's international involvement. The best means of working with China – of aligning China's interests with the world's at large and vice versa – is to engage it across a wide range of collaborative ventures, whether they be challenges pertaining to climate change (where China's own track record in cracking down on pollution may come in handy), public health, and, indeed, the proliferation of terrorist groups and violent non-state actors. Yet such engagement must also take heed of and conform with the core values of both China and its counterparts alike. Collaboration is impossible without countries embracing the tenet to "agree to disagree" where resolution of differences is impossible.

Finally, *keep all lines of communication open*, especially through back-channels and track-II diplomacy. More conferences, panels, and discussions featuring individuals from different stances and countries, including those with conflictual preferences and attitudes towards particular affairs, should be held. Only then could open, unfettered, uncensored debates over critical issues of importance be held, with disagreements and grievances brought to the table in a productive and effective manner. There could well be more that unites us than divides us – but this would be hard to realise, and even harder to have the public acknowledge – without spaces in which reasonable dialogue and conversations can be conducted. It is the hope of this book's authors, that the insights provided herewith has and will kick-start a series of much-needed conversations concerning China and with active Chinese participation.

Understanding China is no mean feat. Yet it is necessary – for all, not just China or other "major powers" – that they do so in order to communicate and resolve the fundamental differences between them. Indeed, any other approach to China would be irresponsible, disingenuous, and most dangerous. If there is indeed a path to building a safer and fairer world, then it falls upon us – as citizens sharing and co-inhabiting this one planet – to work hand-in-hand in bringing about the world we seek to see. China is no enemy; nor is it an infallible paradise. Those who want it to improve and become a better place – not just for its own people, but for the world at large – must continually advocate for this incredibly important and righteous cause.

Note

1 Wong, B. *et al.* (2021) *The Future of US-China Engagement Panel*, *Oxford Political Review*. Available at: https://www.youtube.com/watch?v=MuS1sXG1c6Q

INDEX